TRADITION OF YOG

There are many traditions in classical yog and the
great scope for research. B
what the Mahabharata men

हिरण्यगर्भो योगस्त

Mahabharata later clarifie
Paramatma Sriman Narayan. .... .. the Saiva- Antaryami
and He is the first speaker of yog. Hiranyagarbha Yog has
been maintained in bits and pieces in Pancharatra.
Ahirbudhnya Samhita mentions that He gave discourses on
chitta-vritti nirodha kind of yog which has Abhyasa-Vairagya
and Ishvara- Pranidhana as means. The schemes of Ashtanga
Yog too find a mention here. This is the basis of Patanjali's
Yog. This main stream of yog received many contributions.
Apart from the Pancharatra originated Vaishnava Agamas,
the other major contributions were from Tantras, Shaiva
agamas and Shakta Agamas. Many of the yogic concepts of
Kriya, Mudra and Bandha were given by Shaiva-Shakta
agamas and Tantras. The North Indian tradition of yog was
greatly influenced by these. So much so that Lord Shiva
became the source of yog for them. Hatha-yogic tradition
has strong base in Shaiva cult of yog. The Natha-Sampradaya
puts Adinath (Shiva) as origin of yog. We have great texts
such as Hatha yog pradipika, Gheranda samhita, Shiva
samhita and prolific works ascribed to Gorakhnath.

Dattatreya who advised yog to Sankruti must also be
considered here. This piece of instruction is preserved for
us in the Shandilya Upanishad. Gheranda rishi in his samhita
has the yog where he puts Pratyahara before Pranayama
while usually all traditions maintain the Pranayama to
Prattyahara process. This is quite a significant revolution.

The Bhagwad Gita revived the Karma yog tradition which Bhagwan Himself says was instructed earlier (in Vaikuntha) to Vivasvan (Surya). The Gita mentions the main forms of yoga which are

- **Jnana Yog**
- **Dhyana Yog**
- **Karma Yog**
- **Bhakti Yog**

There is great significance when Vyasa calls Gita as Brahma vidya, Upanishad and Yog shastra in the colophone of each chapter. Each chapter is called as a kind of yog and thus eighteen chapters give us eighteen yogs.

The Yogopanishads posit that Ashtanga Yog is fount-hole of all various yogs. Then there are different yogs in different levels. The first level is Ashtanga Yog. The second level is Mantra Yog of sixteen limbs. The third yog is Laya yog of nine limbs and the fourth yog is Hatha Yog of six limbs. These are graduations and not cults or schools. Classical yog was maintained intact until about late 18th century. Then yog was slowly being compromised and was opened out to greater mass of people.

With the advent of 20th century, classical yog was greatly compromised and pop versions came up to appeal to a greater community and yog now remains to be a consumer product in our era.

Today, yog has only "feel-good" purpose for even those who claim to be students of yog. Another case to bow before time!

कालाय तस्मै नमः।

PRASHANT S. IYENGAR
Pune, July 2015

PRANAYAMA

"Yoga teaches us to cure what need not be endured
and endure what cannot be cured."

—B.K.S. Iyengar

YOG TRADITION OF INDIA

Yog is a pride possession of our great Indian tradition. It is a science, a faculty, a philosophy, a religion and a culture. The science of Yog contains entire thought of man. Yog knowledge can offer the highest goal and bliss of life. An anthology of the discourses were expounded by Prashant Iyengar for the students, scholars and sadhakas of Yog at different points of time. The readers, while learning Mantra Yog, Laya Yog, Hatha Yog, Raja Yog, Kundalini Yog, Nada Yog, Nama Yog as kinds of Jnana Yog, Karma Yog, Bhakti Yog and Dhyana Yog can get acquainted with many facets of Yog, They will learn that Yog is a way of Life. It is the sadhna of life. The engaging style of narration will appeal to the readers' brain and heart while they imbibe the knowledge of Yog, For easy comprehension, the words in the Sandhis are separated in the Sanskrit quotations. The books written by Prasant S. Iyengar selected to be published under the series are:

1. **Ashtanga Yoga of Patanjali:** *Philosophy, Religion, Culture, Ethos and Practices*
2. **Discourses on Yog**
3. **Manual on Humanics**
4. **Pranayama:** *A classical and traditional approach*

PRASHANT S. IYENGAR

PRANAYAMA

A Classical and Traditional Approach

New Age Books

New Delhi (India)

PRANAYAMA
A CLASSICAL AND TRADITIONAL APPROACH

ISBN: 978-81-7822-482-4

First NAB Edition: Delhi, 2016

© Prashant S. Iyengar

Published by
NEW AGE BOOKS
A-44 Naraina Industrial Area, Phase-I
New Delhi (India)-110 028
E-mail: nab@newagebooksindia.com
Website: www.newagebooksindia.com

```
NAB Cataloging-in-Publication Data
PRANAYAMA
ISBN  978-81-7822-482-4
(About the Series, Index)
```

Printed and published by
RP Jain for NAB Printing Unit
A-44, Naraina Industrial Area
Phase-I, New Delhi-110 028. India

Arpan

Late Guruvarya Anna

Late Guruvarya Amma

INDEX

Chapter : 1

PREFATORY NOTE

Pranayama is a compound word comprising two terms,
namely,

PRANA
AND
AYAMA

Prana is the vital energy, which apparently distinguishes
animate and inanimate or living and non-living creation. The
animate things are believed to be breathing, that is having an
in-breath and an out-breath. This breathing is characteristic
to the bio-world or living creations. This breath oscillation in
human beings signifies the existence of prana in the
embodiment. The departure of Prana marks the the end of
respiration and death of the living being.

Prana, however, in yogic texts is defined as
"VAISHVIK CHAITANYA SHAKTI".

This term literally means a "universal power of
consciousness". It is a mystical, philosophical, metaphysical
and quite a mysterious concept. It is fraught with a lot of
obscurity and thus not fit to be deciphered at the outset. It
will hopefully become clear and conspicuous in the course of
time. At the outset, what can be said about it is that 'it is that
(energy) which is centric to all animate creations from birth
and that which incessantly keeps a conspicuous presence until
death.'

It comes with
birth and goes out
with death
and keeps pulsating throughout life
absolutely incessantly;
Its arrival marks the
birth of life and its departure
marks the death of life.

This taking birth and meeting death is called JEEVA-BHAVA or CHAITANYA, an important characteristic of the entire bio-world. That is Prana for a layman. This Prana is not merely for a lively condition of life but all

Actions, reactions
Responses, activity
(Voluntary and involuntary)
are because of Prana.
Thus, we not only
live by Prana but all
that we do bodily, mentally,
sensorially, cognitively, psychically,
emotionally, intellectually
voluntarily and involuntarily
is by Prana.
More or most importantly,
respiration is an invariable
concomittant to Prana.

In philosophy, breathing or respiration is called TATASTHA LAKSHANA or extrinsic characteristic of Prana.

In a way, respiration is TATASTHA LAKSHANA of Chaitanya or even of Prana. This can be a preliminary explanation of Prana.

At a gross level, Prana, chaitanya and respiration are considered indistinct by laymen. But as we proceed deeper to comprehend these concepts through the *shastras*, we will discover the distinctions more clearly. At this stage we will not go into the analyses, definitions and distinctions between Shvasa/shvasayama (breath/breathing) and Prana/Pranayama; since the two are indistinct, the 'ayaama' – meaning regulation of Prana, ends being identified as a 'regulation of breath.'

Thus, the neophyte considers regulated breathing as Pranayama or regulating the breath as Pranayama which is a pardonable mistake. At some point in time, there will be disillusionment.

Today, Shvasayama has becomePranayama; in fact, synonymous entities.

> *However, breathing begins and ends,*
> *while Prana comes and goes or*
> *arrives and departs.*
> *On the point of death, the expression is*
> *"Breathing has stopped but Prana has gone*
> *(or departed or escaped)!"*

The point made here is that breathing is not Prana (or Prana kriya) but breath and breathing are vehicles of Prana. In all practicality, we need not look for distinction in Prana and breath or Pranayama and Shvasayama. It is better and practical to consider Pranayama as Shvasayama, and vice versa. But on a higher level, such an indistinction will be a great lapse and misuse and result in a very great misconception.

It is highly advisable to learn Pranayamic action or regulative action on breath. The breath or breathing tracks are learners' tracks in Pranayama. Thus, we shall be dealing with breath, breathing, breath action, breathing exercises which will be vital training in preliminary Pranayama.

> *For a long time, one should carry out studies*
> *of usages, applications and addressals*

of breath as well as by the breath.
It will be prudent, wise and thrifty
to learn these rather than rush to classical pranayama.
These lessons are best had in yogasanas.

Yogasanas must add this perspective to observe, study, learn and experiment with breath usages and the variegated usages of breath in various aspects of asanas. Asanas as postures require release, activity, motion, movement, posture, steadiness, firmity, flexibility, freedom, access, efficacy etc.. Various kinds of physical postures have different purposes and impacts on the body such as

> *releasing, broadening,*
> *Exercising,*
> *Freedom,*
> *Presentation,*
> *Remedial etc.*

The various postures such as

> *Standing*
> *Sitting*
> *Prone*
> *Supine*
> *Inverted*
> *Backward bending*
> *Forward bending*
> *Lateral bending*
> *Lateral rotating etc.*

provide a fabulous canvas to carry out the study of breath usages, its application and conditioning. So also the rest of the embodiment can learn

> *Usages*
> *Applications*

Conditionings
by making breath the beneficiary.

There must be breath-led dynamics in asanas as well as breath-major dynamics and breath-considerate approach in asanas.This will be a major preparatory of Shvasayama or so-called Pranayama. One must learn the usages of breath for body, senses, organs and as mind conditioners. Asanas provide a very rich academy for that.

Basically it may be deemed that Shvasayama
Can be considered as Pranayama
in the preliminary stages, and overcome the popular
belief that we do not merely live by breath
but breath and breathing is a profound force and
agency worth regulating and controlling because
of it being a very versatile, profound and rich force.

Chapter : 2

INTRODUCTION TO THE ACT OF BREATH AND BREATHING

We, commoners, are busy in our business of life and make provisions for desire-fulfillment, adventure-fulfillment, aspiration-fulfillment and are slaves of our own mind or someone else's mind. Vedanta calls this getting trapped in the net of maya.

Our life revolves and rotates in various wheels such as cycles of day and night and cycles of weeks, months, years, seasons etc. We want to live for experience of life and think that the breathing keeps on and on for that purpose.

We think that we live by breath
And breath takes place for all functions
Of involuntary system in us so that
We can freely be occupied in
our business of life.
Don't we conveniently take our breathing for granted
and keep ourselves engaged in the business of life?

The breath incessantly goes on even in our sleep and slumber as well as in comatic and unconscious state. We do not get the thought of breath unless we go out of breath and pant for breath. Asthmatic patients cannot afford to forget their breath in an acute condition.

The point is that the entire autonomous
system in us depends on breathing and

breath needs no attendance or advertence.
Very rarely, and on very isolated occasions do we take
recourse to voluntary breath. Let us indentify
these are few such occasions.
1) *Lifting a weighty object*
2) *Opening a tightly closed bottle or box*
3) *Taking a high jump.*
4) *Taking a long jump*
5) *To push a heavy weight*
6) *To press heavily*
7) *To make an excessive movement of body*
8) *To take long strides*
9) *To climb up tens and hundreds of steps*
10) *To scale a hill or a mountain*
11) *To climb up a tree*
12) *For heavy-duty body activities*
13) *To get tired by exercising*
14) *On getting tired by exercising*
15) *To recover from high breath rate*
16) *To carry out an olfactory act*
17) *To make a long oration*
18) *To shout loudly or*
19) *To dip in or remain underwater for a long time.*

These are some of the occasions when we become breath-aware, breath-conscious and breath-minded. Otherwise there is an utter neglect.

On the above occasions there is a voluntary, deliberate and purposive breath. On such occasions there are hyper-normal in-breaths or out-breaths or more frequent post-exhalative retentions and less frequent post-exhalative retentions.

It is to be noted that normal, mechanical and
involuntary breathing is of the respiratory system.

But when there is extraordinary volume and mode
involved as in the above cases,
the breathing is not only of the respiratory system.

Generally, the breathing is for biological existence and involuntary system but on those rare occasions the breathing is for voluntary, extraordinary body activity.

The breath rate will change due to some contingency in physiological or psycho-mental condition.

The mode of breathing also changes due to unusual or non-normal conditions in the body-mind complex. The changes in breath–modes are noticeable in mental conditions such as:

1) Quiet-passive condition(Shanta Avastha)

2) Disquiet-restless condition (Ashanta-Avastha)

These two modes of breathing are radically different from each other. These are two opposite poles and breath-modes and the breath rates too are diametrically different which needs to be noted. We very well know as to how our breathing is characteristically different in fearful, painful or dreadful conditions, so also in worry and anxiety, so also in anger and exasperation. All these states and even other states of mind correspondingly impact or influence breathing.

Anyway, it is a very scanty understanding
that we only live by breathing and that only the
autonomous involuntary system works by it.

The basic education in Yog is that one must start using the breath and breathing in various physical and psycho-mental acts. One of the preliminary educations in yog is to evolve an internal activity system presided over and led by as well as conducted by the breath. So also these should be composed by the breath and breathing quite significantly. Since yog must work on the mind-stuff or chitta, all physical, organic, sensory, cognitive, idio-motor, physiological activitation must be either conducted by breathing or composed by breathing or constituted by breathing.

"The acts, actions must be "breath-coated,"
or breath-constituted or breath-based, so that
they ultimately become yogic dynamics."
"Just as there are water-based medicines
or hydropathy, there is breath-o-pathy or
Prana-o-pathy in yog."

In Yog technology, breath is used for the anatomical, physiological body as a conditioner, tuner, toner, exerciser, activator, passivator, stimulator, corrector, culturer etc.

In esoteric aspects, it works as a catalyst and reformer, sublimator and cosmicaliser etc. But this happens in classical Pranayama.

In yogasana itself, the breath acts are used to such an extent that it becomes an internal service agency and even an internal motor or limb system. It is a great exploration to use, apply and devise the breath and breathing as a conditioner of body matter (cellular body).

Thus, the breathing is not merely "done"
but "used, applied, devised and customised."

For Adhyatamic process, breath is an internal conditioner, transformer, transmuting agency, cosmicaliser apart from being a tuner, toner, setter, corrector, exerciser, stimulator, purifier, cleanser etc. It similarly works on mind, psyche and consciousness. Breath only works in a conducive, desirable and yogic way. Thus, it is paramount to learn usages of breath, breathing and breath modes for all such variegated uses.

Since breathing is a very natural and spontaneous act for all beings, there is no need to have any training and learning for it. But at times due to respiratory disorders, it may become necessary. But there is a lot of learning in yog with respect to breathing. Breath is a fabulous, variable, prolific and transcendent factor.

Since it is a very resourceful entity, there is an urgent need for its regulation and management. Regulation becomes important in two cases; one, when the resources are scanty and insufficient, and the other, when it is plentiful. In case of breath, it is a very resourceful and powerful entity.

Now, we come to the most important and awe-inspiring factor for the common, uninitiated person, that

"The reference here is not to the respiratory system which is a part of our systemic anatomy or body, but it has reference to a condition of our body and mind system as a whole.

Our entire existence gets breath-status and becomes breathified, breathicated, breath-profused and breath-logged."

This 'Shvasamayata' or profusion of breath in our embodiment is what qualifies us for pranayama or even so-called Pranayama called Shvasayama. In such an endeavour as Pranayama or Shvasayama, one does not merely breathe by the respiratory system but it is systemic breathing. One breathes by an orchestrated act of the entire exoteric anatomy-physiology and psychology.

Breathing is a concerted effort and not just of the respiratory organs and system.

'The breath must be a concerted effort and have a composite effect.'

The following passage will hopefully open out the above statement.

The breathing here is by, for, in, on and with entire "I", "me" and "mine" in the embodiment.

It is by all the *sapta dhatus* of the body - meaning by the skin, flesh, muscles, bones, tissues, fibres, cavities, organs, senses, mind, psyche and consciousness.

It is by the *saptadhatus*, organs, trillions of cells, corpuscular particles, jnana and karmendriyas, mansendriyas and the totality of man. The entire organic complex such a sliver, stomach, spleen, pancreas, intestines, colon, gall bladder, urinary bladder, duodenum, glands, conative-cognitive organs, idio-motor organs, brain, lobes, cerebro-cortical parts, consciousness, conscience etc. is involved.

Thus, even Shvasayama is so circumspect and this is a condition which is best described as, "The whole embodiment is breathing and is breathed for." This is WHOLISTIC BREATHING.

This enables a profound preparatory for such a concerted, comprehensive act of breathing.

Chapter : 3

PREPERATORY –
A MASTER STROKE!

As suggested earlier, the whole embodiment has to be 'breathified' and 'breathicated.' A neophyte must preferably carry out or even learn these in *shavasana*. (The next chapter will delineate it.)

Later, Pranayama is attempted in seating postures or asanas such as

> *Bhadrasana*
> *Svastikasana*
> *Siddhasana*
> *Padmasana*
> *Veerasana.*

1. One must settle down in a supine asana such as *Shavasana*.
2. Set right or normalise the breathing, body, limbs, senses, organs and get mutually connected in them by using breath and breath-awareness as the sutra (or thread). The whole body–mind-senses complex should be mutually connected and linked, something like "setting up a conference call within."
3. Become breath-aware, breath-conscious, breath-minded and breath-considerate.
4. Use the voluminous in-breath and out-breath to circumscribe the entire embodiment rather than normal, mechanical, habitual and voluntary breath. But use the

deep and voluminous exhalations with great priority and frequency. It should be noted that there are greater exhalative processes here. For convenience, one can use every third or fourth cycle exhalation by making it deeper and voluminous.

5. One must exhale consciously in various body parts and the brain, and feel both, the immersion (*visarjan*) and discharge (*visarga*) in these parts.

   To achieve that, one will have to exhale voluminously in certain confined regions of the embodiment such as
   a) Skull-head-brain-face-senses
   b) Throat and mouth
   c) Chest and thorax
   d) Abdomen and pelvis.

   The discharges and immersion called *visarga* and *visarjan* must be effectively carried out.

6. Then, there must be major abdominal-centric exhalations – long, prolonged, profound and profuse exhalations in the abdominal region is paramount. There must be major abdominal addressals by such exhalations. Thus, there will be abdominal
   evacuations
   discharges and
   immersions.

   In the process, the abdomen and abdominal organs should recede, deflate and get distended but not at all dilate. It should melt away and go to a dissolved state.

7. There must be exhalations but in different confinements as suggested in point 5 above. However, abdominal addressals must be carried out. This is called 'exhalation by confinement'. Teachers must initiate this in students (breath awareness and breath usages give vital training in yogasanas).

8. Exhalation and exhalative awareness should form a confluence as if both are river-like flows.

   "Thus, it is a confluence of breath and awareness."

9. The whole body should get a breath status (a respiratory status). In this way, the breath can have a governing position to carry out the regulative process. Thus, the "I", "me", "mine" will voluntarily agree by being regulated by breath.

10. We need to become a breathing organism and become breath-o-beings rather than human beings.

   Thus, there will be a characteristic change called DharmaParinama in us which is essential for Pranayama or Shvasayama.

11. By extraordinary and unusual volume of exhalation, we will evolve the above "status" or "change" and inculcate a breath-sensitivity culture.

   When a mother handles her own baby, she soon evolves a baby sensitivity culture and not merely baby sensitivity.

This culture is best evolved when we will realise the essential nature of breath and its salient features. This is the topic for our next chapter.

Chapter : 4

THE SOURCE, ORIGIN AND ESSENTIAL NATURE OF BREATH

"The body, limbs, organs, senses, mind, psyche is very much ours, the breath is not ours as much. However, it is very much for us."

"So also the breath is not ours intrinsically and organically; the other things which are organically and intrinsically ours, remain ours because of this breath entity, which is not ours." Let me explain this.

"If the breath isolates us, all that is ours ceases to be ours."

If we take a look at ourselves very objectively, we realise that we are(I+Mine).

The collocation of these two is what we are. The "I" is the subjective entity or pronoun "I" and "mine" comprises of

(My)body
(My)organs
(My) limbs
(My) senses
(My)Karmas (poorva-karma)
(My) class
(My) caste
(My) creed
(My) ethnicity
(My) religion ('ism')
(My) gender

(My) mind and psyche etc.
(My) status and stature
(My) destiny and fate
(My) luck, good/ill luck
(My) fortune/misfortune etc.

All these are our delimitations called *Upadhis* in our philosophy. Vedanta often speaks of delimiting factors such as caste, class, creed, race, age, gender, ethnicity, social condition, economic conditions, customs, conventions, habits, faith, beliefs, status, stature, Karma/fate/destiny, external and internal conditions etc. All these factors have a constant gravity on us and limit our radius, erect walls and boundaries around us.

While essentially man is soul as metaphysics puts it, and we are birthless, deathless, diseaseless, decayless, casteless, classless, creedless and genderless,unconditional without hunger-thirst mutations – Eternal.

Like the infinite space/ether/akasha is delimited in a pot, we are delimited by the above-mentioned delimiting factors. Our "I", "me" and "mine" has such delimitations. Particularly our body and mind are fraught with genetic and genealogical background. We have ancestral conditions. Most importantly, our body and mind have karmic background. So also we have ethnic-racial backgrounds. Even if one rejects these, one cannot escape them. Thus, our body-mind-psyche-consciousness are prone to all the above mentioned delimitations.

None of us are free from these limiting and delimiting factors. None of us are unlimited or un-delimited.

Every cell in us and every corpuscular particle in us has "Karmabandhana" and "Upadhi", but our breath has none of those. Isn't that a marvel?

The breath and breathing do not have any karmic background. Nor is there any shadow of karma in our breath.

Breath is coming in and going out every four or five seconds. The breath does not come in to stay with us or within us. Is it not a marvellous scheme of divinity and the archetypal plan? The breath does not have class, creed, caste, race, ethnicity etc. The Creator has kept the breath outside the karma-gravity, otherwise all other things of Prakruti in us are in karma-gravity. And most importantly and significantly, all fundamentally depend on this "un-sullied breath".

In a way, breath is untouched by *klesha-karma vipaka ashayaa.*"

According to *Adhyatma*, the breath is divine and cosmic, or the Bhagwadiya and Ishvariya aspects. According to spiritual mysticism,

> **"It is the thread (sutra) that links the universal Transcendent Divinity with the Divinity within us."**

Thus, Pranayama is one of the exalted yajnas according to the *Gita*.

The breath therefore is NOT OURS but very much FOR US. And then, "All that is OURS remains OURS, because of this breath which is not at all OURS but for US."

The breath does not even become ours by any remote probability because it does not stay in us for more than a few seconds and is always in an incessant inward and outward movement.

Thus it is the most fundamental foundation and vital force for our living; it has no condition to be the locus of attachment either ways, meaning neither does it have attachment or aversion for that matter within us or vice versa.

Thus, it is free from Maya. It has a source in the supreme cosmic divinity. It can be described as:

Virgin nature
Sublime

Noble
Divine
Magnanimous
Glorious
Godly
Infinite
Metaphysical
Ageless
Endless
Boundless
Immutable
Indestructible.

PARMARTHIC, BHAVYA, DIVYA, DAIVI, BHAGAWADIA, ISHVARIYA, ANANTAetc.

Every breath is like a new-born baby. It is, therefore, ever fresh. It has the innocence of a baby. Just as a new-born baby has potentials to bring about awe-inspiring changes in the family set-up: it can inspire harmony, unity, integrity and oneness and concord, the breath similarly can do that in Pranayama. Just as *dhoop* and *agarbatti* or incense can cosmicalise or sublimate the shrine of God, the embodiment can be become 'KSHETRA' meaning a Holy Shrine, sublimated and cosmicalised via the breath.

'All the matter in us (including mind which is also matter)
lives in us for a life-time and can become life-time residents in us because of this non-resident breath.'

The breath in Pranayama truly works as an incredible purifier. Its presence has a touchstone effect and *Kama-Krodha* (the six Shadripus) flee from our mind. It is a great ennobler, sublimator, cosmicaliser, diviniser and a purifier par excellence.

Sublimity, nobility, cosmicality and trans-mundanity
permeate our embodiment.
We transcend to incredible heights in consciousness.

Look at the marvellous root origins and source of breath;
it is the same as that of "I", "me" and "mine":

> *Past karma*
> *Past sins*
> *Vasana*
> *Maya*
> *Prakruti-vikruti*
> *Delimitations (Upadhi)*

THE BREATH – A GREAT DISSOLVENT

Like water dissolves many things such as sugar and salt,
Shvasa-yama can dissolve the mental matters.The defects of
mind astonishingly dissolve in the breathing of Shvasa-ayama.
The "I"-ness and "mine-ness" dissolve by Shvasa-ayama.

It is an astonishing thing that no past genealogical or
delimiting factors or other aspects of embodiment have allergy
for breath. In fact, our breath is cherished and relished by all
those. Breath is a great catalyst. It is a great counselor in
Shvasa-ayama and it often works to resolve differences and
bring harmony between two or more aspects of the
embodiment.

Shvasa-ayama and Pranayama are great catalytic and
synergistic forces.

All aspects of our embodiment, physical or mental,
Gross or subtle, phenomenal or noumenal,
look to align with the breath in Shvasa-ayama or
Pranayamic processes.

Most importantly, the breath initiates and then converts
the different aspects of embodiment and instates a breathified

condition, as suggested earlier. The breathing of Shvasayama and Pranayama have great leadership qualities.

Often, in worshipful and meditative acts (that is Puja and Dhyana), *Dhoop* or *agarbattis* (incense sticks) are burnt to drive away evil forces from around us; the breathing of shvasayama and pranayama does the same in our mind, psyche, consciousness and chitta. It makes the mind stuff sanctified and cosmic.

Just as the camphor burns, the passions, tendencies and ahankar in puja worldliness get consumed as if breathing is fire itself. All dark clouds of rajas and tamas are cleared for subjective luminosity to blaze forth. To spell out the effect of Pranayama. Patanjali says, तत: क्षीयते प्रकाशावरणम् ।2।52

This helps vaporise the mundanity, materialism and worldliness of life which often overwhelms us.

The Shvasayamic and Pranayamic breathing has tremendous seepage in the entire embodiment. It can get into our corpuscular particles and even the fibres of our psyche, and then transmute, transfigure and transport the yogi to sublime, superconscious states. The yogi can escape not only terrestrial gravity but even the gravity of this universe and experience what mysticism calls,

"Nishprapanchikarana."

Through the practices of Shvasayama, a seeker can easily experience trans-personal and transcendent conditions and taste a sublime, philosophized and cosmicalised culture. The *naishkarmya* attitude sets in the persona of the Bhakti-yogi.

Chapter : 5

PRANAYAMA BEGINS WITH SHVASAYAMA

Ayama is regulation and it entails some education, training and experiment and even some exercises. Pranayama is greatly breath-related.Thus Pranayama training begins with breath usages, conditionings and regulations. Pranayama regulations are to be learnt in and by the breath. Thus, Pranayama invariably commences with Shvasayama. By Shvasayama or Pranayama we mean,

> *Regulation of the breath*
> *OR*
> *Regulated breathing*
> *OR*
> *Breath regulation.*

But then do we merely look for conditioning and regulating or controlling the breath and breathing or do we want to be regulated by breathing and breath?

> *The answer is, "Of course we want both*
> *to be done, but primarily*
> *the latter than the former."*

Thus we need to learn two aspects, that is
1) We, regulating/controlling the breathing and
2) We, getting regulated by breathing.
Secondly, how far and in what way do we want to control

the breathing or be controlled by the breathing and in what way and to what extent do we want to regulate the breathing and be regulated by the breathing? Even a little deliberation tells us that we are primarily expected to go for regulating-regulated conditions than controlled and controlling conditions. Now let us consider the concept of regulation, because that is "ayama."There are three aspects of this:

1) Regulator
2) Regulated
3) Regulating.

The teachers in Pranayama must make the student aware of these three entities, functions and acts. In the following two propositions one must decipher the three entities and ascertain their role, function and act.

1) "I am regulating breathing."
2) "I am regulated by breathing."

Proposal 1 : Here the breath is regulated and the pronoun 'I' with its auxiliaries is the regulator, and movement, motion, mobilization and application of the body-mind-breath complex is the instrumental entity/body exercising the act of regulating.

Proposal 2 : Breath and the allied forces are regulators, the body-mind-breath complex is instrumental and the Pronoun 'I', the subjective entity, is regulated.

In both cases, the preliminaries mentioned in chapter 3 must be observed. The entire embodiment is breathicated, breathified and breath-logged. The body-mind complex has a breath stature. The pronoun 'I' too is transfigured and transmuted as well as transpersonalised. By Pranayama, the pronoun 'I' is to be exaltedly sublimated, relaxed, contented, placid, quiet, serene, pure, pious, balanced, equilibrated, silenced, waveless, ripple-less, unalloyed and transparent.

The process really begins with handling and conditioning the breath, making it deeper and voluminous. Then gradually one learns to make it greatly rarified, gentle and tender. Then in the second phase, the breath becomes conditioner and associated body, matter, senses and mind-matter are set right. The 'I" is effectively set right.

It is paramount to be breath-sensitive. The teachers must make the students observe the natural, mechanical and normal breathing in breath sensitive locations such as the nasal area. The nostrils and area around must also be monitored. The in-breath and the out-breath must be closely felt in relation to nose, nostrils and proximal part. One must be able to judge the velocity, pattern, density, volume and range while breathing in normal and mechanical ways; gradually one can make marginal variations to learn the regulation of breath by the other aspects as well as the rest by the breath.

One must be familiar with the normal, involuntary breathing, then normal conditions, voluntary breathing and marginally modified breathing either in velocity or volume.

"In quack teachings, teachers propose deep breathing because deep and advertant breathing itself has been considered as Pranayama."

Great amount of Pranayama can take place in the range of normal breathing rather than deeper breathing.

The deeper breathing is about 3, 4 or 5 times the normal range.

It is better and advisable to go with a graduated process than by a fast leap.

The point is that breath-regulations should be learnt in the range of normal breathing rather than deep one. There is something like

"Voluntarily-conditioned, normal breathing."

This is unsighted by quack teachers and practitioners. It is quite an exercise to be doing advertant, normal breathing for successive cycles. So also another preliminary exercise is replicated normal breathing. This too is quite a challenging exercise. There is a lot of education in respect of regulation here.

It is important to have a breath-observative attitude, because without such an attitude, regulation is a far-fetched idea.

One must as a preliminary exercise make attempts for observing normal, involuntary, mechanical and habitual breathing. And then characteristically define it in terms of its velocity, density and volume pattern. Try to define the acts, responses, effects and consequences sensed in locations such as the nostrils and so on.

For one's convenience, one may only observe exhalations for a while with inhalations confined to the background and alternatively the other way round. This way one can evolve the breath sensitivities and gradually make marginal changes in velocities, then identify changes, qualitatively and quantitatively, in the body matter and mind matter in locations such as nose and the area around the nostrils.

These marginal variations can be effected in either the volume or velocity or the density of breath, and evolve the literacy for the flow of breath. So also, identify changes in acts, effects, conditions and concequences. This can be done in either exhalations or inhalations alternatively. This will evolve sensitivity, observation, literacy for as well as in breath, which will subsequently help the act of regulation.

One gets a very vital training and education in the realm of breath through the above-mentioned process. It teaches breath-handling skills. Regulatory technique and culture finds this training and education very fruitful. It is also an education of management of, by, in, on and with the breath and breathing. These are studies in the normal breath range. Subsequently, one can carry out comparative studies with marginal changes in velocity, volume and density of breath.

After studies in and around the nasal area, one can later on carry out the same studies and experiments with reference to the chest region, diaphragmatic region and the abdominal-pelvic region.

Once sufficient training has taken place in the above-mentioned ways in shavasana, one can attempt it in a sitting position. The breath additionally can be referred to in the back and spine. However, one should not at all hasten to take up the preliminaries of Pranayama and Shvasayama in the seated position because:

Body attendance becomes very prominent in the seating position. Shavasana or supine positions facilitate relaxation in a big way and help us overcome the difficult condition of maintaining straight and steady positions and conditions of body.

Chapter : 6

BASIC LESSONS IN BREATHING CIRCUITS AND THEIR CONSTELLATIONS

Practices of asanas must handle the above perspective with significant preference. This should be one of the perspectives in asanas – keeping Pranayama and Shvasayama in view. The asanas posturally have a classification such as:

> *STANDING POSTURES*
> *SEATING POSTURES*
> *PRONE-POSITIONED POSTURES*
> *SUPINE-POSITION POSTURES*
> *FORWARD BENDING POSTURES*
> *BACK BENDING POSTURES*
> *TWISTING ROTATING POSTURES*
> *LATERALLY BENDING POSTURES*
> *INVERTED POSTURES*
> *HAND–BALANCING POSTURES*
> *LIMB MOVEMENT POSTURES*
> *TRUNK MOVEMENT POSTURES*
> *KINETIC POSTURES*
> *STEADY POSTURES etc.*

In all these various postures in asanas, one must observe the usage, application, addressals, circuits and constellation of breath in highlighted conditions. One must attempt inscriptive and heavy-duty, i.e. deeper breathing. One will discover a marvel of breath circuits and constellations. One will develop a very rich repertoire of breathing. Similarly, there are different breath usages, applications, constellations and circuits in various body conditions with reference to postures. These are:

EXTENSIONS
ELONGATIONS
STRETCHINGS
CONTRACTIONS
SQUEEZES
ROTATIONS
MOVEMENTS
MOTIONS
MOBILIZATIONS
STEADINESS
STURDINESS
SOFTNESS
HARDNESS
CONVEXING
NARROWING
WIDENING
THICKENING
THINNING etc.

In each of the above cases there are fascinating breath usages, applications, addressals on the postures as well as by the postures. Asanas, thus, are great conditions to carry out breath studies. These have great educative appeal for Pranayama and Shvasayama. The teacher can and must make students aware of this. The teacher must make the students aware of the breathing constellations and circuits in asanas, ranging from kinetic to static conditions.

Just as it is important to be steady in body conditions, in asanas it is also important to have steady, constant and replicated breathing cycles which create a constellation and circuitry. Basically, breath handling is an important aspect in asanas and must be given its due importance.

This will ultimately prove to be a strong preparatory for Pranayama and Shvasayama.

It must be imbibed through the asana practice and study that the breath and breathing is a prolific and versatile force, quite an all-rounder. It almost works with magical and astonishing versatility, has amazing access, penetration in body and even in mind. It is a highly influencing factor with which to work on

> *PHYSICAL*
> *SKELETO-MUSCULAR*
> *CELLULAR*
> *PHYSIOLOGICAL, ORGANIC body,*

And then, even the senses, mind, brain, consciousness, psyche etc. It also effectively works for

> *CONATIVE*
> *COGNITIVE*
> *SENSITIVE*
> *PERCEPTIVE*
> *MENTAL*
> *EMOTIONAL and*
> *INTELLECTUAL*

components in asanas. It is for its prolific versatility that the breath engenders a condition such as being regulating and being regulated.

Thus the neophyte asana practitioner has a great disillusionment and at the same time an invaluable revelation that

"Breathing is not merely for our
living but is a major instrument

and even a spear-heading force for all our activities such as physical, mental, emotional, intellectual, voluntary and even the enriched-response system.

One can discover a strong bond between
'breath and mind.'

As the *Hathayog Pradipika* says,

"Steady breath has steady mind
and
Unsteady breath has unsteady mind."

The science of yog has a theorem, which is

"Quiet mind, disquiet mind
Agitated mind, placid mind
Blissful mind, agonized mind
Serene mind, turbulent mind
Have a corresponding breath;
so also sorrowful and
Delighted mind or every mood
and shade of mind has a
corresponding breath.

Thus, to tackle the chitta (the total mind-stuff), the breath is dealt with by making it

Solar, Lunar (Ida-Pingala)
Central (Sushumna)
Earthy
Watery
Fiery

Airy
Ethereal
Muladharic
Svadhisthanic
Manipurakic
Anahatiya
Vishuddhik
Ajnachakrikric Pranayama.

Chapter : 7

THE BASIC CONCEPT OF SHARIRAYAMA-SHVASAYAMA-MANAYAMA

Pranayama or Shvasayama (or so-called Pranayama) is constituted by three *ayamas* (regulations). They are :

1) Shareerayama
2) Shvasayama
3) Manayama.

In practical and procedural aspect, the negotiations have these three aspects. The classical and traditional Pranayama considers these. But for today's 'pop-yog', these aspects will be beyond imagination. What we have today is "consumer yog", that is

Breath control and
and breath regulations
are considered as Pranayama.
What is practiced today as
Pranayama should better
be called "Shvasayama."
Modern masters must put a question
as to why the so-called Pranayama
should not be called Shvasayama.

Thus, what is being clearly postulated is that

"Shvasayama is not Pranayama."

But in any case, Shvasayama is an important component in learning Pranayama. The Shvasa-kriya in yogasanas greatly contributes in learning Shvasayama, which can virtually become Pranayama.

Having gone through the preliminaries (Chapter 3), the prana, the breath gets substance like (fluid) and does not remain a gaseous element once it enters into our embodiment. It becomes a compound substance having the flow and seepage of a liquid. It becomes a chemical substance and thus can effect bio-chemical changes in us. This compound chemical, that is the breath substance, can now give a touchstone effect to the body. The body is transformed and transmuted into a status called "Kshetra"(mentioned in the 13th chapter of the *Bhagvadgita*). The metaphysical principle of Atma and Antaryamin Ishvara is enshrined in this *Kshetra*.

In Shareerayama, the breath sets right, addresses, transforms and transmutes the associated body. Breath becomes an internal tool and substance to address and culture the associated body. The teachers need to elaborate on the kriyas of breath by conditioning volume, velocity, density, confinement, deploying the breath modes and functions, the graphic modes, breath designs etc. These will be explained in chapters to come.

In asanas itself, one learns to address the associated body by breath and breathing. The breath is a prolific internal agency system, almost like an internal limb and tool system, which also works as an incredible conditioner of body matter.

"Associated breath and breath-led, breath-coated breath dynamics are awesome."

Here, the associated breath and essentially breathified, composite dynamics are to be used as conditioners and regulators of body matter. This is called Shareerayama.

It is absurd to believe that Pranayama can have an unregulated body.

Thus, Shareerayama is important. In Shavasana, the body must lie quiet, serene, ennobled, sublimated, sanctified, aligned and in a well-settled condition. The body needs a regulation for such conditions. Thus,

"when breath and breath-led
dynamics set right, compose, settle,
align, sublimate, ennoble, cosmicalise and pranicise
the body, it is called "SHAREERAYAMA."

One can easily understand that Shareerayama is integral to Pranayama.

So also it can be easily conceived that Shareerayama is vitally important in seating Pranayama.

Pranayama does not tolerate or put up with a steady, erect body merely as a posture. The postural kriyas must facilitate free trafficking of breath and increase seepage and permeation of breath.

Merely a posturally firm, steady, straight and erect body in pranayama is akin to a pot which needs to be filled but is kept upside down under a tap. In Pranayama, if the body is like a sponge then the breath should be like water.

Kneaded condition

For Pranayama, it is necessary to have a kneaded condition in the embodiment. This condition is a preparatory one. The embodiment needs to be breath-profuse or *"Shvasa maya"*. Now what is the kneaded condition here?

The body-mind-breath matters need to get kneaded together like the act of making chappatis (leavened bread). To prepare chappatis, the wheat flour, water and oil need to be kneaded by deft strokes of the hand and fingers. From this dough, the chappatis are turned out. Similarly in Pranayama, there is the preparatory, kneading act, which can be described as strokes of body-mind-breath actions.

Through this 'kneading act', the breath and mind become

integrally one with the body matter which then becomes the 'associated body.'

Here, it is important to understand that the flour, water and oil are not substances which naturally blend or jel together; they are not in fact mixable; they cannot get together at all. Flour is a powdery matter and water and oil are opposite in nature. However, by the marvel that is the kneading act, the dough is produced. This dough is such a composite, unified matter that one can identify neither the powdery flour nor water nor the sticky oil inside. It is the kneading act which has turned out the fourth matter – the dough.

Such a phenomenal act in the embodiment precedes Pranayama.

The body-matter now is the dough of body-breath-mind matter. Such an 'associated body' is addressed in Shareerayama; this associated body is set right or conditioned in Shareerayama.

Let us now get introduced to "Manayama." Manayama means addressing, settling, comparing, setting right, conditioning and cosmicalising the surface mind or peripheral mind. The breath must be able to handle the psycho-mental state. The breath in its associated condition and kneaded condition is a great conditioner of this surface mind. The teachers must impart this training by making students use a profound and unusual volume of exhalation. Such a deep exhalation will invariably make one aware of and help objectify the mind.

There is a theorem in the science of yog :

The fag end of exhalation is the beginning of subjective mind.

An extraordinary depth of exhalation divinises (explores) mineral consciousness or mineral mind.

Mineral mind (or consciousness) is a concept like mineral water. As such water is to be found at deeper planes, similarly such a mind or consciousness is to be found in deeper planes of body or the embodiment. This mind is found or explored or felt in a profound deeper inwardliness and infacedness called "*antarmukhi*" in Adhyatmic psychology.

Voluminous exhalations help access the mind. Then there is the second aspect, the velocity. The breath can be explored in a range from normal involuntary and mechanical to deep breathing. Similarly, one has to work for mind addressals. The teachers must, therefore, induct students to this fact. The breath (exhalations) can be confined to regions like the:

Brain
Throat
Chest
Diaphragm
Abdomen
Pelvis and
Perinium.

Then there are spot locations such as eyes, mouth, sternum, breast, navel etc. These exercises will develop the mind-related sensitivities. Then there are the aerodynamics of exhalations which work as mind conditioners. These are the basic graphic modes such as :

Cylindrical
Obverse conical / Triangular
Reverse conical /Triangular
Circular
Spiral etc.

These exercises need to be imparted repeatedly. Thus by volume, velocity, confinement, graphic modes and aerodynamics, one can use the exhalations as mind conditioners.

Mind conditioning or regulating and sublimating
is one of the most important purposes in all
dynamics and de-dynamics of yog, and the
breath-led or breath-major process
is of paramount importance.

Yog has made a great discovery that breath, breathing and Pranayama are superlative conditions of mind. Shvasayama and Pranayama marvellously work on the various facets of mind such as

> *Body-related or body-rooted mind*
> *Physiology related mind*
> *Organ-related mind*
> *Sense-related mind*
> *Nerve-related mind*
> *Gland-related mind*
> *Brain-related mind*
> *Chakra-related mind*
> *Tattva-related mind*
> *Tendency-related mind.*

The mind, psyche, consciousness, mind-stuff (chitta) are accessed, addressed, and cultured by breath. This is essentially done by addressing skin, flesh, muscles, bones, cells, tissues, fibres, organs, senses, glands, nerves, vessels, nadis, chakras and granthis or the exoteric to esoteric body with the penetration and seepage of 'associated breath' and shvasayamic and Pranayamic breath.

> *Shvasayama can work on the surface body,*
> *mind, anatomy and psychology.*
> *But Pranayama can work on the esoteric*
> *body, chakras, tattvas, granthis and thus*
> *on Karmas-Kleshas- Vasanas – the*
> *metaphysical matter as well as the*
> *meta-psychological mind in the embodiment.*

A beginner too can experience this enchanted state; one can effectively access and sublimate the peripheral mind by relating the breath to the senses such as

> *Eyes*
> *Ears*
> *Nose*
> *Throat (root of the tongue)*
> *Skin*

These are Jnanendriyas such as :

> *Visual organ*
> *Auditory organ*
> *Gustatory organ*
> *Olfactory organ*
> *Tactile organ.*

This is called psycho-sensory mind in modern psychology and it is the greater part of psycho-mental mind.

> *Thus, Manayama is a major negotiation*
> *in Shvasayama and Pranayama and the*
> *teacher can make the student aware of it*
> *and give sufficient training for literacy*
> *to develop such negotiating skills.*

Finally, here we need to consider Shvasayama as a concept. One must learn to use the 'associated breath' for setting right the breath itself. One must be given sufficient orientation so that one is not confounded by the statement or proposition that

> *"Breath sets right the breath."*

When the breath is in a status called associated breathing and even body as 'associated body' and mind in 'associated mind,' the mutually well- connected, well-coordinated, well carried out subserserviencies and community culture in embodiment open out fresh vistas of probabilities and possibilities. One should realise that Shvasayama and Pranayama consist of the following propositions:

1) *"I am setting right, addressing, culturing, conditioning and regulating my body-matter by breath-major dynamics."*

2) *"I am setting right breath (system) by breath-led dynamics."*

3) *"I am setting right or conditioning, sublimating my mind by breath led dynamics."*

Thus the concepts of Shareerayama, Shvasayama and Manayama become greatly important.

Finally, a word about yog's incredible discovery about our complex mind - It is imperative to understand that Pranayama and Shvasayama consider and negotiate the different mental sheaths. We have within us the :

1) *Physical mind*
2) *Organic, physiological mind.*
3) *Brainal (psychological) mind*
4) *Mental mind*
5) *Sensory mind*
6) *Emotional mind*
7) *Hearty mind*
8) *Intellectual mind*
9) *Tendency mind*
10) *Egomind*
11) *Chakrik, pranic mind*
12) *Elemental (pancha- tattvas) mind*
13) *Transmigrating mind*
14) *Divinised mind*

Hope you realise that there is a great amount of conditioning involved. Let us now proceed to open out the topic of regulating, regulator and regulation.

❖❖

Chapter : 8

THE TRIAD OF REGULATION

It is worth noting that Yog is restraint of chitta and seems to be predominantly mind-control. However, Yog does not speak about mind- control, neither does it speak of mind regulation nor sensory control which seems to be a very important point as well. When it comes to controlling or regulation, the science of Yog only speaks about "ayama" of prana.

Yog mentions and speaks about Pranayama which is the regulation of Prana thus implying the regulation of breath. This means:

"By regulating "this one", all the rest are regulated in the embodiment."

"Breath and Prana regulations on the 'I' circumscribe all regulations in the embodiment."

As mentioned earlier, in Pranayama and Shvasayama, there are two aspects:

"I am regulating the breath"
and
"I am regulated by the breath."

Thus, there are dual aspects in Pranayama or Shvasayama. But more importantly, we need to understand the triad in the above-mentioned statements. There is a subjective entity or noun, verb and predicate. Syntactically, no sentence is complete without a noun, verb and predicate. Now, in the two propositions above, there are three aspects and three conditions.

Secondly, when there is something like conditioning, there are three aspects to be considered:

1) Conditioner
2) Conditioned
3) Conditioning.

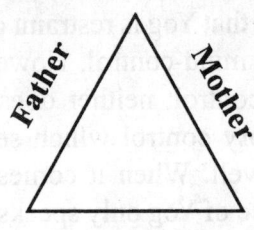

Child

This word is like a triangle with three corners.

Similar is the case of 'ayama' conditionings.There are Ayamaka, Ayamit, Ayaman or Niyamaka, Niyamita, Niyamana or conditioner, conditioned and conditioning. This again is a triangle as shown below.

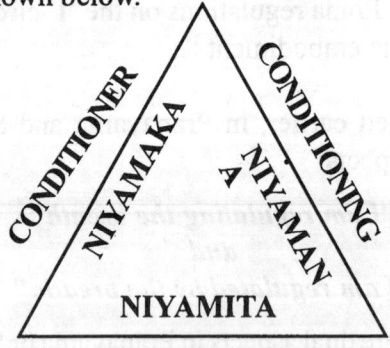

CONDITIONED

Thus, there are three aspects of Pranayama or Shvasayama being such conditioners. Now, let us understand that the pronoun "I" has to go through three phases. The first one is its subjective entity where the proposition is:

Pranayama is being done on ME,

where the Pronoun "I" becomes the beneficiary because it is being set right or addressed.

The other one is:

I am doing pranayama.

Here, the pronoun "I" will be a benefactor or conditioner. The other probability will be that "I" (body-mind complex) will be an agency to set right breath or shvasa or prana. Thus, the "I" will become an instrumental entity. Thus the proposition in the third case will be

"I" (as an instrument) am conditioning/addressing breath or Prana.

Now, let us understand the above scenario with the following table.

CONDITIONER	CONDITIONING	CONDITIONED
1) Pronoun "I"	Pronoun "I"	Pronoun "I"
2) Breath/Prana	Breath/Prana	Breath/Prana
3) Body-mind Complex (Mine)	Body-mind Complex (Mine)	Body-mind Complex (Mine)

Thus we have three aspects, namely,

1) "I" (Pronoun)
2) Breath, prana
3) Rest of 'mine'

All these three need to go through all the three roles, namely, conditioner, conditioned and conditioning. This will give some basic idea of the dynamics involved in Shvasayama or Pranayama. If we ascertain the three entities which are

1) Subjective entity, that is pronoun "I"
2) Rest of "Mine" (body, mind, Psyche)
3) Breath and prana.

Those three have to mutually play a role of conditioner, conditioned and conditioning in relation to each other. These roles have to be rolling and rotating, with each playing the role of the other. This is what the above table is suggesting. They have to, in rotation, play a role of subjective, objective and instrumental entities. In other words:

Pranayama/Shvasayama must take place by rotation:

"by me"
"on me"
"for me."

The "I" must play all the three roles, namely, subjective entity, objective entity and instrumental entity. Strangely the condition

"I have done pranayama"
or
"I am doing pranayama"
or
"I shall be doing pranayama"
or
"I will have done pranayama"
or
"I did pranayama"

are all cases of "No pranayama". There is a greater probability of Pranayama in case the condition is

"Pranayama was done by me"
or
Pranayama was done on "I".

One must try to understand this intriguing and astonishing condition. It might be staggering for some or astounding to some.

A learner, neophyte and student must understand the dynamics, processes and implications of the following proposals which must be rendered by the seeker and student.

"I have done pranayama"
"I have got done pranayama"
"Pranayama was done by me"
"Pranayama was done on me"
"Pranayama was done for me "
"Pranayama was done by me"
"Pranayama was done in me. "

In each of the above cases, dynamics, process, procedure, set-ups, constitutions and nuances must be studied.

The teachers must understand their skills and responsibilities apart from being authentically and classically trained or formally trained practitioners. Teaching is one thing where one has to develop skills over and above just being able to do something well. A good practitioner may not necessarily be a competent teacher. Quacks are rampant today.

Since there was a reference to the "I"here, the following consideration too is important: locus of "I" in (Pranayama).

We are used to relate our "I" to body or mind or mind in a mundane condition. When relating it to the body, we have the following expressions:

I am fat / thin
I am strong /weak
I am well / unwell
I am short /tall etc.

While referring and relating it to mind, we have expressions such as:

I am delighted / sorrowful
I am happy / sad
I am intelligent / stupid
I am quiet / not quiet
I am agitated / passive etc.

But here, we are supposed to have an associated, kneaded, integrated and unified condition in me, mine and breath as seen earlier. The associated or kneaded or composite "I" can be related to

> *1) Associated body or composite body*
> *2) Associated mind or composite mind*
> *3) Associated breath or composite breath.*

These are respectively Shvasayama or Pranayama as under:

> *1) Body–sensitivity culture*
> *2) Mind–sensitivity culture*
> *3) Breath–sensitivity culture.*

Genuine and essential Pranayama or even Shvasayama is done in breathified, breathicated and breath-profused "I". It is this breath persona being imbibed that we have seen in an earlier chapter (4th).

Let us come back to to our triad. We have to characterise the regulator, regulated and regulating. We need to understand their

> *Characterisation*
> *Attributes*
> *Profiles*
> *Qualities*
> *Qualifications*
> *Constitutions*
> *Assisting factors etc.*

Now, let us consider the 'regulator' as a persona. The regulator is like an administrator, controller and ruler. Thus we can understand what qualities, capacities and capabilities it must have. It will further manifest leadership powers, rights, responsibilities, liabilities, privileges, status, stature, personality, profile etc. thus acquiring a governing status and machinery. Even the voice, gestures and mannerisms are to be accounted for, so is attire and appearance.

Jocularly speaking, will we ever come to take seriously an administrator clad in a vest and pajamas, or tolerate a police sergeant appearing in the garb of a pujari (priest), clad in dhoti, uttaraya, a tuft and a mark on the forehead.

So the entity in question requires an effective personality, which includes credentials, qualification, leadership and the whole effective machinery as well as a commanding position.

The regulated then must be a subordinate and demonstrate subserviency against the superiority of the leader. We must be prepared to be administered.

The psyche must learn to accept the regulations of the regulator.

The regulation must be suitable to the conditioner and the conditioned. Also, appropriate tools must be selected and constituted by considering the characteristics, attributes and functions of the conditioner as well as the state of the conditioned or regulated.

For example, a police inspector would need a whistle, a baton and/or a pistol etc. A postmaster or a school teacher would not need those.

Similarly, there are differences between a military officer or an administrator and a political representative or governor and between a CEO of a corporate body and an educational centre such as a university.

Let us now come to the scenario in question:

1) Associated breath as regulator and 'I' or associated mind as regulated;
2) Associated breath as regulator and associated mine (body) as regulated;
3) Associated 'I' (mind) as regulator and breath as regulated;
4) Associated "I" (mind) as regulator and mine (body) as regulated;
5) Associated body (mine) as regulator and the associated breath as regulated;
6) Associated body (mine) as regulator and associated 'I'(mind) as regulated;

These are six kinds of negotiations in Shareerayama, Manayama and Shvasayama. It must be understood that there are separate constitutions of regulation in each of the above six scenarios. The same machinery or set-up cannot be used in all or any of the other cases.

The 'I' will have to assume position in all the three positions such as regulator, regulated and regulation.

Similarly, the associated breath or prana,

will have to work in three positions, namely: regulator, regulated and regulating.

Similar is the case of associated mine (body and mind), which will have to be in the three modes of regulator, regulated and regulation.

One must consider such nuances as:

Breath regulating the "I" and mine
The "I" regulating the rest of mine and breath
The "mine" regulating the "I" and breath.

In each of the three cases, there are basic differences in culture and mode of regulations. We can with a little introspection, understand the cultural repertoire of

Regulator
Regulated
Regulation.

This implies a profound and extensive education to be a versatile and proficient 'regulator, regulated and regulating'. The process of getting educated itself works very substantially for 'man-making for Adhyatma.'

'It can be said that, here, there is everything
From baby-handling to scoundrel-handling.'

For instance, when it comes to regulating the breath itself, it can be like a tender new-born baby. It could be very delicate like an infant. Breath is never pig-headed or mulish or perverted. On the other hand, regulating body-matter might be dealing with the rough and tough and regulating the mind might be quite tricky.

An elephant may require quite a different handling from, say a cow.

There is a big difference between managing a crowd of university students versus a crowd of school children.

The mode, culture and processes change and that needs to be observed.

Yet, it is not as complicated as it may appear because of the breathified and breath-headed condition of the embodiment, a prerequisite condition for both Shvasayama and Pranayama.

Finally, we should consider the triad of:

REGULATOR—REGULATED—REGULATING
AND
BENEFACTOR—BENEFICIARY— BENEFIT
AND
SUBJECTIVE—OBJECTIVE—
INSTRUMENTAL ENTITIES.

Secondly, each of these has the three constituents with varied constitutions. Because of kneaded and associated conditions, we come to the following equations with changes in proportions.

1) REGULATOR = Associated body + associated mind + associated breath
2) REGULATED = associated body + associated mind + associated breath
3) REGULATING = associated body + associated breath + associated mind.

However, the proportions will change in six of the scenarios listed above and earlier. They will be reset for each role and purpose.

Thus, the proportions of the constituents will change the constitution.

To elucidate the above, take the example of a beverage like tea. The ingredients of tea are water, milk, tea leaves and sugar. Suppose a regular cup of tea contains $3/4^{th}$ water, $\frac{1}{4}$ milk, one teaspoon of tea leaves and two spoons of sugar. Now, how will it taste if the cup now contains three spoons of tea leaves and 1 spoon of sugar, $\frac{1}{4}^{th}$ cup water and $\frac{1}{4}^{th}$ cup of milk; or if the cup contains $4/5^{th}$ of milk, $1/5^{th}$ of water, 5 spoons of sugar and one tea leaf?

These different cups of tea can taste like

1) Tea
2) Bitter medicine, like **kadha** *or*
3) Almost honey-like **basundi.**

Different proportions can turn out different substances, from bitter to sweet to tasteless to water to milky proportions of

Associated body
Associated mind

Associated breath
OR
Regulator body/ mind/breath
Regulated body / mind/ breath
Regulating body /mind/ breath.

The next point is that the regulator, when it is the leader, requires communication apart from other qualifications like qualities, credentials, machinery, status, etc. Communication is very important here and communication depends upon factors such as:

1) Who is regulating whom and why,
2) Conditions of conditioner and conditioned,
3) The available machinery,
4) The purpose of conditioning etc.

A police force controlling two million Varakharis (devotees) at Pandharpur on *Ashadhi Ekadashi* exercises a different control than a force interrogating hardened criminals. It is important to understand culture and communication as factors to be considered here. Now, let us come to our scenario:

"I" am doing pranayama,

where "I" is breathified and the rest of "mine" is breathified, too. Now, how will the "I"have culture and communication when associated body is being governed? And how will that "I" regulate associated breath and associated mind? In each of the three cases, the profile, culture, mode, consideration and negotiation of "I" will be changing, which will influence the communicative mode, means, language, dialect, semantics, voice, figures of speech and rhetorics in silent SPEECH (Vachika Kriya in Pranayama or Shvasayama). Basically, "I"(mind) will have a different kind of communication with associated body and associated breath.

In Shvasayama, when the breath is regulator, and the associated body and associated mind is regulated, the whole package will again change:

Language
Dialect
Communicative mode
Semantics
Rhetorics
Figures of speech
Word selection diction etc.

Then, when the associated body is regulator, and breath and mind are regulated, again there will be a turn around in:

Communication
Culture
Language
Dialect
Communicative mode
Semantics
Rhetorics
Figures of speech
Word selection diction etc.

To understand the regulator, regulated, regulating here, we must accord a persona and accord a figuration or characterisation or imaging and imagining. This triad of regulation is akin to the field of dramaturgy; with its roles and enactments involving dialogue, direction, design etc.

Basically, regulator, regulated and regulating are enactments (character roles) for effective communication and something like 'dramatisation.'

Let us now highlight each of these aspects starting with the 'language' aspect in accomplishing Shvasayama and Pranayama.

Chapter : 9

THREE-LANGUAGE FORMULA

In the previous chapter, we indentified the communicative implications in Shvasayama or Pranayama as being an endeavour of regulation. There is a Vachika kriya or an oratory act, which is silent. Communication is usually a two-way process. But because of the 'ayama' being a triad of regulation, there will also be three-language formula.

1. When body-led governor is in governance, there will be a 'body language'that will initiate the communication;
2. When breath-led governor is in governance, there will be a breath language;
3. And when the mind-led governor is in governance, there will be a mind language.

It must be recalled that body, mind and breath will be in a kneaded and associated condition. When the "I" is in governance, there will be one language and when the 'me' (body) is regulator, there will be body language or when the 'me' (mind) is regulating there will be another language; when the breath is regulating, there will be breath language.

There will be three languages because of the three regulators. Hence, the concept of the three-language formula.

We need to understand that when the body is being regulated, there will be some peculiar considerations. There will be a set of considerations, outlooks, priorities and negotiations. While when the breath is regulated, there will be a radically different set of considerations, outlooks, priorities and negotiations. Then there will be a third set when the mind will be regulated.

Basically in Shvasayama or Pranayama,
It is not the case of technically doing ujjayi,
viloma, anuloma,
pratiloma, nadi shodhana, chandrabhedana,
suryabhedana, sheetali etc. but it is all about
regulation and conditioning/s.

Thus, communication and the act of regulating become paramount.

The popular belief that these various Pranayama are done by specific technical modes are naive.

Now, coming to the body-language, here it is not as it literally means. It is not a case of body gestures. It means:

'What the body has to speak (silently)
in Shvasayama or Pranayama to "I", "me" "mine"
(body, mind and breath).

Body (associated) will have its considerations and port-holes with its own set of communications with body and mind as well as breath (all associated).

Thus, what body (associated) speaks and how it silently speaks in the act of governance is 'body-language' here. What the breath speaks and how it speaks silently in the act of governance, is 'breath language' here, and what and how the mind speaks in the act of governance is 'mind language' here.

The practitioner should ask: can the the governor-regulator be dumb and mute? Thus, language and (silent) oration are important considerations here; communication, dialogue, articulation, speech (silent) semantics and oratory skills or diction and voice culture (silent) are all very important.

When language is considered, then dialect, too, becomes important. In the case of body-language, the way it addresses the body, breath or mind will be different. In each case, there will be a different dialect for the way it speaks to body, breath or mind when in governance. Same is the case with mind language. The way it speaks to body or breath or mind will be changing in the act of governance. Thus we will have three different dialects.

Basically, the three languages entail nine dialects in pursuit of regulation or governance in Shvasayama or Pranayama.

All this is by education and training with respect to usages, applications and addressals of the breath and by the breath. The following chapter will induct us into this aspect.

Chapter : 10

GRAPHIC MODES OF BREATHING

In Pranayama or Shvasayama, there are major usages, applications of the breath to set right the embodiment or "I", "me" and "mine." Apart from volume, velocity, density, confinement, modulators which we have considered on an earlier occasion, now we shall also consider different graphic modes. These become conditions of mind, psyche and consciousness. A student or initiate must be taught to draw certain idiographic forms, which become graphic modes.

Just as an artist or painter draws graphic
sketches with pencil or pen or a brush,
the cellular embodiment must be taught
to use the breath as pencil and the body-mind
as a canvas or drawing paper.
The breath will be used as a pencil
for certain graphic modes.

Usually, deep breathing is taught as up-down movements as if they are 'sit-ups of breathing.'

It is quite strange to expect peace of mind by making breath carry out sit-ups. But if one drives breath in different separate tracts for in-breath and out-breath in the anterior and posterior sides of the spine, then it will have different potentials. This will mean drawing oval-shaped circles by our breathing.

'Cyclic breathing can have hypnotic

*effects on the mind which can easily
pacify (or passivate) the mind.'*

There are very basic, primary and simple graphic modes in breath. Basically in shvasayama/pranayama, the breathing is not done.But breath is in 'drive.'

There are basic graphic modes for both, exhalations and inhalations or breathing cycles.

Initially, these must be ideally tried either in exhalations or inhalations. Say, for exhalations (which must be used at the outset), there might be circular graphic modes as well as oval-shaped oblong circles. These may be along the spine or across the spine. One is expected to cast the circle in ways mentioned above by the exhalative breath which is slowly conditioned to be cast in that shape/way. There may be multiple circles drawn in each exhalations or just one such circle by a whole exhalation. Later, it may be tried in inhalation as well.

Diagraphically, it may be shown like this:

The next mode is either columnar or cylindrical in shape. Exhalatatively it may be cast in stages of exhalations or in one go. The breath can come down as columns where the breath will have two dimensions such as width and length. In the case of a three-dimensional mode, it would be cylindrical exhalations as shown below.

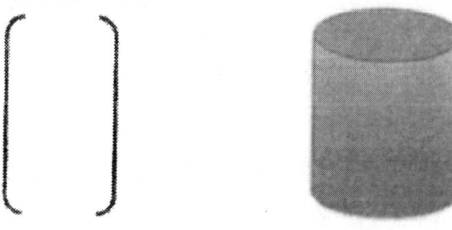

The third basic mode is triangular (obverse) with apex up and base down. This too can be in stages (preferably) and in one go (optionally). This will be stereoscopic exhalation. For two hands of the triangle, there will be a base line.

This may be better called as obverse-reverse conical exhalation/s. The diagraphic mode will be as shown below.

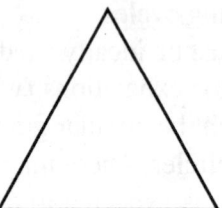

When it is done in multiple stages, the pattern could be like a coniferous tree as shown below.

This can be turned upside down and made reverse triangular or reverse conical; the graphic mode patterns are shown below.

Then, there are other graphic patterns, such as spiral or  in the shape of a rhombus (*Shankarpali*) **as shown** here.

 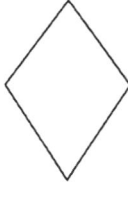

Then comes the concepts of 'breathworkart' or 'breath art' or 'breath craft'; just as there are arts and crafts and calligraphy, here too there can be:

> ***Breath craft***
> ***Breath art***
> ***Breathography***
> ***Breath drawing.***

Since these are all breath-driven modes, one can surmise that there are:

> ***Breath drives***
> ***Breath driving***
> ***Breath driver***
> ***Breath vehicles***
> ***Breath paths (routes) and***
> ***Breath ways.***

Since there is breath driving, there is a need for qualification and skill; so also some trials, attempts, practices and experiments are needed to attain control as well as skill. In case of breath navigation, for all practical purposes, it requires Uddiyana Kriya in breathing.

> ***'Pranayamic breathing implies and entails the***
> ***Uddiyana kriya in both, inhalation and exhalation,***

and for them to become Puraka and Rechaka respectively. Thus, the Kumbhaka makes the Uddiyana kriya and mudra mandatory, without exception.

Now we come to the topic of Uddiyama Kriya for Shvasayama and Pranayama breathing.

Chapter : 11

BREATHING OF
UDDIYANA KRIYA

Almost all the books on Yog make mention of Uddiyana, uddiyana mudra and uddiyana kriya. This kriya is mentioned, taught and practiced as if it is the one and only kriya in practical Yog. There is a mention of asanas, bandhas, mudras, kriyas as the different aspects of yogic technology.

However, most modern tomes on Yog fail to accord a centric position for Uddiyana kriya in Shvasayamic or Pranayamic breathing.

The popular notion is that in Uddiyana, the abdomen is drawn and sucked inward, almost to go flat on the back.This is done after a deep or complete (!) exhalation followed by retention. The abdominal suction is maintained until the retention time. This is called Uddiyana mudra.

The process of suction is Uddiyana kriya and sucked condition during retention (all with respect to the abdomen) is called mudra.

Secondly, the original texts of Yog mention how to do Uddiyana mudra. As a matter of fact, that is also done in case of asanas and Pranayama (as mentioned in *Gheranda Samita, Hathayog Pradipika* or *Yog Samhitas*; however, these texts do not mention how to learn).

However, it is not within the scope Of the classical texts to deal with

the question of how to learn all these things.
This is where tradition, heritage, teacher and Guru
are required. Thus, the legacy and tradition is of
paramount importance.

We are in an unfortunate era where despite our rich heritage, we have a lot of weeds in yog. Quack teachers straight away start teaching how to do various asanas, kriyas, mudras, pranayama and even bandhas and dhyana without tackling the basic question:

"How to learn all those?"
Today any Tom, Dick, and Harry
Can teach any Tom, Dick and Harry.
There are quack teachers who read books
and teach or learn from quacks and teach.
Similarly, Uddiyana is taught. But all this
is nothing but mockery.

Anyway, let us proceed to understand how this Uddiyana was learnt in classical times in a classical way. The textual Uddiyana is usually done in a standing position, standing with feet slightly apart and slightly bent knees, with palms pressed on top of the knees or thighs. Then by slightly hunching the back, an exhalation is done sharply followed by a retention and then sucking the abdomen in. The suction is quite rigorous. But traditionally, the learning process is quite different.

Basically Uddiyana is taught in shvasa kriya of asanas. Particularly the steady postures are used. Uddiyana kriya and mudra is attempted in various, numerous asanas. Those attempts are made in various postures such as,

Standing
Seating
Prone
Supine

Inverted
Lateral bending
Forward bending
Back bending
Rotational etc.

which gives profound education, training and prayoga. One learns the practical negotiations quite profoundly. Variegated dynamics are best learnt that way. Also, Uddiyana is learnt in Prana kriya, Chakrakriya and Tattvakriya in esoteric asanas. All these provide a profound training for Uddiyana. Then, as said earlier, Shvasayama and Pranayama are commenced in supine positions such as *shavasana*. Certain basic breathing exercises are best learnt in supine asanas like suptavirasana, matsyasana, supta swastikasana and supta baddhakonasana.

If uddiyana is attempted in only standing or seated positions, there will be an undue hunch and stoop of the back because of rudimentary conditions in the body; also, the spine is unnecessarily drawn out in such attempts of Uddiyana. Thus, it must be ideally tried in supine positions such as shavasana; here, there is no mal-handling of the back and spine.

As a matter of fact, the kriyas such as Uddiyana, Kapalabhati and Agnisara are best learnt in supine positions, so that there is no back-tampering and spine tampering.

Now, let us consider some basic lessons of Uddiyana kriya and mudra in *shavasana* after extensive orientation and preparations which have taken place in yogasanas.

1) Exhalative Uddiyana kriya

One must settle down in one of the supine positions such

as shavasana and settle down in body, mind and breath in a short while and become steady in that asana. Then, evolve and develop breath awareness and advertence. Become breath conscious, breath sensitive and *breathified*. Thereafter, make a deeper and profound exhalation by supplementary phases. Along with exhalation, one must distend, let go and flatten the abdomen. The abdominal organs too should be deflated. One must learn the correspondence of exhalation and abdominal contraction, suction and deflation. The process of abdominal contraction is called Uddiyana kriya. Basically, along with exhalation and corresponding volume of exhalation, one must learn abdominal deflation.

2) Post-Exhalative Uddiyana kriya

This is the second prayoga or module of uddiyana kriya. Here, one must flush out the exhalation with supplements to complete the possible exhalation. After exhalation, one must start deflating and contracting as well as sucking the abdomen and abdominal organs. This implies retention for uddiyana kriya after the exhalation is over.

3) Inhalative Uddiyana kriya

The uddiyana kriya is commenced with voluntary inhalation. The abdomen goes inwards when the in-breath is taken. Thus the in-going belly and organs are coordinated with the in-going breath. This can be attempted conveniently in every third or fourth breath, which will be a voluntary breath. Those two or three cycles will help recovery and will create a run-up to uddiyana. After the uddiyana kriya ends, one may inhale by relaxing the suction and inhale mechanically and even unconditionally. These are the three basic kriyas of uddiyana.

In the above exercises, one may attempt crescent moon shapes with progressive depth and length. By inhalative and exhalative process, one will learn the uddiyana strokes from bottom to top (inhalative) and top to bottom (exhalative).

4) Pranic Technology in Uddiyana

There is a marvel here. Both, bottom to top strokes of uddiyana and alternately top to bottom strokes can be given in inhalation itself. Thus, both the strokes are possible. Again exhalatively too, there can be both kinds of uddiyana. This is difficult to imagine but easy to execute with pranic technology.

5) Rotary Uddiyana

Inhalations and exhalations can form a circle or orbit and exhalative or inhalative uddiyana phases can be practiced in diagrammatical forms. Some of these sets of diagrams are depicted below.

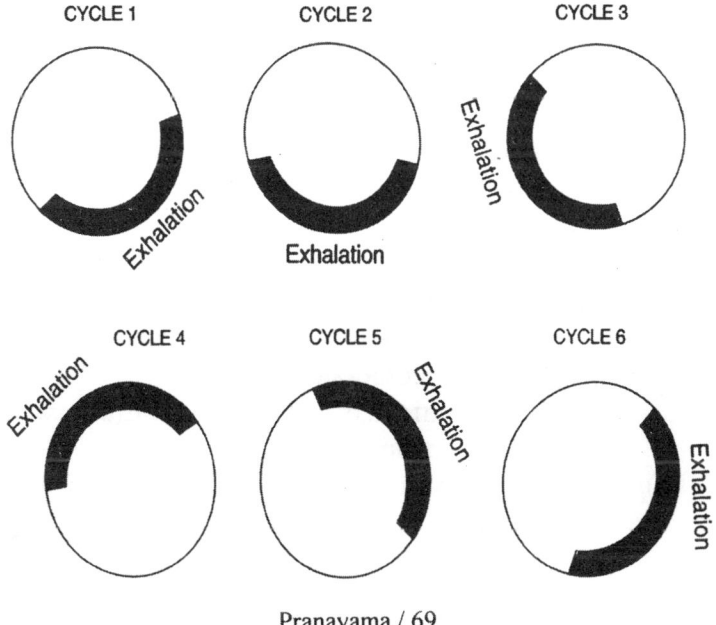

The diagram shows that circular breathing has an exhalation phase shown as a disc inside the orbit. The disc rotates gradually, cycle by cycle. Thus, it creates a rotary movement in a cluster of cycles (such as six cycles in the above diagram).

6) Nauli Uddiyana

In the above five exercises, there were uddiyana strokes along the spine or in an up-down direction. But here, the strokes come across the spine in the abdomen. The strokes will be from right to left and/or from left to right. Thus, the crescent moon will appear across the abdomen. These are the following modes:

A) Exhalative strokes, all from right to left,

B) Exhalative strokes from right to left,

C) Exhalative strokes alternating from right to left and left to right,

D) Exhalative right to left, inhalative left to right, exhalative right to left, inhalative left to right,

E) Inhalative strokes, all from right to left,

F) Inhalative strokes, all from left to right,

G) Rotary uddiyana, clockwise,

H) Rotary uddiyana, anti-clockwise,

I) Exhalations to be alternated with obverse and reverse cones or triangles and uddiyana kriya to be incorporated therein.

J) All reverse, conical, triangular phases with uddiyana incorporated (in exhalations).

K) All obverse conical/triangular exhalations with uddiyana kriya incorporated,

L) All reverse conical/triangular inhalations with uddiyana kriya incorporated,

M) All obverse conical/triangular inhalations with uddiyana kriya.

N) Circular exhalation and uddiyana:
   1) clockwise and
   2) Anti-clockwise
   Also, circular exhalations to be done across.

O) Circular, inhalative and uddiyana:
   1) Clockwise
   2) Anti-clockwise.
   And, similarly done across the torso.

P) Spiral breathing and exhalative uddiyana,

Q) Spiral breathing and inhalative uddiyana,

R) P and Q can be driven in opposite directions; so that clockwise and anti-clockwise strokes can be attempted.

NOTE : With each of these uddiyana kriyas, there can be a retention (kumbhaka) attached and a mudra executed. Then, countless modes of uddiyana kriya will be available to a sadhaka in Pranic kriyas. These will be further described later.

CHAPTER : 12

UDDIYANA MUDRA

Having tried and practiced various exercises of uddiyanakriya as described in the previous chapter and in shvasakriya of various asanas, one can then try retention and mudra as well. But before attempting those, one must be used to uddiyana kriya.Then this mudra must be attempted in a supine pose such as shavasana. After a profound exhalation, one must hold the breath and go for abdominal suction, contraction and deflation. Quacks will call this outer retention as 'Bahya Kumbhaka.' Then, one should attempt what this science is called, 'Panchavayu Uddiyana.'

These are four kinds.

1) Making an exhalation with reference to head, brain, face which is a head-brain confinement in exhalation. After such an exhalation, attempting uddiyana is called udanic uddiyana or udan-vyana uddiyana.

2) When the exhalation is by chest confinement and uddiyana has been done, it is Pranic-uddiyana or prana-vyana uddiyana.

3) When exhalation is confined to the navel band followed by uddiyana mudra, it is Samanic uddiyana or Saman-vyana uddiyana.

4) When the exhalation is in the pelvic-perinium confinement area and is followed by retention, itis called apanic uddiyana or apana-vyana uddiyana.

Various graphic modes described in chapter 10 may be used in the above modes or even the numerous pranic modes. It must be noted that the above classes are pancha-vayu modes; the reference here is to prana-vayu (not oxygen), apana-vayu, samana-vayu, udana-vayu and vyana-vayu. But these are not five pranas and unless the pranakriyas are used, the pranas will not be activated or applied.

Most importantly, it is pertinent not to mix up vayu kriya and prana-kriya and not to confuse the five vayus and five pranas with each other, despite them having the same names. The prana and Vayu are substantially different.

As there are four kriyas and mudras of five vayus, there are four kriyas and five mudras of uddiyana of five pranas as well,

These are:

1) **Prana-**Vyana uddiyana
2) **Apana-**Vyana uddiyana
3) **Udana-**Vyana uddiyana
4) **Samana-**Vyana uddiyana.

These four ultimately become 350! The clarification for how we come to this number will come later. Once the pranic-uddiyana kriya and mudra are commenced, then the vista of Shatchakra uddiyana kriya and Panchatattva uddiyana kriya opens out.

The pranic Uddiyana, tattvik Uddiyana and chakrik Uddiyana are all aspects of essential yog.

Uddiyana kriya and mudra become profound by Agnisar kriya and Kapalabhati kriya, which we will see in the next chapter. Here it is just coming as a vital piece of information to expose the reader/sadhaka to a repertoire of uddiyana.

1) Prithvi-tattva prana kriya uddiyana
2) Prithvi-tattva uddiyana
3) Aap-tattva prana kriya uddiyana
4) Aap-tattva kriya uddiyana

5) Tej-tattva prana kriya uddiyana
6) Tej-tattva kriya uddiyana
7) Vayu-tattva prana kriya uddiyana
8) Vayu tattva kriya uddiyana
9) Aakash-tattva prana kriya uddiyana
10) Aakash-tattva kriya uddiyana
11) Muladhar pranakriya uddiyana
12) Muladhara chakra kriya uddiyana
13) Svadhisthana pranakriya uddiyana
14) Svasisthana chakra kriya uddiyana
15) Manipuraka pranakriya uddiyana
16) Manipurika chakra kriya uddiyana
17) Anahata pranakriya uddiyana
18) Anahata chakra kriya uddiyana
19) Vishudhi pranakriya uddiyana
20) Vishudhichakra kriya uddiyana
21) Ajna pranakriya uddiyana
22) Ajna chakra kriya uddiyana.

So also in Pranayama, there are:
1) Chandrabhedhana uddiyana
2) Surya bhedana uddiyana
3) Ujjayi uddiyana
4) Bhramari uddiyana
5) Pratiloma uddiyana
6) Sheetali, Sheetakari uddiyana.

As Agnisara and Kapalabhati kriyas compliment uddiyana kriya and mudra, we shall first take up the agnisara kriya next.

Chaper : 13

AGNISARA KRIYA

Agni is vitally important in the metabolism of the entire bio-world. Agni is an invariable concomittant of life. Food ingestion is another characteristic of life. Food needs a certain temperature to aid the process of digestion. The cells in the belly have a certain temperature thus giving rise to the term 'gastric fire.' In the food that we eat, the cooling or heating process is vital in making it edible. The gastric fire has an indispensable role. Temperature variations are important in human food. Thus, cooling, boiling, burning, roasting and frying are all agnikriyas; agni kriyas encompass the whole range from freezing to boiling. (Refrigeration too is a form of agni kriya, where temperatures are taken to sub-zero levels.)

The human abdomen is an astonishing chemical complex. All eaten food is processed here under a mixture of air, temperature and chemicals. Aap, agni and vayu have an incredible role on the food that is eaten. The food is turned into enzymes and nutrients by abdominal processing where the gastric fire must work efficiently and flexibly as well as suitably for ideal metabolism.

For efficient cooking, a well-equipped kitchen is necessary;
Similarly, the cook within the abdomen is equally important or even more important. Our systemic kitchen will be working round the clock from birth to death. It is a true marvel of nature.

The belly works in three shifts, without a break or summer holidays, and processes, converts, degrades the food or decomposes the food for excretion.

The systemic body process changes and transforms the food for body matter which are skin, flesh, muscle, bones, marrow, tissues, fibres and cells.

According to Upanishadic wisdom, food is also transmuted for essence of mind.

अन्नमयहि सौम्य मत: ।

For Adhyatma, the intake of pure, sattvic food is important. While Yog does the super processing to transmute the food, yogasana, pranayama, kriyas, mudras and bandhas are all part of its technology. And additionally, yog-dharma plays an exalted role.

Uddiyana kriya is one of such kriyas, which work on this perspective. Agnisara kriya is another such kriya, which uses vayu and agni tattva by dynamics and prana. Agni tattva is important in such processing to modify the agni aspect. Agni kriya can work on:

Earth matter of body-mind
Water matter of body-mind
Air matter of body-mind
Akash (space) matter of body-mind.

We can easily imagine that fire either moderates or fuels the inner metabolism; temperature modulation can work in elements such as earth, water, air and space. Agni dwindling and escalating can work on itself. Thus, Agni-sara kriya becomes an all-important kriya. From a physical, scientific point of view one can consider the following conditions :

(Earth+/- Fire) : like Earth heated or cooled, that is not by physically modifying the temperatures, but arriving at the characteristic changes by temperatures;

(Water+/- Fire) : similarly water, heated or cooled, effects similar characteristic changes...

(Air +/- Fire) : similarly air, heated or cooled, effects characteristic changes and not physical changes...

(Fire brings about just an increase or decrease in temperatures) In case of

(Akash +/- Fire) : Akash is given the same treatment.

The *sara* too is very significant. It is "Agnisara" meaning the essence of agni. The process for the neophyte is as follows.

Make a complete exhalation and hold the breath and in quick succession suck, relax, suck, relax, suck, relax the abdomen during the retention. There can possibly be

10   20   40—50—80—100 such strokes.

When the retention time comes to an end, the kriya should be suspended and inhalation taken; after a couple of normal breathing cycles, there will be a second round of it. A cluster of 5, 6, 7 or 8 rounds can be performed.

This kriya sets right the agni in body as well as in mind and modifies it for different manifestations.

Some Basic Exercises :

As in Uddiyana kriya, the preliminaries are to be learnt in supine positions such as shavasana. Here too, the preliminaries are learnt in shavasana, so that the head, back and spine are steady and not vigorously oscillated. Again, it may be mentioned here that no text speaks of this but the age-old tradition of learning and teaching had this.

Thus this is totally unknown. More importantly in classical tradition this kriya is already inducted in some of the yog asanas. Apart from some of the steady supine poses, it is attempted in some of the forward bending, twisting, back bending and inverted asanas. Thus the real broad preliminaries are accomplished in asanas itself. Here the attempts must be in *shavasana* rather than the seated positions where the trunk, back, shoulder and head will be unduly jerked and jolted.

As said earlier, it can be done by settling down in a supine position such as *shavasana*. Then, after exhaling completely, one should hold the breath, and the abdomen should be given successive strokes like:

Suck-relax, suck-relax, Suck-relax...

Then, taking note of the rhythm, one can slowly decelerate until it becomes 'slow', again come to its original tempo and accelerate thereafter, until it becomes 'fast'. Gradually, one must be able to render it in: Slow, Medium and Fast tempos.

In slow tempo, the suction will be deeper and in the faster tempo it will be surfacial and superficial. The effect of the three tempos will be different and thus, tempo is the first variable of agnisar kriya. The second variable is Desha (or region).

Here, in the exhalation which proceeds
the kriya, one can opt for breath-confinement
in regions such as brain, chest, abdomen and
pelvis. This is the second variable of Agnisara kriya.

The third variable is the Graphic mode.

Here, the preceding exhalation should be given a graphic mode (or shape) such as cylindrical, obverse conical, reverse conical and circular.

Then the fourth variable is a large package of nearly 350 Pranakriyas. This is an essential agnisara kriya. There can be Panchatattva agnisara, and Shatchakra agnisara kriya. These work in a major way for culturing the *chitta*. But it subserves an ulterior purpose as well. It has remedial value as well. It can be a good exerciser and conditioner of digestive and excretory organs. It thus comes in the consumer package of yog in the modern world. There is a similar kriya called Kapalabhati, which is a kind of pranayama in neo-yog. But it is one of the Shatkriyas of classical and textual *Hathayoga*. These kriyas are neti, dhauti, basti, nauli, Kapalabhati and tratak, but in pop-yog, but Kapalabhati becomes pranayana in neo-yog.

Chapter : 14

KAPALABHATI

At the outset, we must understand the distinction between Agnisara and Kapalabhati. There are similar jolts to the abdomen here as in Agnisara. The suction and relaxation of the abdomen takes place as in Agnisara kriya. In Agnisara, there is a post-exhalative retention and during retention the kriya of abdominal suction and relaxation takes place in quick succession. However, in Kapalabhati, it is as follows:

Exale, suck
Inhale, relax
Exhale, suck
Inhale, relax
Exhale, suck
Inhale, relax in quick succession.

The rapid breathing is like a kerosene pump, which is operated in quick succession. The Kapalabhati breathing should not be complete and full. Kapalabhati breathing is like a kind of bellows-breathing. Like Agnisara kriya, this too can be done in three tempos –slow, medium and fast. This too has pranakriya, tattva kriya and chakra kriya.

A neophyte may have confusion between bhasrika pranayama and Kapalabhati kriya. The following may be considered here.

1) In Bhasrika, the breathing process and momentum will jerk and jolt the abdomen. But in Kapalabhati, it is uddiyanik.

2) In Bhasrika, the volume of breathing is important. Nostrils are heavily involved in forceful breathing. The inhalations are sharp and short but in exhalation they are sharp, but very very short and thick. In Kapalabhati, both are short and thick but not necessarily voluminous. Most importantly, there is an uddiyanik stroke, deliberately given, during exhalation.

3) In Bhasrika, the exhalations are made from the head or brain; thus it feels light after a few rounds. In comparison, Kapalabhati does not come from the brain. Bhasrika creates a discharge in the brain, while in Kapalabhati, the discharge is in the abdomen.

4) Bhasrika stroke begins with the exhalation, while Kapalabhati begins after the exhalation.

5) In Bhastrika, exhalation is a response to inhalation, while in Kapalabhati, inhalation is in response to exhalation.

6) A round of Bhasrika makes the brain light, while in Kapalabhati, the abdomen initiates the exercise.

7) Bhasrika deals with voluminious inhalation and exhalation but that is not the case with Kapalabhati.

8) The three speeds are important in Kapalabhati but not in Bhasrika. There is no speed variation in Bhasrika pranayama.

In Bhasrika, almost 2 rounds can be attempted in the beginning and may be increased later as per necessity.

Some primary lessons in Kapalabhati :

As in Uddiyana and Agnisara, Kapalabhati is best learnt initially in a supine position. Unless one is very well versed in these kriyas, one should not attempt these in a seated position. Here is a short example of how one can start one's practice.

One should lie down in a supine position such as shavasana and settle down in body, mind, breath and the cells of body in about 3 to 4 minutes. Evolve the breath awareness. Then, to commence this kriya, make sharp, deep, profound exhalations and operate the abdomen like bellows. In each exhalation movement, the abdomen will be given an uddiyanik stroke.

In inhalation, the uddiyana will be relaxed. This needs to be done successively for 15, 20, 25 or 30 times. When the uddiyana strokes start fading out, a break can be taken. After a few recovery cycles (normal breathing), one can restart after a deeper exhalation. This is the second round. In the beginning round 8, 10, 12 cycles can be attempted and later increased.

There are characteristic variations in Kapalabhati kriya. Thus, Kapalabhati can be performed after exhalation in brain confinement or chest confinement or abdominal confinement or pelvic confinement. This is one set of variables. Then, there can be graphic modulations preceding exhalations. This has been discussed earlier in chapter 10. These are:

Cylindrical exhalation
Linear exhalation
Columnar exhalation
Reverse conical/triangular exhalation
Obverse conical/triangular exhalation.
Spiral exhalation
Circular exhalation and
Alternated conical exhalations.

These will form another set of modulators in the Kapalabhati kriya.

There are pranic modes for exhalations. Since uddiyana is a kind of crator-like shape or valley in the abdominal cavity, this can be done along and across the abdomen. This can be supplemented with changing the supine asanas as well as the arm positions.

One can have the arms above the head, spread sideways and arms down as in *Shavasana.*

One can also change the strokes of exhalation thus causing modulations in Kapalabhati kriya. At a later point in time, one will understand

Pranic Kapalabhati
Kapalabhati of Panchatattva
Kapalabhati of Shat chakras.

These are essential paradigms.

All these kriyas can take place first in normal breathing, watching its velocity and density pattern, and then with heavy-duty, inscriptive exhalation as well as feather-touch, tender exhalation.

Now, we have a new topic to consider: tender and silky and/or sublime breathing.

Before going to the next chapter, a final comment on Kapalabhati kriya. As mentioned earlier, it takes place after exhalation. But there is also a tradition which suggests that this kriya (only in the preliminary stages) may be attempted after inhalation. This is an option, however, only for the isolated few. This kriya, according to the classical tradition, must take place only after exhalation.

Chapter : 15

FINE, REFINED, SOFT, SILKY, TENDER, RARIFIED BREATHING

The names of the different Pranayamas can give great insight into their qualitative dynamics and aspects. Two pranayamas specifically, Anuloma and Pratiloma, very importantly have *loma* in their names. (Pranayamas such as Bhasrika, Bhramari and Sheetali Pranayamas are exceptions.) *Loma* means hair; pranayama is compared to the fineness of a strand of hair. The breath should become fine, soft and tender to influence the hair. Earlier, we had considered velocity as one of the variables in breath conditoning. Extremely low-velocity breath tends to be thin, fine, soft, silky and tender. In Pranayama, a major component is to be regulating the breath and in turn, to be regulated by the breath. There are a few primary exercises with respect to velocity apart from:

> *Volume*
> *Density*
> *Confinement*
> *Aerodynamics*
> *Graphic modes*
> *Postural modes and*
> *Pranic modes.*

Velocity is a major factor to be exercised, practiced and studied. One has to use the breath as a kind of exclusive conditioner and make it low velocity, tender, soft, delicate, fine, refined, silky and rarified. This conditioning is an important one.

In quack practices, deep and slow (or thin) breathing itself is pranayama. Slow (or thin) breathing implies a great ability to control. Thus, it entails great intent, effort, practice, advertence, mindfulness and undulating conditions in mind. Teachers often instruct their pupils: "Slowly inhale"or "Slowly exhale."Slow breathing is to be suggested. Let me give you an analogy here; what is the difference between "slowly cycling"and "slow cycling."

Slowly cycling is either laziness or fatigue or casual cycling. While 'slow cycling' is actually an event and implies a great amount of skill and control as well as mental concentration. It needs a lot of learning, education, practice, experiments with great intent and priority. Pranayama teachers need to emphasise on this. Slow breathing, initially, is a mindful exercise; with practice, one can evolve fine or refined breathing effortlessly.

At this point, we need to understand what kind of matter is breath. It is such an entity that if you bring in one quality, a set of other qualities follow. If you slow it down, it becomes fine. If you try to make it tender and gentle, it invariably becomes slow. Therefore, such a conditioning has multifaceted advantages.

Here are some observations with respect to our breath matter:

1) Thin breath (rarified) is not a rapid-fire breath,
2) Thick breath is not slow,
3) High-velocity breath is high-density breath.
4) Slow breath is not high in density.
High-velocity breath = High-density breath
Low-velocity breath= Subtler breath.

So far as breath and breathing is concerned, it is predominantly dealing with gaseous matter. Solid, liquid and gaseous are three kinds of matter. The solid and fluid matters have an inherent density or viscosity.

In a 20-litre container, you can fill maximum 20 litres of water. But what about air? It can exert a pressure of 1/10000 lbs per square inch to even 1000 lbs or more per square inch.

That is the uniqueness of gaseous matter. One has to learn and develop the physical and mental control to breathe slowly; gradually with practice, more soberly and slowly. Over a period of time, one should learn to handle or manage a greater volume of breath with tremendous control and at a lower velocity or pace have a tender and silken quality to that breath.

When a layman is asked to take a deep or voluminous breath, he or she makes it sharp and thick. But a mature student of Yog tries to combine both these aspects – that is extraordinarily low-velocity-density breath with an unusual and extraordinary volume. This pranayamic breath is compared to the act of threading a needle: it is subtle, thin, tender and basically requires steadiness, skill, integration, involvement and concentration. The threading act requires good eyesight; similarly to culture our breathing, we need inner mind or sight to evolve this subtler breathing.

Now, we will delve into this very important aspect of how to train for this subtle breathing. Also, it needs to be noted that this subtle breathing has to be attempted and negotiated in locations such as :

1) Pelvic-perineum region,
2) Umbilical-abdominal region,
3) Diaphragmatic region,
4) Thoracic region and the
5) Facial-nasal region.

Such a practice becomes great education in 'breath driving' or breath negotiations. One must realise that inside us there is a delicate and subtle 'breath vessels network' which is something like the blood vessels network. Such a network will require acts like 'cabling the breath' and/or 'cabling the entire fibrous network' with the precision of 'threading the needle.'

With practice, one has to overcome haste and develop the tenderness and delicacy of mind, a quiet and serene condition of mind.

Our breath teaches us a very valuable lesson for us to imbibe Yog, yogic mind, yogic culture, yogic philosophy, yogic religion and yogic conduct.

It will teach us patience, steadiness, steadfastness, composedness, innateness, single-pointedness, circumspectness and such associated qualities.

Chapter : 16

NOT TO HASTEN TO SEATING PRANAYAMA

Pranayama begins as shvasayama. All preparatories and preliminaries of Pranayama are in shvasayama and by shvasayama.

Sometimes, children are taught to fashion alphabets on a slate rather than on paper. The surface of a slate can be used again and again many times by effacing it; similarly, pranayamic experimentations, learnings, practices are carried out on and through the breath. This will ensure that our rudimentary attempts do not have lasting effects.

Most beginners dread as to what will happen if something goes wrong. Breath is renewed roughly 21,600 times every day. Thus, any wrong has a lasting effect of little more than a few seconds. Breath is renewed and there is no pile up of waste or build-up of 'gas baggage' since there is a recycling process of supreme nature.

Thus, Shvasayama is the best process for learning the mysterious Pranayama.

After all, Prana is a deducible aspect but invisible, ungraspable and an imperceptible principle, how can one regulate it?

The other question is that when yog does not speak about 'Ayama' (control) of the body, mind, psyche, senses, tendency at all, why it brings the aspect of *ayama* for Prana only.

There is no express and explicit Sharira-ayama or Chitta-ayama or Indriya-ayama, Vasanayama, Kleshayama. Why only Prana-ayama? There are yama and niyama but no 'ayama' except for prana.

One of the reasons is that by prana being regulated, everything else is being regulated, and by Prana not being regulated, nothing is regulated in the true sense.

There is a great and incredible study of prana in the science and philosophy of yog. Thus, it has this impeccable theorem:

'Pranayama is Sarva-ayama
and no ayama is essentially
an ayama unless it is Pranayama.'

The pranic studies in yog have an incredible depth.

Prana is a mysterious energy often overlooked by modern sciences; they have no clue or notion about its powers.

Prana, according to mysticism, is a Shakti
Or an Adi-Shakti which, even metaphysics,
is clueless about.

Can mortal man achieve *ayama* of an immortal, eternal and indestructible power? This is the central question.

In a way, pranayama is not done by us. A later chapter will consider this aspect of 'who does Pranayama.' We have yet to consider what is Prana and its ayama; that is why it all commences with shvasa and shvasayama. This basic training and education and Prayogas are extremely important. It is an extensive process.

Firstly, the body needs to be
steady, relaxed and passive,
as well as comfortable.

Hence, the supine position or *shavasana* is ideal.

Thus, even if texts have not considered *shavasana* to learn the precept of Pranayama, tradition has laid great stress on it and the classical tradition has particularly recommended shavasana for such training.

There should be no haste to commence pranayama in the seated position. If that is done, then most of your awareness, advertence, cautions and efforts will be allocated and directed towards the position and the breath will be almost neglected. This is unjustifiable and hence the classical tradition recommends and it suggests to

> *Opt for supine position until a thorough*
> *proficiency is attained in Shvasayama*
> *and Pranayama, rather than a hurried attempt to*
> *try and adhere to a seated position.*

Attempting Pranayama with an unsteady and weak spine (imprecise state of spine and the nervous energy) is absolutely unjustifiable and improper. Doing with such neglect will be dangerous and harmful.

The spine, back and trunk are best cared for in a perfectly supine posture such as shavasana. This is the main reason why shavasana is advocated so strongly. The head too is rested and steady which is equally important. In the seated position, the brain and neck are unsupported and thus unsteady. There is no point in waging a war with the spine, back, neck and head under the pretext of pranayama. Hence this caution "not to hasten for pranayama in the seated position."

Now, coming to another aspect, one can regulate something which is in one's voluntary control. In other words, only controllable things can be regulated. When pranayama is considered as 'regulating prana', is it really possible? Can we regulate prana under whose mercy we exist? Certainly not. Pranayama really does not mean *'regulating prana'*

but it really means

'to be regulated by prana.'

The mystery and travesty is that we are, in fact, regulated by our vasanas and karmas. But when the prana regulates us, the vasanas and karmas are temporarily DETHRONED and prana is given a CORONATION. This is one of the centric theorems which comes in the 'Yog Vasishtha.' It says

"Pranayama immerses vasana."

The point in that implied meaning is that Pranayama is

'TO BE REGULATED BY PRANA
And NOT regulating prana which
is an extremely far-fetched idea.'

Of course, when we deal with prana, pranamaya kosha and pranayama in later chapters, this will become evident. Here, it may be hinted that one of the main pranakriyas is the Vachika kriya of *Madhyama Vaani*, meaning the kriya of silent oration – that is silently uttering literal letters, beeja mantras or mantras or *naama*. Without this aspect of silent speech called Madhyama vaani, no prana kriya is ever possible, even as an exception. The organ of speech (*Vaacha*) is presided over by the goddess Saraswati. Thus these are called Saraswat kriyas.

Therefore silent, oral speech called Vaachika kriya becomes Saraswat kriya (meaning kriya presided over by goddess Saraswati, the goddess of knowledge and wisdom).

Saraswat kriyas initiate prana kriyas and prana kriyas result into pranayama, by which we are regulated.

Man can only dabble, splash, immerse and douse in nature-made or god-given things. Thus Yog does not empower man to regulate prana but be regulated by prana and leave it to Saraswati, the goddess of knowledge and wisdom.

Anyway, a lot of education is required with respect to

Usages
Applications
Addressals

by associated breath and breathing as well as the

Usages
Applications
Addressals

on the breath, and for the breath. This is an extensive and exhaustive as well as elaborate process and the best way to have that education is in a supine position such as shavasana and

NOT TO HASTEN TO
SEATED ATTEMPTS.

Once the basics become profound, one can venture to sit and have further education, training and experimentations, like:
1) To sit steady, straight, erect, firm
   and related in trunk, preferably
   taking support of the wall.
2) To sit firm, steady and reinforced
   using the breathing as a fortifying agent.
3) Assume the above position breath-by-breath and by the breath with breath-coated bio-mechanics and Psycho-dynamics, as well as breath-based bio-dynamics and psycho-dynamics.
4) Evolve vigilance of and for the spine as well as the whole back
5) Maintain the waist, pelvis and keep them well-elated.
6) Keep the abdominal walls, diaphragm and chest erect.
7) Decompressed condition of all latitudes of the trunk.

8) Maximum spacing between thighs of swastikasana or padmasana and waist.
9) Sit as the *Gita* postulates in the sixth chapter: "Samanakayashiro grivaa."
10) To sit in the *tri-unnata* state as the *Shvetashvatara Upanishad* says.
11) The neck and head are usually erect and straight. But for certain specific purposes the chin may be brought down to fit in the notch.
12) Assume swastikasana or bhadrasana or siddhasana or simple seated postures.
13) Padmasana may be taken if long seating is possible but not out of fascination.
14) Shoulders must be rolled back and down so also in a broadened condition.
15) Breast bone (sternum) must be lifted and steady.
16) Palms must be rested on the knees on their back, Jnana mudra is not necessary when learning preliminaries.
17) Alternately palms may be kept one over the other facing upwards at the centre of crossing of legs.
(left palm is kept over the right palm).
18) Mouth, jaw, face must be relaxed.
19) When the jaws relax, there will be a slight space between upper teeth and lower teeth; they should not touch each other. The lower teeth should be slightly behind the upper.
20) Lips in a state touching, not touching. There should be no pressure nor should they be stuck.
21) Facial muscles should be dropped down and relaxed.
22) Eyelids in a state touching, not touching.
23) Eyeballs must rest downwards and not make their presence felt in the sockets while the eyes are closed.
24) The tongue should be restful and in seating positionthe tip of the tongue will gently touch the backof the upper teeth.

25) The mouth should be in such a state that the saliva will not ooze from the mouth. So disturbances will be prevented.

The teacher must prepare the student to such a condition that he/she will not need constant reminders to sit erect. This is done by evolving breath awareness and breath activities in various asanas in their

Doing
Evolving
Correcting
Maintaining and

Releasing phases. So also one should evolve freedom, ease, efficacy and steadiness in asanas. Patanjali himself prescribes that

'Asanic proficiency
is a qualification for pranayama.'

As often said, breath usages, applications conditionings and culturing is an important aspect of accomplished yogasanas. The trunk, the spine as well as the waist have great education in asanas in relation to breath as well as the other way around.

A teacher, classically trained and educated, makes the student aware of it. Then there is great training with respect to esoteric kriyas of the spine in asanas.

Then the breathing, uddiyana, agnikriya, Kapalabhati, all these appear to be like vast oceans.

No doubt higher, essential and the esoterics of pranayama are in seated conditions. However, this does not belittle the preparatories, which take place in supine positions and *shavasana* in particular.

Chapter : 17

INTRODUCING MUDRAS AND BANDHAS

The beginner in pranayama must be familiar and aquainted with some of the basic mudras and many of the secondary mudras as well as bandhas. All these are available today in some of the texts in *Hatha Yog*.

All the teachers of pranayama refer to
Mulabandha mudra/bandha,
Uddiyana mudra/bandha
Jalandara mudra/bandha.

Modern quack teachers have confusion about the three bandhas and mudras. Some of them are so ignorant that they hold with conviction that these three bandhas and mudras are one and the same. These three bandhas and mudras are incomparably different. Modern teachers teach mudras under the name of bandhas. Now let us take a classical and pedantic approach.

The main statement here will be:

'No one can ever teach
anyone the three bandhas,
nor do they need to be taught.

It is not even formally learned nor need to be learnt. A proficient and accomplished yogi is a beneficiary of these.'

The mudra-traya (three mudras) never become bandha-traya (three bandhas). What is attempted, learned and taught are only the three mudras.

No syllabus includes the three bandhas
in the classical gurukula process.

The bandha-traya (or the braid of the bandhas) only come in kumbhaka pranayama of accomplished yogis Like Yagnavalkya, Matsyendranath, Gorakanath, Jnaaneshvar and such siddha yogis. Let us now see how these three mudras are not bandhas.

Each of these mudras can be performed singularly and independently. This means that there can only be mulabandha mudra or uddiyana mudra or jalandara mudra. However, these cannot exclusively be mulabandha or uddiyana bandha or jalandara bandha. Bandhas mean it is a composite position and these come in quick succession or simultaneously. Thus there is a reference to them as bandha-traya. There are only three bandhas in yog technology and science. Mudras, however, are many.

Bandhatraya can come only in kumbhaka pranayama, which is the body of puraka-kumbhaka-rechaka or puraka-rechaka-kumbhaka (bahya and antara kumbhakas) of a proficient siddha yogi and never ever for an aspirant or a sadhaka in yog. Bandha-traya cannot take place after exhalation or after inhalation. (NOTE: It must be noted here only as a piece of information that mere inhalations are not puraka, exhalations are not rechaka and retentions are not kumbhakas as often mentioned in their literal translations. This will be elaborated in a later chapter).

The bandhatraya can not be done after an exhalation or after inhalation when there is no pranayama. The mudras, like the asanas, may be practiced separately; for example, the uddiyana mudra or the ashvini mudra or the shanmukhi mudra can be practiced individually and separately. But the bandhas are inclusive aspects, and if they are practiced separately then they morph into mudras.

A student in Shvasayama and Pranayama needs to learn jalandara mudra, uddiyana mudra and mulabandha mudra amongst other mudras. But one should not have a mistaken notion that what is being attempted in one of these are bandhas. Hence an earlier statement, clarifying that there cannot be attempts or trials or learning endeavours of bandhatraya. A seeker could ask which of the three mudras must be learnt first. An answer has already been suggested by discussing uddiyana mudra first in a previous chapter.

Thus, the mudra process in shvasayama and pranayama will be led by uddiyana mudra, followed by the mulabandha mudra and the jalandara mudra. Later, uddiyana, mudra and jalandara mudra can be attempted in the seated position. These attempts are done after profound exhalations. The order of these mudras can be in the two following ways:

1) Uddiyana followed by Mulabandha and Jalandara in quick succession, and

2) Uddiyana followed by Jalandara and then Mulabandha.

In some of the specific aerodynamics, the process may be:

MULABANDHA MUDRA

UDDIYANA MUDRA

JALANDARA MUDRA

OR

MULABANDHA MUDRA

JALANDARA MUDRA

UDDIYANA MUDRA in quick succession.

Basically, a beginner must ideally attempt Mulabandha mudra and jalandara mudra separately immediately following UDDIYANA MUDRA.

Thus we have:

UDDIYANA JALANDARA MUDRA
OR
UDDIYANA MULABANDHAMUDRA

Now, there are two kinds of important uddiyanas:
1) Uddiyana mudra kriya starting from the anal mouth. This is mulabandhik uddiyana kriya.
2) Uddiyana kriya starting from the upper part i.e. the diaphragm, which will be Jalabandarik Uddiyana Kriya.

Thus, there are either pelvis-anus originating uddiyana kriya mudra or diaphragmatic uddiyana kriya mudra. In other words, the roll-up of uddiyana can commence from the lower end or the upper end.

When we later on become familiar with the Prana kriyas, we will be able to see this difference more clearly. The formulae for the two Prana kriyas are:
1) LUM—VUM—RUM—UDDIYANA
2) RUM—VUM—LUM—UDDIYANA.

In the first, the roll-up will start from the pit of the belly and in the second, it will start from the brim of the belly. The former is launched from the region of the perineum and the latter from the rib cage (or thorax). Teachers must sensitise students to these two trainings.

Generally students are made aware of only these three pranayamic mudras. However, there are many other mudras mentioned in *Shiva Samhita* and other texts; some of these are:

JNANA MUDRA
PRITHVI MUDRA

AAP MUDRA
TEJ MUDRA
VAYU MUDRA
NABHO MUDRA (THESE ARE ALL OF THE HANDS)
ASHVINI MUDRA
SHANMUKHI MUDRA
KAKI MUDRA
KHECHARI MUDRA

and many more.

The keen student can look into hathayogic texts for further information. At this stage we need to consider uddiyana kriya and mudra with reference to shvasayama and pranayama, which we will address in the next chapter. As implied, uddiyana kriya-mudra becomes the most important one.

Chapter : 18

UDDIYANA KRIYA AND MUDRA

Many students are confused regarding the difference between uddiyana kriya and uddiyana mudra. In a sense, all mudras have a kriya, a process. Thus uddiyana mudra has a process, which is generally launched wih a voluntary exhalation, suction, squeeze and elation of the abdomen. The kriya is the process initiated by several and composite or successive actions for uddiyana to happen. Uddiyana mudra is a locked and sealed condition of the abdominal suction as long as retention (breath) lasts. Thus, uddiyana mudra is an arrested condition of abdominal suction. It is a mudra in both senses, that is, gesture and seal.

Sucked abdomen and deflated condition is a gesture and the retention causes a lock or seal or arrestation. This will persist as long as the retention lasts. When the retention time is over, the grip of the mudra should be slowly relaxed. Then the inhalation can follow. Alternately, the mudra can be released along with a controlled and steady inhalation. One can try a second attempt after 3 or 4 normal or recovery cycles. Then there can be another round consisting of 10 or 15 or 25 such mudras.

TWO-FOLD UDDIYANA :

The uddiyana kriya and mudra are two-fold or of two types basically.

1) One mode of uddiyana kriya commences after a complete exhalation followed by retention and uddiyana mudra. This

is called uchhavasa purvaka;

Another kriya–mudra here would be after exhalation; a post- exhalative uddiyana kriya and mudra. Therefore, there will be a demarcation such as Exhalation → kriya → retentive mudra.

2) In the second mode, the kriya will commence along with exhalation. The kriya will continue after the exhalation is over and then with the retentive phase the mudra can be maintained. This is uchvasa-sahakriya and mudra. This can ideally be done with continuous flow with relevant demarcation. This is exhalation uddiyana or concomitant uddiyana.

Now follows a brief description of the kriya process. In the first type, one must lie down in shavasana and settle down and go through the preliminaries explained on an earlier occasion as part of the preliminaries and preparatories of shavasanapranayama. Then, take a deeper and resourceful inhalation, and exhale slightly, sharply; a deeper exhalation (possibly in stages). At the end of this, begin the kriya by deflating, contracting and squeezing the abdominal band; suck the abdomen towards the rib-cage or diaphragm. Stick the abdominal organs to the back and towards the dome of the diaphragm. Maintain the suction-contraction-deflation during an external retention (not a bahya kumbhaka). This is uddiyana kriya and if it is not maintained without variation until the retention is on, it is a mudra. There should be no slackening or dwindling of the above characteristics. Such an arrestation in abdominal conditions is called uddiyana mudra. When the retention time is over, the grip on the abdomen should be slowly and gradually released in a controlled manner and NOT SUDDENLY.

This inhalation can be repeated after a few normal or recovery cycles and a second attempt may be made as described above.

In the second type, the mudra can be slowly revoked in a controlled or in a piecemeal manner or in multiple stages of inflation. This too should be a gradual and not a sudden release. In the second mode of uddiyana kriya–mudra, one should take a little deeper and sharp as well as substantial inhalation. Then a controlled and deeper exhalation should be commenced with uddiyanic mannerism or uddiyanic kriya. This kriya will continue well beyond exhalation; thus the kriya can be continued even after the exhalation is over. The mudra must be immediately followed after the kriya is over in the retention phase. The above-mentioned abdominal conditions should be instated and maintained without any compromise during retention. When the retention time is up, the release or the revoking of uddiyana can take place in a graduated manner as described above. Then one should recover with a few normal cycles of breathing and go for the second round of uddiyana. There can be a cluster of 8, 10, 12, 15, 20 or 25 such uddiyanas commensurate with one's capacity.

FURTHER SUB-DIVISION OF THE TWO MODES

The above two modes have a subset comprising of multiple and aerodynamic modes; these are also known as graphic modes.The pre-uddiyanic exhalation can have the following graphic modes. These will significantly modify uddiyanic kriya and mudra.
1) Columnar exhalation.
2) Cylindrical exhalation.
3) Reverse conical/ triangular exhalation
4) Obverse conical / triangular exhalation
5) Anterior to posterior
   a) Columnar exhalation
   b) Cylindrical exhalation
   c) Obverse conical exhalation
   d) Reverse conical exhalation

e) Alternated obverse/reverse conical exhalation.
6) Top to bottom, obverse-reverse conical,
7) Spiral exhalation,
8) Circular exhalation,
9) Exhalation ending with obverse cone,
10) Exhalation ending with reverse cone,
11) Various (350) pranic modes,
12) Crescent-moon exhalation,
13) Chakrakriya exhalation,
14) Panchatattva kriya exhalation.

The various postural conditions will further add to your repertoire and make the uddiyana kriya and mudra rich and profound. This evidently is a profound syllabus of uddiyana.

METERED UDDIYANA

This is another very important consideration. It is called "Matra-baddha Uddiyana."

This prayog is very important for pranayama in 'classical mode.' This is a mathematically framed uddiyana. It is also rhythmic and important in classical pranayama. Importance of this mode is beyond any doubt. There is a set proportion for the following phases.

1) Preparatory inhalation
2) Preparatory exhalation
3) Uddiyana kriya
4) Uddiyana mudra and
5) Revoking of mudras

Now, let me introduce you to a preliminary lesson here.

Mentally count to ten rhythmically and complete the preparatory inhalation in that time;

In the same rhythm, complete the exhalation in ten counts;

In ten counts, commence and complete uddiyana kriya (suction-deflation of abdomen);

Hold the retention for ten counts with the mudra.

Slowly release the mudra in another ten counts.
The above five phases will be in proportion of:
10 : 10 : 10 : 10 : 10
meaning
1 : 1 : 1 : 1 : 1
This will be 'Samavritti uddiyana.' Subsequently, other proportions can be attempted when one is qualified and capacitated. There can be various proportions such as:

a) 1 : 2 : 1 : 2 : 1
b) 1 : 2 : 3 : 4 : 5
c) 5 : 4 : 4 : 3 : 3
d) 2 : 1 : 2 : 1 : 2
e) 1 : 2 : 1 : 4 : 2 etc.

These are 'Visham-vritti uddiyanas' which can be handled with high proficiency and skill levels. Thus the uddiyanas become metered and help evolve control and capacity.

Now let us proceed to discover further more classes or modes of uddiyana which makes this topic extremely fascinating.

Cut Uddiyana modes :

The classical approach is very thorough education. It is not, as quacks like to believe, merely

> *"hunching the back after*
> *exhalation or during exhalation*
> *and by pressing the hands on knees*
> *or thighs, to suck the abdomen and*
> *to hold till retention comes to an end"*

In fact, there is profound training in the classical approach. It is an extensive and elaborate process, which commences in asanic practices. There are several postural modes of uddiyana commenced in asanas. These postural asanic groups are:

Standing postures
Seating postures
Forward bending postures
Back-bending postures
Lateral-bending postures
Rotational postures
Inverted postures
Supine postures and
Prone postures.

All these will cause modulations in uddiyana kriyas, modes and mudras. As seen so far uddiyana kriya and mudras is changed by posture and breath (exhalation) modulations or variables such as:

Volume
Velocity
Confinement
Deployment
Aerodynamics
Graphic modes
Design modes
Pranic modes etc.

Wehave seen some other modes of uddiyana, also called

"Cut Uddiyana"

These are, in a way, the aerodynamics of exhalation.

TYPE 1

This is with reference to diaphragm at the base of the thorax. One is supposed to make a sharp exhalation, which is perpendicular from diaphragm to back. It is a sort of waterfall-like or avalanche-like exhalation. It may appear like the Niagara of breath. This should be followed by uddiyana kriya and mudra. One should understand the graphic mode of uddiyana, which will be peculiar.

TYPE 2

Here the exhalation will be like shutter-down exhalation from the top of the chest to waist or diaphragm to waist. This sharp exhalation should be followed by uddiyana kriya and uddiyana which will again be peculiar and grossly different than the above type and the ones to follow. If uddiyana is a sort of valley or crater, each of these other types will be different types of valleys or craters.

These are sort of bladed uddiyanas.

TYPE 3

Here, the exhalative cut is angulated from diaphragm to shoulder blades rather than perpendicular. This is followed by uddiyana kriya and uddiyana mudra. This will be another type of valley.

TYPE 4

Here the exhalative cut is made with downwards angulations. From the diaphragm, the cut comes towards the waist. This is followed by uddiyana kriya and mudra. Thus yet another uddiyanic valley or crater is created.

TYPE 5

This one has two blades like the two sides of a triangle or a reverse capital V.One blade will angulate towards the chest and the other one towards the abdomen. By different angles, the uddiyana will be modulated. Following diagram will indicate those.

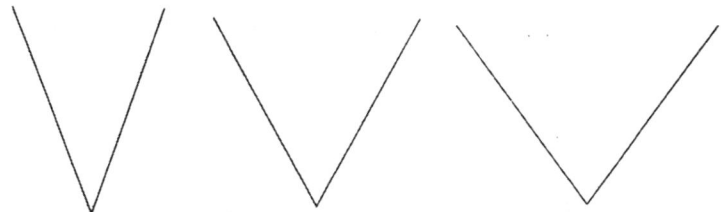

Here the angle increases and the base becomes broader. The cutter can be placed across the diaphragm. Thus the angulations will be towards the right and the left side of the trunk.

TYPE 6

Here the breast-bone line should be extended down in the abdominal location and type 5 can be rendered below the diaphragm.

Crescent Moon Uddiyana Kriya:

Uddiyana kriya can take a crescent moon form or shape:

This will be cast along the spine or even across the spine, which will be described later as nauli-uddiyana. The crescent-moon uddiyana kriya has progressive uddiyanas. There are basically three modes.

1) Inhalative uddiyana kriya
2) Exhalative uddiyana kriya
3) Dual uddiyana kriya.

1) Inhalative Uddiyana

This uddiyana kriya is related to inhalative breath. Along with a deeper voluntary inhalation this uddiyana stroke is given inhalation and is done in multiple stages here, stage-by-stage the uddiyana stroke of the crescent moon is given in progression. Mild uddiyana to strong uddiyana or small and tiny uddiyana to a larger uddiyana; thus the uddiyana will grow as depicted in the following diagram.

The wavelength will progressively grow in the phases of inhalation. Graphically it can be alternately done as follows (refer to the diagram):

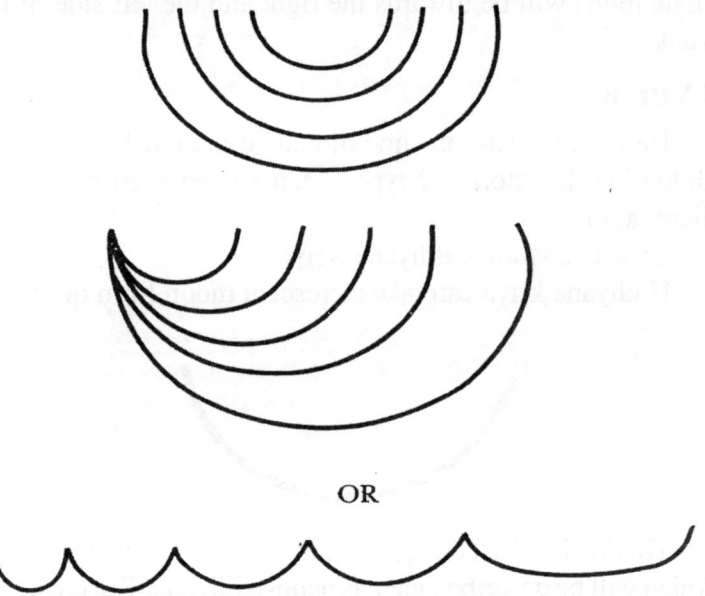

OR

This will be training for making the inhalation attain a physical and graphic component of "Puraka"(of course, puraka and inhalation distinction will be opened up at a later point in time in a new chapter.) Here, the abdomen will be excavated by uddiyanic strokes. There is graphically a waning moon condition, thus the "Chandrakalaa uddiyana."

There is another mode of inhalative cresent. Here the breathing goes on in a cyclic manner i.e. inhalation – exhalation – inhalation-exhalation. But during each inhalation, the crescent-moon uddiyana will be cast with progressive depth and size. Each exhalation will efface the uddiyana. Here too one can evolve an uddiyanic set from small to large size.

2) Exhalative uddiyana

The above process can also be rendered in exhalation. The crescent moon should be cast during exhalation and again similar modes can be worked out during exhalation. This will be training for the physical and graphical components of rechaka. Thus it means that all exhalations are not 'rechaka.' This will become clear in a later chapter.

3) Dual Uddiyana kriya

The breathing is going on a cyclic way. Mild crescent will be drawn by inhalative strokes and immediate exhalation will draw a larger crescent and this process will continue until the largest uddiyana appears. Thus a cluster of breathing cycles will complete the uddiyana suction. It can be depicted as below:

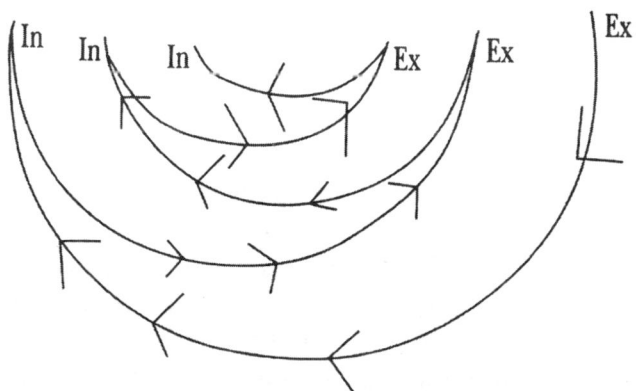

Since both the inhalations and exhalations draw a progressive crescent it is called Ubhayanvayi chandrakala uddiyana meaning dual-crescent uddiyana.

Nauli Uddiyana Kriya

Nauli is one of the kriyas in Hatha-yogic practices; where the depths are struck along the right column and left column of the belly in rapid succession. However, in classical process uddiyanic breathing is learnt by casting an uddiyanic crescent across from the right to the left side; and left to right side. In earlier exercises, the crescent moon was up to down and down to up in the belly along the spine. Here however, it is across the belly. Here the movement is like nauli uddiyana. The crescent may be drawn on one and the same latitude of the abdomen such as navel or there could be progressive ascending and descending movements from the pit of the abdomen (pelvis) to the top of the chest.

Again it has three modes such as the earlier up-down uddiyana. These are:
1) Inhalative nauli uddiyana
2) Exhalative nauli uddiyana
3) Dual nauli uddiyana

Let us describe these three now.
1) Inhalative nauli uddiyana:
   There are two sub-divisions here
   a) Inhalative from left to right.
   b) Inhalative from right to left.
   These uddiyanas will appear from mild to intense mode or smaller to larger size (in an arc). The breathing will happen in a cyclic process. With inhalation, one must cast the uddiyana and the following exhalation should efface those.

OR

   The inhalation can be in stages and the uddiyana can be waxing progressively.
   c) Exhalative nauli uddiyana too has subdivisions as discussed above for inhalations. These can similarly

be in cyclic breathing or in exhalative process of one deep exhalation.

d) Dual nauli uddiyana uses both the phases of breathing i.e. inhalation and exhalation. These will cause orbital movement. Then these can either be clock-wise or anti-clockwise. Here again there will be progressive sizes of uddiyana.

e) Ascending, descending movements is another module here. The nauli uddiyana strokes can traverse from the pelvic pit to the brim of the thoracic, to and fro. This gives a feeling of dancing movements on the stage of the trunk.

f) There is an uddiyana kriya which is called Sarvatomukhee meaning having face on all sides and in all directions. There will be almost normal breathing. There will be multiple cycles of such normal breathing. But these cycles will be graphically in crescent-moon shape. Here, a confinement such as the pelvic or abdominal region, may be selected. One should give free movement to crescent-moon graphic movements all over the region, corner to corner. Crescent can move in all directions such as:

Up to down
Down to up
Centre to right
Centre to left
Right to left
Left to right,

all over the region, in all-facedness. Just as the fish moves in water in all directions, the crescent moon of breath can go in all directions of space in a chosen location. The crescent-moon breathing effects concavity; in the middle of this there will be uddiyana kriya by that.

Children love to doodle and dance in free,

empty spaces. They dance all over the empty space, similarly the breath is made to move all over the space of the chosen location.Then the whole trunk can become a playground for such breathing.

We have gone through a long chapter of uddiyanic breathing – a part of 'ayama' or regulations. Now, we arrive at an important aspect of 'regulation'.

Regulations are not always by directives, control, rules, regulations and/or regulative codes and principles and enforcements. The way to regulate a baby, a child and/or an adolescent is different.

The way a wild beast is controlled
and regulated and a puppy or a
kitten are all different. A snake is charmed
and then regulated.

The breath and prana/s cannot be regulated necessarily with a stick, or a whip lash or such things. Regulating the breath is totally a different proposition. We are entirely under the mercy of our breath. Our subsistence depends upon breath in each moment of our biological life.

Then, what is the regulation here?
Why is there a regulation here?
How is the regulation described here?

Let us look at this in our next chapter.

Chapter : 19

CONCEPT OF REGULATION OF PRANA AND BREATH

First, we shall consider the concept of regulating the breath in the case of Shvasayama. Here, we are not regulating something which is unruly, nor is it even a case of controlling something. Regulation or control comes in respect with a commodity which is either in acute scarcity or super-abundance. Neither is the case here.

According to modern science, we have about 21,600 breath cycles per day; we are said to be in the breath rate of about 15-16 per minute. Secondly, breathing is part of the involuntary system and it goes uninterruptedly 24/7 without any kind of holiday or strike.

'Nothing is as conscientious as our breath.'

Then where is the need of regulating it when it is so regular? Anyway, breath is not a commodity which entails any regulation because of actual or probable scarcity or superabundance; nor is it irregular and unruly for which purpose it needs a regulation or control.

Moreover, how can the most unconscientious and irregular, erratic, spasmodic and unpredictable "I" be the subjective entity, a regulator or a regulating authority? How can the characteristically unconscientious "I" be regulating the most conscientious entity, our breath?

It is quite an enigma and unintelligible as to why Yog speaks about regulating the breath. The mysterious thing is that (as said on an earlier occasion):

Breath regulation is primarily to regulate ourself.

Our biological and psychological condition is such that by breath being regulated, we are biologically and psycho-mentally (or even totally) regulated.

More importantly, by yogic practices and yogic lifestyle, one realises the fact that our every manifestation is breath-based. Yog technology and science makes one realise this reality that behind our every psycho-mental, physical or psychic act, the breath is a major factor. The breath is a highly versatile force with an endless repertoire. It is an extremely resourceful aspect in us which is ever fresh, ever new, renewing itself moment to moment and thus, a tireless force. Because of its unimaginable and endless versatility, it becomes necessary to be regulated in yogic discipline and yogic practices or for that matter yogic life style.

Just as Deism declares with
certainty and conviction that the
Almighty is behind all phenomenon,

our microcosm attests to the fact that breath is there behind every action, reaction, response, happening, change and transformation within our embodiment.

According to Yog psychology and and physiology, breath is a major composer for our states of mind. Thus, the breath is a regulator of our organic self. Breath is a regulator-conductor of our mind, psyche, consciousness and chitta and even the entire organic being. All these need regulated condition and

BY REGULATING ONE (that is our BREATH)
ALMOST EVERYTHING IN US IS
REGULATED, ORGANICALLY
AND AUTOGENOUSLY.

Thus yogic science advocates breath control. Breathing is almost a master key to unlock all the mysterious enclosures of mind and psyche and even the mysterious mind.

Secondly, as mentioned, the breath plays, dances and doodles like children in open spaces and grounds.

The breath must be played with and be played by which is one of the ways to regulate the breath. The breath should be charmed like a snakecharmer charms a snake; not thrashed and whipped (like circus animals) and hunted down. The breath is charmed by breath 'plays' and breath 'games' rather than creating gym conditions.

Breath art, breath craft and breath plays are primary-modes to regulate the breath. Thus, one needs to play with the breath and make the breath play with/in our embodiment.

Before one comes to the regulation (ayama) of prana, one has to understand that the prana is a vital energy and force within us. Everything is under the mercy of prana. Prana is a divine-force in us; it does not really need any regulation as such but by its 'ayama', everything in us is well-managed and well-regulated.

Most importantly, the prana cannot even be indentified, recognised by lay people like us. Prana is very difficult to grasp, unidentifiable, intangible, unobjectifiable and inaccessible. How is it, then, that yog suggests its regulation?

How can we regulate something which is imperceptible, unimaginable, ungraspable, inaccessible and intangible? Prana is a metaphysical principle too. So how does one regulate it and why does science speak of its regulation particularly when there is no need, no way and no possibility? Also we, ourselves, are disqualified to be regulating it, so the question arises: who will do it?

At a later stage, we shall also see an intriguing aspect: "I do not do pranayama, when pranayama is done."

When pranayama is being done, we regulate our breathing by the path yog technology gives us. But even here, the subjective entity or the pronoun "I" is not the doer; it is not even the empirical "I" but a composite and associated 'I'. This has been considered in one of the opening chapters. Anyway, in pranayama what one needs to do is use the systems and organs, which are in voluntary control such as body, mind and breath dynamics. But these are not significant components of pranayama. Additionally, what one needs is the Vachika kriya (madhyama vani). This is silent speech and takes recourse to silent sound forms of:

SAMANTRAKA
OR
AMANTRAKA Modes.

These silent utterances are charmers of prana. They trigger and activate prana nadis. They carry out Pranayama.Thus, we are a very indirect, instrumental aspect when pranayama is done or pranayama really happens. Mysticism calls it *Sarasvat kriya*. The speech (*vacha*) is presided over by the Goddess Sarasvati, and the process under HER presidency qualifies to be having the Pranayama realised. Thus in a way, 'forces consecrated by Sarasvati carry out pranayama.'

By prana being thus regulated
everything in us, of the nature of body,
mind, senses, speech, psyche, consciousness
and vasana are regulated.

BY ONE (prana) BEING REGULATED, EVERYTHING IN THE EMBODIMENT THAT NEEDS REGULATION, IS REGULATED.

Chapter : 20

COMMENCING SHVASAYAMA IN THE NEXT STAGE

With this orientation and background, one has developed sufficient knowledge and awareness about breath, breath studies, shvasa kriya studies and the yog dharma mentioned in previous chapters. Now, one arrives at another beginner's step.

Pranayama does not commence with pranayama at all. It starts in what is called shvasayama.

For a neophyte, shvasayama itself is pranayama. Patanjali says;

"**Thereafter**, when the in-breath and the out-breath is (conditioned) or interrupted or stopped, is pranayama."(Y.S./ I - 49) तस्मिन्सति श्वास प्रश्वास गति विच्छेद: प्राणायाम: ।

Here, the in-breath and/or out-breath are conditioned, meaning their movements are altered or modified or interrupted or halted or suspended. This is one of the most effective means of regulating the breath.

The most important point is the reference to not just any given breath or any breath but a particular breath/breathing which Patanjali denotes with the term 'thereafter' in the sutra.

Now, this first word in the sutra is impregnated with mountainous purport. This condition is laid for the entire foundation and launch pad of Pranayama. This foundation is very deep and extensive.

In short, 'thereafter' means when
the fruits of classical yogasana are actualised.
This fruit is when the chitta is insulated
to all the dualities called dvandvas.
These are the opposites which vex the
mind and psyche. These are our tormentors
and oscillators. These need to be kept at
bay by insulating the chitta. Thus the mind
is neutral and in an unalloyed condition.

Thus the mind is exaltedly evened out. The chitta is in perfect equanimity. When the chitta is in such samattvam, there is a corresponding breathing pattern. This is really the normal breathing which is radically different from the natural conditions of mind which is constantly vexed by worldly conditions of dualities such as,

Pain and pleasure
Sorrow and delight
Elation and depletion
Up and down
Loss and gain
Like and dislike
Attachment and aversion
Love and hatred
Clemency and inclemency
Honour and dishonour
Hot and cold
Sweet and bitter etc.

This is our state in worldly life; we are with ups and downs and oscillations. Thus the breathing is treading on a 'dirt track.' It is highly spasmodic and sporadic. Such breathing is akin to being highly seismic or like being in a high seismic zone.

However, when the chitta is totally or at least greatly insulated to such dualities, the breathing is smooth, leveled and/or even. This is really the normal breathing which is subjected to *gativichcheda* meaning modification in:

Volume
Velocity
Density
Divisions
Shaping
Fabrication
Customisation...

Then begins the pranayama suggested in the sutra here.

The above-mentioned insulated state is achieved by a yogasana called SHAVAASANA. This is the corpse pose. Like a corpse, one must be totally neutralised and unaffected by dualities. Let us look at the following descriptions of shavasana.

If we attach electrodes and sensors to our body – in fact various parts of our body including brain, skin, muscles, pulse points – all such meters should register 'zero fluctuation.'

In shava-asana, one is supposed to emulate a condition proximal to it. It is a grand hibernation.

Now, how will the breathing be in such a state? This breathing needs to be given gradual and marginal conditionings, which will be a starter pranayama. According to Patanjali, pranayama is launched in a state of chitta which is 'Dvandva anabhighataAvastha', while in pop-yog and consumer packages of yog, the so-called pranayama is for quiet and peaceful mind. Pop-yogaa-pranayama is for vexed mind or tormented mind.

Neo-yogic pranayama is launched
on a battered and tormented mind
while classical pranayama in Patanjali's
scheme comes for a mind which is in
perfect equilibrium. This is a notable fact.

When the mind is profound, shavasana is exaltedly quiet, serene, noble, tender, spotless, taintless and in an unalloyed condition. It is like a serene and quiet lake.This, then, has a corresponding mode of breathing. This breathing is subjected to conditioning called *Gati vichcheda* by Patanjali. The details of this *Gativichcheda* come in the following sutra. There are various modules of conditionings approved by tradition. These are opened out in the following sutras. We shall consider them in due course.

The certain regulative modes, already discussed on an earlier occasion, are to be attempted on such qualified normal breathing.

Just to recall those modes here briefly:

there are marginal changes in velocity and volume in confined breathing modes;

then, there were certain basic graphic modes such as cylindrical, columnar, reverse/obverse conical or triangular or alternated and anterior to posterior modes.

Today, when neo-cults and different styles of yog consider pranayama as a respiratory or breath conditioner, the following fact is worth considering. Respiratory organs consist of the nostrils, air pipe, lungs and the bronchial/air sacs. If the entire area of the air sacs in our lungs are opened out, it admeasures 1,500 sq.mts, or an area as large as a tennis court. Our lungs can contain up to 3500 cc of air while our normal breathing is about 500 to 750 cc. A yogi can take the breathing capacity to some seven times the normal breathing amount. One can imagine what such voluminous breathing can do. There are 180 million air sacs in the lungs. Thus, there is an exchange of gases in these many air sacs. There are nearly 15 cycles of breath a minute. The exchange of gases in those nearly 180 million air sacs rapidly increases. With each breath, the diaphragm goes up and down in exhalations and inhalations respectively. The entire rib-cage goes up and down and lungs deflate and inflate in exhalation and inhalation respectively. Just imagine the volatility and dynamism of this incessant activity which takes place 24 hours, day in and day out. The diaphragm, while going up and down, creates a pressure on the abdominal organs and releases the pressure fifteen times per minute. This keeps the billions of cells awake and active in the abdomen as well. It is also intimately connected to the nervous system, which has a network of over 5,000 miles and the circulatory system which has a network of over 60,000 miles.

The breath greatly keeps the autonomous system operative, triggering the nervous-circulatory system and keeping the abdominal-chemical complex active.

One can easily infer as to how extensively and substantially the deeper breathing would work on this complex. It would exalt the oxygenation and de-carbondioxide filteration process. It would impact the bloodcells, nervecells and bodycells. The systemic body would work exaltedly. The physical system, skeleto-muscular system, physiological system, cellular system, metabolism, psycho-neuro-mental systems, endocrine system, cellular metabolism all would be made greatly efficient and effective. It would improve co-ordinations, responses etc...

In shvasayama or pranayama, there is

Breathified
Breathicated and
Breath status or condition in the embodiment.

There is a unified, kneaded condition which is unique here. Otherwise, elsewhere, even when there is deep breathing, the mind and senses are outsourced and in divergent activities. Here, there is an exalted unity, clearly demonstrating what shvasayamic and pranayamic breathing can do.

Yog has a unique concept of body-wide or embodiment-wide breath circulations/network and pranic circulation or network.

Outside yog, we are in a federal structure. Even if we are seriously involved in an activity with total involvement, yet our involuntary system is out of this 'involved state.' The digestive, circulatory, excretory and other systems are again out of this 'total involvement.'

One can imagine how much of us
is excluded in such a 'total involvement';

However, such divergent, fragmented and federalised conditions are greatly mitigated in shvasayama and Pranayama. That is why it is the path of 'yog' – union.

Pranayama is an exclusive way
of improving the pranic unction to
the entire exoteric body-mind system
as well as the esoteric system;
a more particularly, pranacised
embodiment is essential for yog to actualize.

In case of unqualified yog seekers, the whole embodiment needs to be breathified and breathicated.Thus, shvasayama teaches one to perform 'breath-based activities' through yog technology. Then, the qualification for yog appears. So also, power, prowess, capacity, ability etc. begins to surface. For those who are familiar with (modern) science terminologies, the following will make it clearer,

By deeper breathing of shvasayama
The diaphragm is acted upon in an
unusually exalted process.
This is the seat of the solar plexus.
Thus there is added stimulation to solar plexus.
That is why there is exalted purification,
empowerment, energisation in the
embodiment. Hence there is a greater
manifestation of power, energy, zeal,
zest, will, volition, glow etc.

Thus, there is great manifestation in physiology, psychology, neurology, psycho-physiology, psycho-neurology, cellular metabolism, endocrine system etc. There is an unusual and exalted co-ordination in these systems. That is why there are these exalted manifestations required for yog (jnana, vairagya, sheela, dhairya, veerya etc.) will get exalted. Sublimation, purity, piety and sanctity get exalted too. Ultimately, there is an exalted manifestation of unity.

Our normal breathing merely works for our biological living and for the involuntary / autonomous system; it is merely for our subsistence and an 'ordinary functional state' of our embodiment.

But in shvasayama/pranayama, there is exalted orchestration in our systemic body and above all, activation of our esoteric system.

Thus, Jnana shakti, vivhar shakti,
Pratibha shakti, Karma Shakti,
Creative power, intuitive power
psychic powers escalate to a very
astonishing magnitude.

In pranayama, there is escalation in pranic energies (pranic Shaktis). There are two kinds of such energy escalations:

1) Psycho-physic energy escalations or capabilities to work on minimum energies.
2) Nirodha-escalating manifestation or restraint-escalating manifestations.

Thus there are two such pranayamas, by the former there are efficient and effective manifestations of energies and better or even exalted conservations in energy so that the biological, physiological and psycho-mental activities are carried out with astonishing economy. So also resources are greater now and we transform into a power house of energy. Yogis are tus capable of performing super-human feats.

On the other hand, the restraint potential or restraining potential astonishingly escalates. Thus, yogic dharma and yog-shaktis get a quantum leap.

Spirituality is on the rise.

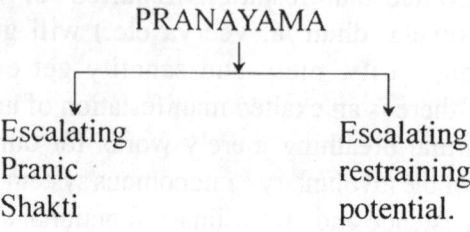

PRANAYAMA

Escalating	Escalating
Pranic	restraining
Shakti	potential.

The restraint-escalating pranayama is consummating which is the culmination of essential pranayama. The prana-shakti-escalating one is the earlier phase of pranayama before reaching the culminative phase.

In the prana-shakti-escalating pranayama, there are three pranayamas.

1) Bahyya vritti Pranayama
2) Abhyantar vritti Pranayama
3) Sthambha vritti Pranayama

The first one is a manifestation where the external or outwardly movement of prana takes place by exhalations. The internal or inwardly movement of the prana which takes place in inhalation. The third one, Sthambha vritti, is a retentive phase, which again has two types:

1) Retentive, coming after inhalation, which is called Antar kumbhaka, and
2) Retentive coming after exhalation, which is called Bahya kumbhaka.

When the restraint-escalating-pranayama is taken up, there are four pranayamas. The first three are mentioned above. But there is an additional fourth pranayama, which is called Kevala Kumbhaka.

It is, perhaps, time now to get a very basic and primary understanding as to what is prana since we are beginning to consider pranayama. Let us make some preliminary observations:

Prana is not the shvasa or the breath or breathing. Prana, in fact, is the so-called vital energy, the universal cosmic energy or Shakti, which has an inward and outward movement in us as long as we are living;

Pranayama is the practice in which we ceremoniously receive this cosmic universal Energy;

Pranayama is the linking process of the Sthula Sharira and the Sukshma Sharira, which is an essential aspect of spiritual Sadhana or Adhyatma and Paramartha Sadhana. There is an in-flow and out-flow of the Vishva Chaitanya Shakti with our breathing.

Thus we are not merely taking in oxygen while we are inhaling and expelling carbon dioxide in exhalation but simultaneously we have an inward and outward flow of the

universal cosmic energy because of which we are not only living and being animate but have the manifestation of our consciousness (Chaitanya).

Pranayama solemnizes these inward and outward movements of this divine, cosmic universal energy. In pranayama, this inward and outward flow of prana (divine, cosmic-universalenergy).

There is binding together of our gross body-mind duo with the psychic, transmigratory and astral duo – the linga sharira – in an exalted way. Without the gateway of pranayama, there is merely the coexistence of the two, and this is the basic quality and characteristic defining a living body.

Prana is thus the binding agent between the subtle, Astral, linga-sharira body with the gross body-mind duo. Therefore, the end of this binding process is called death (mruttyu).

Pranayama is an exalted association of gross and subtle body, namely, the sthula and sukshma sharira.

Dhyana and Samadhi is an exalted binding of sthula, sukshma and karana sharira/s.

The association between gross and subtle body is because of Prana (and not the breath). Pranayama exalts this association and the dissociation is death. This pranayama handles the flow of breath and establishes a state of citta called 'Dvandva Anabhighata'.

This chitta has no touch of volatility, turbulence, agitation, irritation, worry, anxiety, passion, disturbance or oscillation etc. This is the basic requirement to launch Pranayama. Let us now consider all such preparatory and qualifying blocks.

Chapter : 21

INSULATION TO DUALITIES IN CHITTA

We have now understood that before we make a beginning in actual and practical pranayama, one needs to have an insulation in chitta. It is not just an empirical state that gives one a temporary, bubble-like state of quietude, unagitated, unanxious, tender, serene, sober, placid and an unalloyed state of mind. But this state of mind, which is bio-chemically, psycho-neurologically, psycho-physiologically reinforced by processes such as *yog asanas*.These are not superficial, clinical or even cosmetic conditions. The chitta then must have such a lofty culture; such a state should be in the entire ocean of chitta and not just in the conditions of the surface mind.

MIND IS INFINITE

Even from the view of modern psychology, the mind has several layers such as:

> *Conscious*
> *Sub-conscious*
> *Intra-conscious*
> *Super/supra-conscious.*

These are almost unfathomable in depth; yet, these too are a shallow pond compared to the discoveries in Yog, adhyatma and Vedanta or in the Darshanas.

Thus the condition such as *dvandvaanabhighata* in the mind stuff must be in all levels of our ocean of mind. If the mind itself is infinite, then the chitta is of greater infinitude. At the base of the ocean-like chitta, there are:

Vasanas (tendencies), beginningless vasanas, endless vasanas,manifest-unmanifest vasanas – anaadi klesh vasanas, anaadi Karma vasanas, anaadi Jeeva vasanas.

Infra psychosis of all 8.4 million life-classes, The archives of all our past incarnations and experiences, the transmigrating, external mind.

Such deep-reaching effects are possible only by yogasana-technology and shavasanic laya-kriya in particular. Empirical and psychological measures are too shallow and truly bubble-like.

Abating a storm in a tea cup is not being suggested here.

Thus we have to understand that merely the psychological mind-generated mind stuff is absolutely insufficient mind or even the brain-neurology-generated mind is absolutely insufficient.

Without recourse to yogic techniques, any deeper addressals are improbable and impossible.

Modern psychology is absolutely blind to the deeper planes of the mind that yog and adhyatma speak about.

> *'Our peripheral mind*
> *or appearancive mind*
> *or brain-generated mind*
> *is but a pebble on a mountain*
> *(while our chitta is the whole mountain).*

The 'dvandva-anabhighata' conditions are pre-conditions for the whole mountain and not just a pebble on the mountain. The astronomical dimension chitta is in chip-form in not only the brain but in the:

> *Shat chakras*
> *Hridaya granthi*
> *Brahma granthi*

Rudra granthi
Vishnu granthi

Unless one is able to carry out the kriyas of asanas in the realm of prana, chakra and granthi, one does not qualify for pranayama. And until such time, only shvasayama is probable and possible.

The chakras constitute the pranayama kosha and the pranayama needs to take place in that kosha and not merely in the *annamaya kosha*.however, Shvasayama will work on the *annamaya kosha*.

The very term Pranayama impressly and expressly, implicitly and explicitly suggest that it is by, for, on, in and with the *pranayama kosha*.

Therefore, conceiving what is prana-maya kosha and understanding prana-kriyas become extremely essential and paramount. The earlier prescribed insulated state has to appear in *Annamaya* and *Pranamayakoshas*. However, for Shvasayama, such a condition in ANNAMAYA-MIND is sufficient. The adhamadhikari, meaning the one on the lowest rung of qualification can begin with Dvandva-anabhighata-avastha in *Annamaya* mind.

Annamaya mind is the temporal, empirical, psycho-mental, psychoneurological mind of thought, sensation, perception, cognition, intellect, emotion, memory etc., faculty-generated phenomenal and neurotic mind.

While Pranayama-mind is our Vasanas-Sanskaras stored in the shat chakras – muladhara, svadhisthana, Manipuraka, anahata, vishuddhi, ajna and also the mind rooted in the locus of prithvi, ap, tej, vayu and akasha which again have affinity with the chakras. The first term in sutra "There after" has such deep purport.

❖❖

Chapter : 22

BREATH REGULATION

The second term in the sutra is 'shvasa prashvasa', meaning in-breath and out-breath; and the third term is 'gati vichheda', meaning interruption, variation and the alteration in the flow of those breaths.

First of all, this breathing qualifies when the chitta is in a state, which is insulated to the oscillation between dualities. (For Shvasayama, such a state is in the tangible mind.)

Such breathing basically consists of

In-breath (shvasa)

And Out-breath (prashvasa).

By implication, this state is the link-phase between the two breaths. The breathing of such a state of mind (quiet, serene and sublime) clearly consists of the following stages:

Inhalation : Roll over to exhalation

Exhalation : Roll over to inhalation

Inhalation

It is perfectly a cyclic breathing.

The basic *gati vichchedas* are as follows:

1) Normal inhalation/normal exhalation
2) normal inhalation/ sharper exhalation
3) sharper inhalation/normal exhalation
4) sharper inhalation / sharper exhalation
5) sharper inhalation / rarified exhalation
6) rarified inhalation /normal exhalation
7) normal inhalation / rarified exhalation

8) rarified inhalation / rarified exhalation
9) normal inhalation/dotted exhalation
10) sharper inhalation / dotted exhalation
11) rarified inhalation / dotted exhalation
12) dotted inhalation / normal exhalation
13) dotted inhalation/ sharper exhalation
14) dotted inhalation /rarified exhalation
15) dotted inhalation / dotted exhalation
16) dotted inhalation / normal exhalation

Thus, there are almost 16 basic *gati vichchedas*.
These can be diagrammatically depicted as follows:
The following table will help comprehend and conceive the seemingly confounding concept of *gativichcheda*.

INHALATION	EXHALATION
1) Normal	Normal
2) Normal	Sharper
3) Normal	Rarified
4) Normal	Interrupted
5) Sharper	Normal
6) Sharper	Sharper
7) Sharper	Rarified
8) Sharper	Interrupted
9) Rarified	Normal
10) Rarified	Sharper
11) Rarified	Rarified
12) Rarified	Interrupted
13) Interrupted	Normal
14) Interrupted	Sharper
15) Interrupted	Rarified
16) Interrupted	Interrupted

There are also gradual and graduating modifications like normal, subnormal, hyper-normal and marginal changes in volume and velocity.

Besides, there are confinements, and graphic modes and very many permutations and combinations worked out as some basic exercises to understand the concept of gati vichheda.

Now, before going to the last word in the sutra, which is 'Pranayama,' let us look at certain textual definitions. Of course, the first and foremost is by Patanjali.

1) Thereafter, interrupting or modifying the flow and/or volume and velocity of breath is Pranayama (YS/ 2/49);

2) After experiencing the culminative condition of Mastering the asanas, there follows achamana which is a ritualistic sip of inbreath and immersion of the vayu of body which is exhalation in Pranayama. They are respectively called shavasa and Prashvasa, and the gati vicheheda is absence of both, that is pranayama (Vyana).

'Pranayama is puraka, rechaka and kumbhaka.'
(Yogi Yajnyavalkya)
'Restraining the prana and apana is Pranayama.'
(Linga Purana and Markandeya Purana)
'Regulating the whole body's vayu is Pranayama.'
(Soura Purana and Kurma Purana)
'Rechaka, puraka, kumbhaka is pranayama.'
(Amrutanada, Darshana Upanishad)

Panayama seems to be taking place in breathing organs or the respiratory system; it seems to be regulating the breath in its system but if we look closely at the effects, results, consequences and impact, they are all on

"CHITTA"

the entire mind-matter, mind-stuff and consciousness. The effects are:

"Steadiness of the chitta
Purity-piety of the chitta
Sanctity-sublimity of chitta
Placidity of the chitta
Cosmicalisation of the chitta
Transparency of the chitta
Sooth & benevolence of chitta etc..
Attitude-preparation and qualification
for Dhyana etc.

Thus, Pranayama is greatly for evolvement and transmutation of chitta. This is what is called Pradhana-artha or the main effect of Pranayama. By implication, it is for Jnana (adhyatmic wisdom)and then there are several secondary purports of pranayama such as siddhis and glories. This provides a channel and perspective for students of yog.

Thus any and all kinds of gati vicheheda
Of in-breaths and out-breaths are not
Pranayamas but only those which contribute
For the above mentioned major purport;
Pranayamas are those which have positive and conducive contribution to harvesting the crop of yog-dharma in one's consciousness.

Thus breathing feats or gymnastics are not pranayama;
Someone can demonstrate the ability
To have a very long inbreath or an out breath or a very, very long retention. There are many miraculous feats performed by the so-called yogis such as

Having a vehicle pass
Over the chest, or surviving in
Confined spaces for hours and hours,

performing super-human, power-strength displays,
bending metal etc.

These are all astonishing feats performed by street-performers, so-called yogis, and lay-men start believing that these are the main effects of pranayama.Thus many take up the pursuit of yog for such ulterior motives and material benefits.

The by-products have become main products because of human psyche and indiscrete propagation.

Earlier, yog was not really meant for consumerist minds and not at all was it a 'career'option. Let us take a pedantic approach to understand what pranayama is. Basically, we cannot just look into its defininition and ascertain its meaning and characteristics or its salient features.

We also have to consider the context in which Pranayama is mentioned in the *shastras*. There are also some other considerations like the 'qualifications' for pranayama, the prerequisites as well as the end result or fruits of pranayama.

Pranayama comes for setting right, culturing, purifying, sublimating the consciousness or chitta. It must primarily turn out yog, dharma, nirodha, dharma and jnana-vairagya in mind stuff.

The chitta must have:

Yogic parinamas (Dharma, lakshana and Avastha) on chitta. It has to become

a conditioner of the external and internal, the gross, subtle and phenomenal within as well as the organs and senses of mind.

The following verse from the Varaha Upanishad makes it clear:

इन्द्रियाणां मनोनाथ: मनोनाथस्य मारुत: ।
मारुतस्य लयो नाद: तन्नादलयभाश्रिय: ॥

The word *Maruta* is for pranayamic breath. This breath is a means for *Laya* or absorption. Thus, Pranayama clearly has a meditative purport.

Until now, we have considered all words in the relevant sutra of Patanjali except the last term, Pranayama. In the following chapters, we shall focus on this. First, we will have to see the difference between: Inhalation and Puraka, Exhalation and Rechaka and Retention and Kumbhaka.

Inhalation, exhalation and retention do not make Pranayama but puraka, rechaka and kumbhaka make Pranayama.

It is generally confounding and confusing to hear or read a statement like that.

Inhalation is not puraka,
Exhalation is not rechaka
and
Retention is not kumbhaka.

Pedantic studies offer this realisation quite easily but rampant quackery prevalent in today's practices makes one develop faulty conceptions. The next chapter will divulge further and provide a rationale.

Chapter : 23

INHALATIONS-EXHALATIONS ARE NOT PURAKA-RECHAKA

In modern times, there is a dearth of traditional and classical as well as formalised gurukula mode of education. Today, the modes are broadly :

Yog classes
Yog studios
Yog workshops
Yog retreats
Yog shibirs/camps
Yog certification courses
Yogic diploma courses and so on.

Then there are so-called yog ashrams where yog practices or teacher-training courses and social-work mode of yogic package sare promoted. There are hardly *vidhyarthis* in the subject of yog. Everywhere, there seems tobe rampant quackery. There are many misconceptions.

1) Deep and advertant breathing makes the puraka-rechaka pranayamas.

2) Using a few physical and skeleto- Muscular and breathing conditions make the in-breath and out-breath rechaka and the in-breath puraka,

3) Mindfully and advertantly filling up the lungs witha quiet and relaxed mind is puraka and emptying the lungs in a slow and controlled manner is rechaka.

4) Slow, soft, deep, advertant steady body-mind breathing is puraka-rechaka pranayama.

5) *Seated, yogic meditative postures such as the ones the* Gita *prescribes in the sixth* chapter and breathing in the manner described above is puraka-rechaka Pranayama.

6) Or using the fingers on nostrils and blocking one nostril(by deviating or manipulating the septum) is pranayama... and so on.

Whenever there is an inhalation in the context of pranayama it is called Puraka and an exhalation, rechaka, and a retention, kumbhaka. This is an absolutely wrong notion. Now, let us make a very primary definition of pranayama and puraka, rechaka and kumbhaka here.

(Also of interest here is that the shastras mention two classes of Pranayama. When puraka, rechaka and kumbhaka are done with a mantra, then it is Samantraka Pranayama and when there is no mantra involved, then that is Amantraka pranayama.)

The in-breath and out-breath as well as retention that is carried out by certain shastra–ratified techniques, processes studded by certain cultural-religious norms set by Yog and a strong philosophical base will make the in-breath and out-breath puraka and rechaka and the retention, kumbhaka. There is a very prominent physical component of UDDIYANA in all the three cases.

Therefore uddiyana-kriya becomes a very prominent physical component of puraka-rechaka-kumbhaka or pranayamic breathing. Thus, there was elaborate treatment to

Uddiyana kriya
and
Uddiyana mudra,

in the preceding chapters. It is mandatory that pranayamic in-breath and out-breath must have uddiyana-touch or uddiyanic influences as an important bio-mechanical component. In retention, there is uddiyana mudra. Of course, apart from the uddiyanic component in breathing, there are more important components such as:

The cultural, philosophical and religious fabric in breathing.

These are the fabrics of yog-sanskruti, yog dharma and yog-tattvajnana. Patanjali implies these things in using terms such as

Bahya vritti
Abhyantar vritti
Stambha vritti

for rechaka-puraka-kumbhaka respectively. He adds the suffix 'vritti' which is very significant. It needs to be told today that in classical pranayama, conditions such as : Inhale as much as you can, exhale as much as you can and retain as long as you can are not suggested at all.

Pranayama does not look for such capacity or anyone quality; rather, the quality of all the three aspects is important.

Vritti is more important than vidhi in pranayama.

We need to consider another thing here. The teacher often speaks about or suggests

full & complete inhalation
And
full & complete exhalation.

This means 'as much as you can.'But this is absurd. Breathing involves the matter of air element. Air is such a matter that there is nothing like 'full.' Air always fills up a container of any shape and dimension. If lungs are containers of breath(air) there is never such a condition as full. Even in a rubber tube, we can fill up within a wide range of pounds or kilos of air. It can be from 1 to 50 lbs or in a strong tube it can be between 1 to 500 lbs even if the container tube is of the same size.

Air is a compressible matter.
Human lungs can take 350 cc
or even up to 3500+ cc
in the case of a yogi.

Secondly, there is always some residual air in the lungs and thus, a complete exhalation is sheer rhetoric.However, lowering this limit is one of the effects of the technology of pranayama.

Another important distinguishing factor between deeper inhalation and pranayamic inhalation is as follows.

In deeper inhalation, the thoracic Region is made to participate, addressed and involved in a significant way, while in pranayamic inhalations, the location in hip, buttocks, anal, ileum, perineum and pelvic–abdominal region are also accessed. Is this not a significant difference?

Inhalation in pranayamic process is called 'apana kriya'.The region of apana is below the navel and upto the anal mouth region.

A beginner must practice inhalation
and exhalation, both with pelvic-abdominal
confinements. It should be recalled here that
major abdominal addressals were suggested in
shvasayama.Thus, one must learn and practice
for a long while. This breathing should have pelvic
initiation, initiative, participation, involvement,
addressal, effect and so on.

It is time that we begin to understand the concepts of puraka-rechaka. Basically Pranayama is addressing, setting and resetting the Pranayama kosha (we shall consider this in a later chapter).

Thus the puraka, meaning nourishment or complementariness, is for that Pranayama kosha. It is called "pranayamakriya" in its process.

Inhalation is an oxygenation process
In puraka kriya or nourishment of our
Psychological and biological self.
Thus, it is a nourishment to us, while
Pranayamic puraka is nourishment
not to us but to OUR Pranayama kosha.

Thus, inhalation (deep) is our nourishment but puraka of Pranayama is nourishment to our 'pranamayakosha.'

It should be noted that spiritual
sciences do not call our nourishment
as puraka or puranakriya. However,
nourishment of something that is ours,
the pranayama kosha, is called Puraka.

Pranayama kosha is, in fact, Deva-mayakosha in us. It is the abode of the devatas (33) in us. It is the atmosphere of devaloka in us since the devatas who preside over our 14 indriyas reside there as well as the Adishakti-rupas. Their nourishment is our true nourishment.

It is truly our nourishment when
the deities in us are nourished. This
is the concept of adhyatma. If
'we' are nourished directly, the
demons are nourished.
Philosophically, we must be indirectly
nourished, through the devatas.
Thus, pranayama becomes an exalted
Adhyatma Sadhana, which is propitious to
the Adhidaivik constitution in us.

Basically the nourishment here is not for our biological aspects. Similarly Rechaka or rechaka kriya or purgation is with reference to the Pranamaya kosha and not with reference to us. Similarly retentions with reference to in-breath and out-breath is not kumbhaka. But kumbhaka happens after puraka which is called antara-kumbhaka and that which happens after rechaka is called bahhya kumbhaka.Thus, kumbhaka needs on either side, puraka and recheka and not inhalation and exhalation. It is not because of the oxygen that is taken in that it is called puraka nor that carbondioxide is expelled in exhalation that it is called rechaka. In inhalation, we primarily take oxygen which is important for our biological existence. While in exhalations, we expel toxic carbondioxide, heat etc. These are worthy of expulsion. Yet these inhalations and exhalations are not called puraka and rechaka respectively.

The purana-rechana is not with reference to biological or empirical 'I' but a more sublime, transcendant and ethereal 'mine'. Pranayama is thus for a superior entity in us than us.

As suggested earlier, apart from higher cultural, philosophical and religious components, there is an uddiyanic process for in-breath and out-breath in Pranayama for puraka and rechaka. Then in both the kumbhakas there is invariably a combination of

Mulabandha mudra
Uddiyana mudra
Jalandara mudra.

for the unproficient practitioners. Normally, these are done consciously and voluntarily. While in the case of accomplished and proficient yogis, these three happen as bandha-trayas (a triad of bandhas).

Bandhatrayas only happen in
Kumbhaka pranayama of an
accomplished siddha-yogi.

These are never done voluntarily. Moreover, there is no case of:

Exclusive mulabandha
Or
Uddiyana bandha
Or
Jalandara bandha.

Bandhas do not take place without a kumbhaka condition. There can never be an exclusive practice of the bandhas.

Bandhas are never ever done,
or learnt, or taught or practiced.

Rather, bandhas are an outcome of the proficiency

Achieved by a yogi in pranayama.
There is no sadhana for/of **Bandhas.**
There are no voluntary executions
of the bandhas. Bandhas are purely
happening for a very proficient
yogi in a triad.

Chapter : 24

RETENTIONS ARE NOT KUMBHAKAS

Just as the in-breaths and out-breaths are not puraka-rechaka, similarly the retentions are not kumbhakas. Retention of breath can take place voluntarily or involuntarily. Retention is where the respiration is held for a while, like when we take a dip in the water. Similarly, retentions are sometimes with respect to our bowel movements or our bladder (urination) or some physical feats or emotional turmoil or fear, excitement etc.

Such voluntary retentions are there for extra-ordinary physical acts or sometimes in voluntary acts as well.

But in shvasayama, the retentions come for some higher purpose. They are there for pranayamic training as well.

In quack practices, such shvasayamic retentions are considered. But they are not kumbhakas or stambhavritti pranayamas. These require either puraka or rechaka to proceed or follow. Since in shvasayama, there is neither puraka or rechaka, the kumbhakas cannot take place.

Puraka creates certain manifestations
In chitta by way of escalations or
augmentations; there are additions in those qualities.
Those are called Abhyantara vritti
Pranayama. By puraka, there will be additions and
by rechaka, there will be some deductions in chitta and
the Pranayama kosha.

These deductions exalt the conditions in chitta and the Pranayama kosha. Thus, the puraka-rechaka effect balances in conditions in the chitta and the Pranayama kosha and evolve yog–dharma.

These additions and deductions are important for they address important things.

These plusses and minuses are important; a combination of puraka- kumbhaka is Multiplication and rechaka-kumbhaka is division. Thus, these have quantum benefits.

NOW, WHY IS IT 'KUMBHAKA'?

'Kumbha' as a water container does not merely 'retain' water or store water or hold water. It contributes immensely. Unlike today, where the water containers are made from steel or its alloys or plastic, traditionally, the water containers were earthen or copper or silver.

The conventional water pots killed the worms and purified the water thus enhancing intrinsic value. That apart, the worth of such stored water increased the utility value.
It could be conveniently
used at any time. The water became
pure to be safely consumed, as well as
become chemically better by interaction
with earth or copper or silver (which
glass, plastic, etc. do not do).

Thus, the worth and value of water is increased by the kumbha.

Similarly, post-puraka kumbhaka increases the worth and value of Prana by a quantum leap (multiplication and not just addition).

Similarly, the post-rechaka kumbhaka does something equally profound.

Just as a copper vessel/pot kills the bacteria and purifies the water, rechaka does that not by just deductions but by division. If rechaka works as a subtracting act, the kumbhaka after rechaka, works for multiple divisions. Therefore, puraka works for additions and rechaka for subtractions, while antarakumbhaka enhances multiplications and bahyyakumbhaka divisions.

The word kumbhaka used for so-called retentions in shvasayama and pranayama work for quantum results. This can be explained in another way.

Like in electronics, there is the conceptof condenser and a component called condenser, which escalates power.

For example, in an electronic flash gun, 6 to 8 dry batteries of 1.5 volts release that meagre power for 8 to 10 seconds; the condenser collects this and then gives a burst of 1000 to 1500 watts of dazzling flashlight.

Similarly, the puraka→kumbhaka holds the puraka emission during the time of retention and becomes an incredible power subsequently in the form of multiplication, while the rechaka → kumbhaka works in the form of division.

Thus, there are incredible power manifestations in internal and external kumbakas or sthambhavritti Pranayamas.

Just as puraka-rechaka are said to be having physical-mental techniques, breath techniques as well as the cultural, philosophical and religious fabric, so also the kumbhakas have:

1) Physical component of uddiyana mudra or (bandha traya) as well as mulabandha and Jalandara mudra.
2) Yogatantra of puraka and rechaka and prana kriya, chakra kriya and tattva kriya.

3) Samantraka, Amantraka Pranakriyas.
4) Yogic principle (ethos)
5) Yog philosophic and religious principles.
6) Yogic cultural component.

Usually, for internal retention a complete inhhalation is suggested. But Antarakhumbaka in classical mode is never done after such a condition. That is why the *Shastras* always speak of proportions in kumbhaka pranayama.

Then, there are the samavritti or vishama vritti pranayamas; their proportions in antara kumbhaka are:

2 : 4 : 6
1 : 3 : 2
1 : 1 : 1
2 : 2 : 2 and so on.

And bahyya kumbhaka are:

2 : 4 : 6
1 : 3 : 2
1 : 1 : 1
2 : 2 : 2 ...

During either of the kumbhakas, there are mudra-traya or bandha-traya in case of unproficient and proficient ones respectively.

The volume of inhalative breath in Antara-kumbhaka depends upon the possibility of uddiyana kriya during its performance. Therefore, inhalation should not continue before antara kumbhaka if the uddiyana is nullified or defacilitated.

Unproficient ones cannot be inhaling more in the uddiyana condition. But the proficients ones can do it. Therefore, the exercise of inhalative uddiyana is very important before kumbhaka is attempted even in Shvasayama. Then at the end of such inhalations, one needs to perform mulabandha mudra (anal, perineum and hip contractions) and jalandara mudra (suction of thoracic region towards throat and the chinlock by head-down position). Kumbhakas should not be attempted or for that matter, even Retentions should not be attempted without the chin lock (the chin goes into the notch at the throat).

Mudra-traya should be attempted in retentions while bandha-traya will happen for a proficient yogi. At this point it becomes important to consider the role of

Kriya
Mudra and
Bandha

which we shall do in the following chapter.

Chapter : 25

KRIYA, MUDRA & BANDHA OF KUMBHAKA OR RETENTION

As reiterated earlier, the three bandhas cannot be performed and displayed nor can it be taught or learned. There is never a possibility of noting :

> *'This is uddiyana bandha*
> *or*
> *'This is mulabandha'*
> *or*
> *'This is jalandara bandha'.*

However, it is possible to attempt, do, perform, display and have a condition such as

> *This is mulabandha mudra*
> *or*
> *This is uddiyana mudra*
> *or*
> *This is jalandara mudra.*

In quack practices, which are rampant in yog today, mudras (three) are taught as bandhas and there is no distinction between the three mudras and bandhas because of sheer ignorance. As has been said often, what can be attempted, displayed and learned and taught are:

> *Uddiyana mudra*
> *Mulabandha mudra*

and
Jalandara mudra.

The bandha-trayas are happening for a proficient yogi who is in pranayama of puraka-rechaka and not inhalation-exhalation of students, seekers or experimentors in Shvasayama; those attempting shvasayama will thus be qualifying to learn mudras in general and mudratrayas in particular.

Yog shastra mentions several mudras such as:

Sinha mudra
Yog mudra
Brahma mudra
Shambhavi mudra
Kaki mudra
Maha mudra
Maha vedha
Shanmukhi mudra
Ashvini mudra
Vajroli mudra
Shajili mudra
Amaroli mudra
Khechari mudra
Mulabanda mudra
Uddiyana mudra
Jalandara mudra
Viparitakarani mudra etc...

Those who are shastradhyayi or even curious ones can look into Hatha yogic texts such as *Shiva Samhita* and *Gheranda Samhita* which mention the mode and usages. One should be aware of the Shat kriyas of Hatha Yog such as:

Neti
Basti
Dhauti

Trataka
Kapalabhati and
Nauli.

The bandhas are only three.Now we shall finally look at the distinctions between mudra-traya and bandha-traya.

1) There are mudra practices (mudra-traya) but there are no bandha practices (bandha-traya).

2) Isolated and singular bandhas are never there but are always there in a triad. However, mudras can be done singularly or separately.

3) Mudras can be practiced separately as asanas are practiced while mudras such as uddiyana or ashwini can be incorporated in asanas. Students, seekers, unproficient ones can attempt mudras (mudra-traya). But bandha-trayas occur only in kumbhaka pranayama of a proficient and master yogi. In the Shvasayama or pranayama of unproficient practitioners, there will be retentive pranayama-shvasayama (but these should not be called kumbhaka). What will occur here is mudra-traya and not bandha-traya.

4) Bandhas will evolve at various stages or hierarchies.

5) Bandhas or mudras have a two-way process:

a) Mulabandha → Uddiyana → Jalandara.

or

b) Uddiyana → Mulabandha → Jalandara.

6) Mudras do not need pranayamas for attempts because there are mudra-sadhanas outside the realm of pranayama. However, the bandha-trayas are integral to pranayama;

7) Mudras have kriyas (even mudra-trayas) but bandhas do not have kriyas;

8) There are uddiyana kriyaàuddiyana mudra, Mulabandha kriyaàmulabandha mudra, and jalandara

kriya à Jalandara mudra;

9) Mudra-trayas are post-exhalative acts but bandha-trayas come both, post-exhalatively and post-inhalatively;

10) However much mudras may evolve, they will never become bandhas;

11) Mudra-trayas are vitally important for seeker students..

12) The mudras are evolved by evolving kriyas.

13) Mudras cannot actualize without kriyas.

14) There are raw, rudimentary and ripe mudras but that is not the case with the bandha-trayas.

We have partially considered uddiyana kriyas in an earlier chapter. The discerning reader should now re-read that and then proceed.Now, we will proceed to take up the Mulabandha-kriya → mudra process.

Chapter : 26

MULABANDHA KRIYA →
MUDRA

Basically, Mulabandha kriya and mudra prayoga (attempt and usages) are in seated postures done for pranayama. However, there must be innumerable prayogas of uddiyana kriya and mudra for qualification. And as seen earlier, these attempts are in many different yogasanas; also various exercises and prayogas in supine asanas.

The procedural reality is that uddiyana will become more and more proficient; the mulabandha or mudra results in this one mode of commencing the mulabandha mudra. The second one comes later where mulabandha mudra is taken up directly rather than indirectly. Here, contraction, squeeze, suction is effected in pelvic-perinium-anal region. This contraction at the base subsequently causes uddiyana mudra.

The mulabandha kriya should be commenced with a post-exhalative retention. One must learn this post-exhalative suction, contraction, squeeze, ejection at the muladhara region i. e. the hip, buttocks, anus, perineum region. This entails a sharper, thicker and forceful as well as deeper exhalation.

Extensive uddiyana kriya and mudra
or more pervasive uddiyana kriya-mudra
includes the mulabandha kriya and mudra.

EXHALATIVE MULABANDHA KRIYA–MUDRA

Let us consider some exercises here.

a) Make an exhalation by effecting evacution in the following order –head, brain, throat, chest, diaphragm, abdomen, navel, pelvis, hips, buttocks, anus. Then append it with retentions and this will result into Mulabandha mudra.
b) Make a profound exhalation in the abdomen and pelvic region. Follow it with a retention. This will result in a mulabandha mudra with concommitance of uddiyana mudra.
c) The above two modes should be attempted with exhalations ending in the pit of the trunk (at anus and hips by obverse and reverse triangular/conical shapes).
d) Attempt the first two modes with spiral mode of exhalations and attempt the mulabandha mudra.

SEATED EXHALATIVE KRIYA & MUDRA:

After sufficient attempts in supine positions, one can take up seating-position uddiyana, mulabandha kriya-mudra post-exhalatively. Then these suction, deflation, squeeze and ejection can be attempted with sharper inhalations after deeper and sharper exhalation. Let us make a manual of seating, post-exhalative mulabandha and uddiyana kriya and mudra.

1) Sit straight, steady and firm by breath and awareness. Evolve the seating. Have rich breath–awareness and breathified and breathicated sitting.
2) Take deeper and resourceful inhalation in stages so that it will be very voluminous.
3) Exhale voluntarily with erect and upright trunk. This may also be in stages.
4) After such exhalation with uncompromisingly straight and erect body, append another phase of exhalation by keeping the palms on knees, slightly pressed and slight hunch in the back. One may slightly lean forward too. Such postural modulations will facilitate deeper exhalations.

5) When such an exhalation too ends, attempt a retention and immediately suck the abdomen inwards, backwards and upwards. Do this kriya of suction by intently pressing the palms on the knees. This will be mulabandha mudra (of course with uddiyana).

6) Thereafter, overcome the hunch of the back. Become straight and erect and even with some concavity at lumbo-sacral region. Then, get the head down from the nape of the neck and effect a chinlock (jalandara mudra). Roll the shoulders back and elate the thorax. When the kriya ends, arrest the condition, which will be mudra.

7) Hold on to the mudra-traya as long as the post-exhalative retention can be effected.

8) Then gradually release the grips of mudra and take an inhalation. Alternately the mudra can be released inhalatively as well.

9) Have 2 to 4 recovery cycles of breathing and go for second attempt from stage one mentioned above. There can be 8 or 10 or 12 attempts in one round. Multiple rounds may be attempted after going past orientation and even preperatories.

Evolve the ability, qualification, calibre, skill, nuances by such practices, frequently for months and years.

INHALATIVE KRIYAS AND MUDRAS :

1) To assume seating as mentioned in the above process.

2 To exhale in the confinement of the brain region quite profoundly.

3) Then inhale in stages in the order: upper chest → lower chest → diaphragm → abdomen → pelvis.

4) While the inhalation comes to abdominal region the uddiyana kriya should be commenced. This will also include the Mulabandha mudra.

5) At the end of inhalation, one must suck the abdomen back and up and hold the breath. Suck the pit of the trunk abdomen towards the diaphragm.
6) While the retention is on, one must lift the chest, roll the shoulders backwards. The sternum should be lifted and the breath held for a short while; do not attempt to hold as long as one can until some proficiency and ease is attained.
7) During the short retention, the neck should be elongated from the base. The chin should be elongated forward and then brought down to go into the notch. The jaws, mouth, teeth, tongue should be soft and relaxed.
8) After the very short retentions, the neophyte should release all mudras and grips along with exhalations.
9) In kumbhaka or retention after inhalation, the inhalation terminus should be the diaphragm and not the throat or above.
10) Uddiyana mudra must be maintained quite prominently.

There is an alternative process for a beginner. There are distinct differences with the above process.

1) In the above process, the process commenced with profound and sharpen exhalation of brain confinement. Alternately, here it is pelvic exhalation.
2) Take an inhalation of illium-perineum region and pelvic-abdominal inhalation in stages. This should be a slightly sharper and thicker inhalation.
3) While inhaling, contraction, suction, squeeze and elation in pelvic-abdominal region should be effected. This will be mulabandha and uddiyana kriya.
4) With the last stage of inhalation, the abdominal organs should be unified with the diaphragm (with suction). Simultaneously the thorax should be sucked up and

the shoulder rolled back, sternum lifted and chin lock effected as mentioned in the process above. Thus there will be Jalandara mudra. The retention should be nominal and titular but not to its testing capacity and might. Then, the step 8-onwards process should be handled and few cycles of normal breathing be done as recovery breathing.

Both the above-mentioned processes must be attempted in different graphic modes discussed in one of the earlier chapters. Particularly the reverse-conically commencing and obverse-conically ending inhalations will give immense benefits.

Mulabandha launch
and
Jalandara terminal

Process of kriya mudra-traya :

However, each mudra may be singularly attempted beginning with and ending with obverse cones alternately. Anyway, these mudras viz.

Mulabandha
Uddiyana
Jalandara

These kriyas are commenced as aspect of yogasana itself. Then there is a perspective such as usage and application, addressing and conditioning by/on/in/for breath and there are several shvasa kriyas executed in asanas. Then there are:

Yogasana kriyas
Yog kriyas
Prana kriyas
Tattva kriyas
Chakra kriyas

Laya kriyas

practiced in asanas amongst the 18 great kriyas of yog asanas. Thus much of the training of the mudras is applied in asanas itself. Then as a preliminary in Shvasayama, many breathing exercises are handled. These were discussed in one of the previous chapters.

Thus much of the prayogas of mudra-trayas are taken up. It must be noted here that extensive uddiyana kriyas are taken up in the first place. By its proficiency, mulabandha mudra begins to arrive on the scene. When both these mudras are in practice one should attempt Jalandara mudra in a wide range of inhalative Shvasayama and Pranakriya in Shvasayama. These attempts are in seated Shvasayama exercices.

Initially, these mudras will be raw but then gradually become ripe. Thereafter, the attempts must be made with very fine, subtle, thin, rarified, tender, and gentler breathing. It should be brought to notice here that the term

'GATI VICHCHEDA'

in the sutra, expressly comes for the retentive phase after inhalation and exhalation. For long, we have been considering it by reference to mudras in particular. Incidentally, there was a passing reference to puraka and rechaka. Thus we considered partially internal, external and the arresting manifestations (bahya, abhyantara, sthambha vritti) in this chapter and some foregone chapters. But yet we have not come to explore the term "Pranayama" in the first sutra referring to pranayama. It is now overdue and we should not further postpone it. Let us commence it in the following chapters.

❖ ❖

Chapter : 27

PRANA AND PRANAMAYA KOSHA

This is an important, vital and fundumental consideration in the very classical approach in yogic pursuits. In neo-yog, this has received deplorable neglect. Shvasayama has been and is being given the status of pranayama. Even the modern masters of yog are unaware of:

Prana
and
Pranamaya kosha

and it has only remained as a topic in theoretical adhyatma. Anyway Prana(for which there is no word in any other language), is a metaphysical principle; it is thus a noumenal and not a phenomenal entity.It is energy having a cosmic source. Yog-shastra defines it as

Vishva chaitanya shakti
Meaning
Universal cosmic energy.

When seekers in yog do something akin to pranayama, they merely deal with one's own personal breath but do not question as to how it is an *ayama* of universal cosmic energy.

Moreover, in a consumer package, one
tries to set right one's own chaotic
Breath. Thus Pranayama

is not merely setting right the chaotic
personal micro-mind by breath.

What one voluntarily does on the breath has no logical rationale to be called pranayama. In what way does this so-called pranayama have to do with prana which (according to the Shastras) is *vishva chaitanya shakti?*In our classical approach, it becomes paramount that we consider what is prana and its ayama.

The question remains as to what is prana. There is a very basic primary information about prana as 'that energy because of which we are living and animated.' All signs of sentiency are because prana is instilled in us;and when life ends, what departs for transmigration is prana.

Prana comes and goes,
Not coming to birth
and having a death later.

But Adhyatama does not give such childish answers. Adhyatma speaks about

Adhibhautic
Adhidaivic
Adhyatmic

aspects in man.

We are manifestations of bhutas or elements which is adhibhautic, constituted by celestial forces called our Adhidaivic constitution and with an Adhyamatic Pratishtha (status).

Thus man has a macrocosm within oneself; and because there is a universal principle residing in us as "Antaryamin", all these sub-serving deities have to huddle around Him. Therefore, according to Adhyatama, all the 33 deities rally around Him and have their residence within us. These are the entire celestial clan of beings called Devatas. There are 33 classes of celestial deities.

These are:

Ashta vasus (8)
Ekadasha rudra (11)
Dvadasha Aditya (12)
Indra (1)
Prajapati (1)

Similarly, 49 maruta ganas and celestial yaksha, rakshasa, kinner, vidhyadhara, Gandharva also reside in us. Now why are all these celestial beings crowding in us? It is because of the

Antaryami Amruta,
That is Purusha as Antaryami in us.

Now since the celestial beings have to reside in us there has to be a celestial atmosphere for them within us.

Thus there is pranamaya kosha
Within us which has celestial
Atmosphere. The gods, demigods,
semi-gods reside in us.

Just as man has to carry oxygen (our atmosphere) in outer space—gods need to have theirs within us. That atmosphere is made up of prana or pranic profusion. Thus it is called Prana maya kosha meaning prana profused sheath.

Prana is the 'oxygen of gods.' It is there in the atmosphere but minimal. In and by pranayama, breathing becomes rich in prana. Therefore, there is better replenishment of prana for pranamaya kosha. This is one of the reasons why Gita says

"The body should be understoodas a Kshetra
(Holy place) Arjuna."(13 Chpt.)

There is Teertha-kshetra in our body because Ishvara resides in it as antaryami and his secondaries reside in us.

Teertha-kshetra (or holy place) has a holy atmosphere, holy dwellers, holy things and hence this kshetra is richly sublime. These are not malign forces but all benign forces and there is no discord but full concord here. Everything is godly and cosmic, sublime and noble in this Pranamayakosha swarga within us.

There is no malice, hatered, aversion,
psychosis, neurosis, malefide conditions and
the three gunas,namely, Sattva, Raja and Tama
have no contrariety. The five elements of
contrasting characters such as
> *Prithvi – hard*
> *Aap– cool and soft*
> *Tej – hot parching*
> *Vayu – soft and fluid-shaped*
> *Akash – attributeless*
all have harmony and perfect concord. They
are no longer pancha mahabhutas or even
pancha tattvas but become panchadevatas.

Everything is pure, pious, sublime, noble, heavenly and sanctified

Because Pranamaya kosha is Deva-Devata-maya kosha.

It is because of this that 'the body is a kshetra' (*Bhagvad Gita*). There is the shrine of 'Divinity' and a complex of Divvya desha (temple complex).

Pranayama kosha is composed of five pranas, namely,

> *Prana*
> *Apana*
> *Samana*
> *Udana*
> *Vyana.*

And six chakras:

Muladhara
Svadhisthana
Manipuraka
Anahata
Vishuddhi
Ajna.

The Hatha yogic texts and Tantras describe the chakras as the place where manifestations of adishakti such as yakani, dakani etc. as well as Brahma, Vishnu, Mahesha, Ganesha, Sadashiva Guru reside in chakras as chakra–devatas. The 14 senses (five conative, five cognitive and four internal of mind) have 14 devatas as presiding deities. Thus, there is a god-complex within us. This swarga in pranamaya kosha and pranayama is for them. It is by 'them.' It is not for 'us' and by 'us'. At this point, we come to a question: who, then, does pranayama? Let us consider this in the following chapter.

Chapter : 28

'I' DOES NOT DO PRANAYAMA

Classical yog is an 'anushthana', which is expressed in the 28 sutras of the second chapter. *Anusthana* is ritualistic, worshipping form where god is worshipped as 'God.' The principle of worshipping is देवंभूत्वा देवं यजेत् ।

Which means becoming godly and divine to worship Divinity. One must take up godliness to worship god. It is a

Sublime
Transcendent
Ethereal and
Noble

state of oneself. According to religious consciousness, one should not be petty and paltry. One should not be insignificant, helpless and hapless. One should not be miserable, guilt-stricken and petty. One should not feel impoverished and destitute. We must be absolutely unusually sublime to be worshipping Divinity. We need to be ideally transcendent and not enmeshed in delimitations such as:

Caste	**Class**
Creed	**Race**
Ethnicity	**Gender**
Status	**Stature**
Condition etc.	

Our empirical 'I' is in such grave delimitations. We must be exceedingly pure, pious and sanctified. Such should be the 'I' which really is not the 'I' of the business plane of life. It is 'I' less 'I'! It is a very transcendent 'I' and not at all with the taint of any of the delimitations mentioned above.

Such is the required 'I' in pranayamic endeavour. Rather, for all aspects of yoganga-anushthanat,such an 'I' ('I'-less 'I') qualifies for pranayama. Thus the preliminaries must work in this direction.

Breathified and breathicated 'I' has such a transcendent condition.

It is 'Daivi' (divinized) without any "I"-ness at all.

Basically we are in a 'kneaded' condition under breath-awareness; this is a major condition. So also the pranicised condition of the embodiment is a major characteristic. What is noticeable is that the 'I' is free from *Annamaya* gravity. In our worldly life this is the gravity which works on us and even 'I' and 'me.' Thus, we are engulfed and permeated by all those delimitations mentioned above.

When one escapes this *annamaya* gravity, our 'I' or 'me' does not remain 'this' (meaning the 'I' claim).

Thus, it is 'that I' which does pranayama and not 'this I' which is busy and preoccupied by the entire worldly life. In mysticism, this 'I' is said to be 'nobody to anybody and everybody.'

It is not man or woman, young or old, neither father nor son nor mother or daughternor wife or husband, so also birthless, deathless, diseaseless, decayless and transcendent.

Don't we exist in a metaphysical, meta-psychical status in a dreamless sleep? Are we man or woman, or young or old, stong or weak in such a state?

Is not the first moment on awakening after sleep or the last moment of a wakeful condition before going to sleep? Are these not transcendent conditions? It is a twilight condition before the rise of 'I'ness or asmita. It is a pure state of being before any becoming. It is the field of mind before any blade of vasana or sanskar. In yog-psychology, this is called 'escape of annamaya gravity.' The teachers in yog must make the student understand this and give some clue of this experience in *shavasana*.

Pranayama needs such a culture of psyche, consciousness and mind-stuff.

> *It is yog–dharma and yog-sanskriti.*
> *One must come out of shareera-*
> *dharma and annamaya-dharma*
> *which has an inseperable*
> *background of:*
>> *Genetic background,*
>> *Genealogical background*
>> *Ethnic background*
>> *Karmic background etc.*

But when one is under pranayama gravity it is almost a

> *'no-gravity gravity.'*

Therefore, it is a transcendendent condition.

In other words, it is 'Adhyatma-shastra.'

In adhyamatmic status, we are nobody to nobody and nobody to anybody and everybody.

> *Such is the subjective entity which*
> *does pranayama. It is not 'WE' or 'I'*
> *that does it.*

Not much can be said about such a mysterious 'I'. Words have great limitations.

Chapter : 29

MORE ABOUT PRANA AND PRANAMAYA KOSHA

Pranayama is by, for, on, in, with 'Panchapranas'
These five pranas are:

Prana

Apana

Samana

Udana

Vyana

At the outset, what needs to be said is that there is a distance of several light years, billions of astronomical units between

Pancha-pranas

and

Pancha-vayus.

The panchapranas are essentially prana while panchavayus are essentially vayu (gas). Thus, panchavayus are elemental while the panchapranas are not at all elemental.

Thus panchapranas are Abhautika while the panchavayus are very Bhautika.

Though there is a radical difference between the panchapranas and panchavayus, they have the same nomenclatures. But pedantic is precise in addressals. He refer to the five pranas as prana—apana—samana—vyana—udana and refer to the panchavayus, without fail as Prana-vayu,

Apana-vayu, Samana-vayu, Udana-vayu and Vyana-vayu. He does not fail to add the noun 'vayu' when referring to pancha-vayus. Thus when referring to Panchavayus, it is important to mention their family name – Vayu. But the Pancha-pranas are without such a family name. The prana, apana etc. are common in both groups because of their regions in the body. First of all, let us consider the five vayus which are within the body. All internal movements are because of these vayus.

The first one is Prana-vayu. This is not oxygen as physics says. Oxygen in vernacular in called Pranavayu, but what is being referred to here is not oxygen. Thus, vernacular people should not confuse the two here. Prana-vayu is the vayu that dwells in the heart region. All the movements in this region are conducted by the vayu called Prana-vayu. Thus the region of the prana-vayu is the heart region.

Apana-vayu dwells and moves in the region below the navel region (pelvis and hip to the legs and feet). The Samana vayu is between the heart and the navel. The Udana vayu is in the region above the heart up to the crown of the head. The Vyana is vyapaka that is all over the body and particularly in the peripheral layer of the body. Out of the five vayus, the prana-vayu has a set of upa-vayus meaning subsidiary vayus. The following are its names and functions:

1) Naga-vayu – belching, vomitting
2) Krukar-vayu – hunger and thirst
3) Kurma-vayu – flickering of the eyelids.
4) Devadatta-vayu – yawning
5) Dhananjaya-vayu – form of body

These are also colloquially refered to as the five upa-pranas. Now, the functions of the five pranas are as under:

Prana : breathing and coronary-pulmonary activity;

Apana : Movement near the anal region and the generative organ as well as other movements in the lower extremities.

Udana : Movement of visual and auditory organs; so also the neck and shoulders;

Samana : Digestion and circulation of nutrients through the blood.

Vyana : Throat region and all peripheral condition.

An ancient commentary on *sankhya-karika* called *Yuktidipika* conveys the following about these Pranas:

Pranavayu: External function— serves and acts like a policeman or officer; Saluting the superior officer – Internal function – Respiration,

Apanavayu : External function – taking stance before an action such as crouching before a leap; Internal function – excretory movement and the procreative or generative act,

Samanavayu : External function – co-operative endeavours; co-opting, collective, social activity; Internal function – distribution of bio-energy equally in the body and the distribution of nutrients via the circulatory system,

Udana vayu: Internal function –arterial pulsation, blood supply to the brain and brain conduction; External functions –activity by impulses, aggression, reactivity and exhibitiveness.

Vyana vayu – Internal functions – Body-wide nerveconduction; External function – love, affinity, affiliations, affection, warmth,emotionality.

These five vayus constitute the four kriyas in yogasana-pranayama technology. Since Vyana is all-pervasive, it becomes a common factor in all vayukriyas. These kriyas are as follows:

Prana : Vyana kriya (heart/thoracic)

Apana : Vyana kriya (buttocks and below)

Samana : Vyana kriya (heart to navel)

Udana : Vyana kriya (heart upwards)

This means Vyana has equal concommittance in all the vayu kriyas.

Coming to our speech (vaikhari vani), it is said that oblation of prana into apana vayu is speech. Because our oratory speech is only along with exhalation. *Prashnopanishad (1/5)* divulges this relationship between prana and vacha.

Then just as there are pancha-vayus, there are panchapranas. They have their loci in some locations as have the vayus. Infact, these vayus or pranas are not five substances. But they have five names because of their operations and operative centres. The prana is one but has five different names because of its five functions and operative centres; it is just like our planet, which has one ocean but we have given itdifferent names for our convenience; they also indicate to us where they are.

For example, the Pacific Ocean is between the two coasts of far-East Asia and the west coast of the two Americas.

Or the Atlantic Ocean is between the east coast of the two Americas and the western side of the European and African continents.

Or the Indian Ocean is between Australia and South Asia-Africa.

Similarly Prana is one but has five names and loci, as mentioned above.

Prana is the source energy in all bio-manifestations; just as Nuclear, solar energy or even electricity have several different manifestations, similarly prana manifests in living beings.

One and the same prana manifests in different ways from plants to ants and from ants to elephants. All their animative acts are Prana-vilas. The monsterous feats of an elephant or the awesome acts of birds and other creatures are a prana-vilas.

In us, one Prana manifests in all our physical, mental, intellectual, sensory and psychic activities.

*Prana is manifestation of Adishakti in us.
Prana as a matter of fact is manifestation
of 'Shakti' in us. What the Adi-shakti
in us does, is through prana.*

The Saptashati eulogises prana:

या देवी सर्वभूतेषु.... नमो नमः ।

The Upanishads praise prana unanimously:

*'Prana is Aditya,'
Prana is effulgence of fire.' (Prashna/1/7)*

*'Salutations to Prana which governs all this universe.
All beings are supported by Prana.' (Atharva Veda/11/4/15)*

"All this is by Prana." (Ath.Ved. 11/4/15)
"Prana is Rudra." (Chan. Upa. 3/16/3)
"Prana is Aditya." (Chan.Upa. 3/6/4)
"Prana is Vasus." (Chan. Upa. 3/16/1)
"Prana is Hari." (Shatapatha B. 6/5/1/5)
"Everythingin the three worlds is sourced in Prana."
(Prashna Upa. 2/13)
"Prana is my king (Vajasaneya/20/5)
"Prana is all power and prana is immortal."
(Briha.Up, Chand. Up)

One of the approximately 32 Brahmavidyas according to
the Upanishads is Prana-vidya;
It says,

*"One who realises that Prana is the senior-most
and the supreme-most becomes senior-most
and supreme!"*

The Vayu devata is greatest amongst the devatas; the
Upanishad says:

नमस्ते वायो.... ।

(TaittiriyaUpanishad)

The Brihadaranyaka Upanisad says:

"JUST AS PRANAMAHMA IS TRUTH
PRANA TOO IS TRUTH." (2/2/20)

Just as in the Lord's prayer, we invoke God with the words, "Oh Lord! You are our Father, you are our Mother...

It is said about prana too: Prana is father, mother, brother, sister, preceptor... (Chandogya Upanishad/7/15/1)

The Kaushitaki Upanisad has a passage which inquires into the supreme Good. It has an illustrative story –

It so happens that once the deities within us have a conflictas to who is the supreme one within. Each claims its own superiority and the result is a grave quarrel. So they all decide to set up a tribunal under Prajapati Brahma. Brahma very deftly sidesteps judging. He wisely suggests:

"Why not let each one depart from the body to judge their impact and effect? See what happens in their absence. Then one should return after six months for another one to depart. This way, you will solve your own problems."

They are convinced and shortly, each one starts departing for six months to return and for the next one to depart.

Thus one deity departs to return after six months. The man gradually becomes blind, deaf, dumb, intellectless etc.

But the man lives, survives. However, when prana finally decides to leave, all deities feel choked and uprooted. They collectively beseech prana,

"Oh Prana! please do not depart."

Thus they get their answer. They all shower bounties and offer their greatness to prana and willingly give a crowned position to Prana.

The Upanisad finally declares,

'PRANA IS BRAHMAN.'

Chapter : 30

MORE ABOUT PRANAMAYA KOSHA

Students of yog and yog-sadhana are oriented with the Pranamaya-kosha for Prana kriya in yogasanas. Just as the body has 60,000 to 70,000 miles of vascular network and 6,000 odd miles of nerve- network, there is a pranic network too according to esoteric physiology. It is an endless network. From the esoteric heart emanates 101 nadis of which 100 nadis have 72,000 branches each. The navel is another nadi centre. Then each of the six chakras are again a source of countless nadis.

Yog-technology deals with unknotting several knots in the nadis which are because of klesha, vasana etc. and other impurities. The nadis need to be set right, cleansed and purified. This is greatly important in spiritual evolvement.

> *Like the coronary heart blocks*
> *which create fatal problems to life, the*
> *vasana granthis too create such blocks*
> *in the prana-nadis thus preventing*
> *sublimement, ennoblement, transfigurations*
> *and transmutation necessary and*
> *inevitable in spiritual evolution.*

The Pranamaya kosha is constituted by the five Mahapranas (Prana-apana etc). Then there are the shat chakras and Granthi-trayas of esoteric physiology.

These granthis (nadi junctions) are:

Brahma granthi,
Vishnu granthi and
Rudra granthi.

The Pranamaya kosha is the reason why the entire universe exists as a miniscule universe within us. Our entire "Prarabdha plan" (destiny plan) is in this Pranamaya kosha. It has the blueprint of our entire life with all its minute details. The shatchakras are "Shakti sthanas"; mula shakti is set right to suit our destiny plan in these six chakras. The one and the same *mulashakti* (vital energy) manifests in each one of us differently.

The sun has a constant temperature of around 6,500 degrees Celsius but we experience different conditions and temperatures on the surface of our planet from dawn to dusk and from winter to summer. Similarly, the *mulashakti* manifests differently in each one of us.

Adishakti has 51 shakti-peethas, each one having a shabda or Akshar.

The pranakriya takes place using the Madhyama vani while breathing. In Madhyama vani, the swara-varnas (vowels and consonants) are silently uttered along with voluntary breathing. The shat chakras have 50 petals which again have 50 letters. These are as follows:

VISHUDDHI CHAKRA

अं आं इं ईं उं ऊं
ऋं ॠं लं लृं एं ऐं
ओं औं अँ:

Anahata Chakra

कं खं गं घं ङं
चं छं जं झं ञं
टं ठं

MANIPURAKA CHAKRA

डं ढं णं तं थं

दं धं नं पं फं (10 petles)

SVADHISTHANA CHAKRA

बं भं मं यं रं लं (6 petles)

MULADHARA CHAKRA

वं शं षं सं (4 petles)

AJNA CHAKRA

हं सं (2 petles)

One can see that all the literal letters are here and pranakriya uses all svara-varna-vyanjanas with a few exceptions. Long sound-forms are used in pranakriya to create resonance in prana-nadis.

A neophyte is supposed to use the following single-lettered, silent sound-forms which are vaachika kriyas as well. Following is the list of these letters which do not use the short and half sound forms.

अ आ ई ऊ ए ऐ ओ औ अं अ: ॥१०॥

क का की कू के कै को कौ कं क: ॥२०॥

ख खा खी खू खे खै खो खौ खं ख: ॥३०॥

ग गा गी गू गे गै गो गौ गं ग: ॥४०॥

घ घा घी घू घे घै घो घौ घं घ: ॥५०॥

च चा ची चू चे चै चो चौ चं च: ॥६०॥

छ छा छी छू छे छै छो छौ छं छ: ॥७०॥

ज जा जी जू जे जै जो जौ जं जः ॥८०॥

झ झा झी झू झे झै झो झौ झं झः ॥९०॥

ट टा टी टू टे टै टो टौ टं टः ॥१००॥

ठ ठा ठी ठू ठे ठै ठो ठौ ठं ठः ॥११०॥

ड डा डी डू डे डै डो डौ डं डः ॥१२०॥

ढ ढा ढी ढू ढे ढै ढो ढौ ढं ढः ॥१३०॥

ण णा णी णू णे णै णो णौ णं णः ॥१४०॥

त ता ती तू ते तै तो तौ तं तः ॥१५०॥

थ था थी थू थे थै थो थौ थं थः ॥१६०॥

न ना नी नू ने नै नो नौ नं नः ॥१७०॥

प गा पी पू पे पै पो पौ पं पः ॥१८०॥

फ फा फी फू फे फै फो फौ फं फः ॥१९०॥

ब बा बी बू बे बै बो बौ बं बः ॥२००॥

भ भा भी भू भे भै भो भौ भं भः ॥२१०॥

म म मी मू मे मै मो मौ मः ॥२२०॥

य या यी यू ये यै यो यौ यं यः ॥२३०॥

र रा री रू रे रै रो रौ रं रः ॥२४०॥

ल ला ली लू ले लै लो लौ लं लः ॥२५०॥

व वा वी वू वे वै वो वौ वं व: ॥२६०॥

श शा शी शू शे शै शो शौ शं श: ॥२७०॥

ष षा षी षू षे षै षो षौ षं ष: ॥२८०॥

स सा सो सू से सै सो सौ सं स: ॥२९०॥

ह हा ही हू हे है हो हौ हं ह: ॥३००॥

ळ ळा ळी ळू ळे ळै ळो ळौ ळं ळ: ॥३१०॥

क्ष क्षा क्षी क्षू क्षे क्षै क्षो क्षौ क्षं क्ष: ॥३२०॥

Now look at this marvel.

Suppose 320 modes are used for inhalations and 320 modes are used for exhalations, then there will in all probability be an astonishing (320 x 320 = 102400) modes.

These are only single-letter usages. If one uses the double or triple letters, the growth will be exponential. The pranakriya in pranayama is supposed to start with "Svara-varna-Vyanjan."

These are the 330 literal letters, which are used in Vachika kriya (Madhyama Vani) while breathing in pranayama. The *naama* (nomenclatures of Divinity) can be similarly used in breathing.

These will form the Amantraka pranayama which the science of Yog mentions.

When the beeja mantras or other mantras such as Gayatri, Panchakshari, Shadakshari, Ashtakshari, Dvadashakshari etc. are involved, it becomes Samantraka pranayama.

Shastras mention two classes of pranayama, namely,

Amantraka
and
Samantraka.

The above is a primary definition of the two pranayamas. Without Pranakriya, the yog technology does not work on essential and core aspects of yog. This is true of pranayama as well. Without pranakriya, the endeavour would be only shvasayama and not at all pranayama. Without Pranakriya in breathing and pranayama, there will be no accomplishing of

Pancha-tattva kriya
Shat-chakra kriya

which is paramountly important in man-making in pranayama and even chitta-parinama in pranayama. In yogasanas, Pranakriya, Tattvakriya and Chakrakriya work in a limited way but these are vital preliminaries after which pranayama can work on a higher and finer plane. The Chakra-Tattva kriya duo in Pranayama works exaltedly on infra-psychosis of klesha and Vasana. Yogaasanas with these kriyas carry out the vital preliminaries and pranakriya in Shvasayama can work on those moves subtly. Pranayama will work exaltedly, and will also work on the infrastructure of the chitta or mindstuff.

Pranamaya kosha is also the loci of Tattvas.

As believed generally, prithvi, aap, tej etc. are not only the elements or materials of body but also of the mind. These elements can have positive or negative as well as base or lofty and noble effects. Let us briefly consider this.

Physicality and 'mindality' of Prithvi tattva :

Element of earth is behind solidity in the body. The shape and form of body limbs and organs depends on this element.There can be excessive hardness, or inflexibility in the body and its parts. Calcifications etc. are mutations of the earth element. Good flexibility, mobility and lightness or buoyancy is a result of better management of this element of the body.

This element can have such a similar manifestation in the mind. Rigid mind, uncompromising mind, stone-mind, stone-headedness, mental heaviness, uncompromising obstinacies are negative manifestations in the mind-matter. On the positive front, there can be relentlessness, courage, steadfastness or mind like the rock of Gibraltar, mental toughness etc. Resoluteness is another quality that it can bestow. There are situtations in life where we are expected to be tough like stone in a meritorious condition. That is the grace of this element. The excess deficiencies and optimal levels of its manifestations are possible in mind matter as well and hence this element needs to be ideally managed.

On the physical/biological plane, this is a significant element. Health sciences advocate a balanced level of iron in the body and body chemistry; so also the minerals. But this earth is quintiplicated earth and not the only element of earth (50% earth and the other 50% is all the remaining four elements). Students of philosophy need to be familiar with the concept of:

Quintiplicated earth and elements called Panchikruta tattvas, which work on phenomenal plane. This is a topic of Metaphysics.

Therefore, a seeker of pranayama needs to be literate about metaphysics in general and quintiplication in particular.

Merely taking supplementary calcium and iron is not managing the element in the body; one must understand that this quintiplicated element in the body must be addressed.

Moreover, in Adhyatma, Paramartha and yog, there are prithvi tattva kriyas for metaphysical qualities such as

Magnanimity
Generosity
Tolerance etc.

The earth is so magnanimous that when we plant some 200 grams of seeds in an acre of land, we reap a golden harvest worth several quintals of grain. Mother Earth can be more generous than our biological mother. Biological mother may disown her child for some exceptional reasons but Mother Earth supports one and all. She is bountiful and generous to one and all.

This makes the use of the Prithvi tattva kriyas and the prithviprana kriyas very important in pranayama. By taking recourse to the beeja mantras in which "Lum" is the sound form used in puraka (addition), Rechaka(subtraction), Antara kumbhaka (multiplication) and bahya kumbhaka (division), the mathematical and quantitative management of this element is carried out.

As suggested, there are two kriyas with reference to the element of earth which, of course, for a yogi is Anusthana in Prithvi-devata and not prithvi-tattva. In the material world, it is

Prithvi MAHABHUTA (or the great spirit)
In metaphysics and philosophy, it becomes
Prithvi TATTVA (principle)
But in religious consciousness, it becomes
Prithvi DEVATA (deity).

There are two kriyas in asana-pranayama with reference to Prithvi . They are

1) Prithvi Prana kriya
2) Prithvi tattva kriya.

The prithvi prana kriya is by the letters:

ल ला ली लू ले लै लो लौ लं: ॥९॥

In Puraka-rechaka and two kumbhakas, the prithvi tattva kriya is by the letters, which lead up to beeja mantra. They are -

लं लां लीं लूं लै लैं लों लौ लं: ॥९॥

The beeja mantra, however, is:

लं

These are again used in Puraka-Rechaka and the two kumbhaka Pranayamas. So also, what mightily contributes for this is

> *Uddiyana kriya, mudra*
> *Mulabandha kriya, mudra*
> *Jalandara kriya, mudra*
> *Agnisara kriya*
> *Kapalabhati kriya, mudra*
> *Bandha-traya.*

These Pranayamas, kriyas, mudras and bandha-trayas will be instrumentalities for managing Prithvi.

PHYSICALITY AND 'MINDALITY' OF AAP (or water)

The element of water, aap, is again a material substance for both our physicality and 'mindality'. There can be excess or deficiency of this element resulting into positive or negative impacts in its manifestations in the embodiment. We are all aware of the dangerous proportions of

> *Water retentions*
> *and*
> *Dehydration, both of which can prove fatal.*

The body is said to contain some 80% water and its normality is vital. The very concept of bio-chemistry shows the pre-eminence of water or liquid and/or chemicals in the body. The brain too has electro-chemical states. Thus it is needless to speak elaborately on the relationship between the human body and the element of water or even the watery constitution of the body.

The mind, too, is equally under the influence of water.

Hypo-hydrated mind is a dry, cruel and emotionless mind. While hyper-hydrated mind is timid, weak, sentimental and unduly emotional. An ideally hydrated mind has exalted human qualities such as generosity, magnanimity, compassion, sensitivity, friendliness, humaneness, philanthropy, altruism, love, affection, warmth, devotion, reverence etc.

Therefore, it becomes evident that one needs to carry out aap management or tuning and fine-tuning of aap in the mind-stuff. A substance like water flows down slopes and can be channelised or even pumped up; so also the aap in the body and mind can be so managed. In life management, the mind at times needs to be hardened and at other times softened and made tender, at times, numbed, at others, sensitized, at times the mind needs to be thickened and at other times, thinned down. Thus Yog considers this and provides these two –

Jala prana kriya
And
Jala tattva kriya

for its management. This is by inhalations, exhalations and retentions, Puraka, Rechaka and kumbhaka, uddiyana kriya and mudra, Kapalabhati and Agnisara kriyas in Pranayama. So also Bandha-trayas for a proficient yogi. The letters for the two kriyas are as follows:

Jala–prana kriya:

व वा वी वू वे वै वो वौ व: ॥९॥

Jala tattva kriya:

वं वां वीं वूं वें वैं वों वौं वं: ॥९॥

The beeja-mantra, however, of this element is:

"वं"

PHYSICALITY AND MINDALITY OF TEJ

Fire is the third element. In case of our body, one is aware of disease and morbidities due to imbalances in this element. There are conditions of fever to sun-stroke on the one hand,

and chronic cold conditions etc. on the other. Fire is very important for animation, metabolism, activity, digestion etc. Even the appearancive beauty depends upon fire. The glow and charm or beauty of the human face is by the proper expression of 'Tej.'

Temperature regulation in our body is vitally important and the hypothalamus in the brain regulates it.

Even austerities are rightly called Tapas which suggest temperature levels in the embodiment. We understand the figurative meanings of a

"Hot blooded"
and a
"Cold blooded act."

There are similarly hot and cold conditions in the mind, which have both the meanings viz. positive and negative. The shadripus too manifest a fire such as:

Kama—agni
Krodha—agni
Lobha—agni
Moha—agni
Mada—agni
Matsara—agni

They really burn the man to ashes. But on the positive front again, there are agni such as

Jnana—agni
Yog—agni
Vairagya—agni,

all of which exalt the process of spiritual evolution. It was said earlier that Tejas, which is an exaltation of agni, is an important component of the Adhyatmic process. The locus of agni tattva is in the Manipuraka chakra which is the location of the gastric fire or Vaishvanara agni; 'RUM' is the beeja mantra for it. It is significant that the theist and deist prefer the name of Sri Rama, which is again nama of Agnitattva. Raama–nama is significant in the early hours before dawn. Swami Ramdas in his *Manobhoda* says,

"प्रभाते मनी राम चिंतीत जावा..."

According to Ayurveda too, the night hours have Kapha escalation and on waking, it is best countered with agni tattva. Raama–naama is thus significant for this purpose.

Yog has Agni tattva kriya in its technology to tune, fine-tune, and manage Agni tattva. This is done in pranayama by inhalation, exhalation, retentions, purakas, rechakas, kumbhakas, Uddiyana kriya mudra, Mulabandha kriya mudra, Jalandara kriya-mudra, agnisara and Kapalabhati kriyas and in other Tattvas kriyas. Here again, there are two kriyas:

Agni Prana kriya
and
Agni tattva kriya.

These are used with the following letters:

र रा री रू रे रै रो रौ रः ॥१॥
This is Agni tattva kriyas

रं रां रीं रूं रें रैं रों रौं रं ॥१॥

The Agni prana kriyas are:
The beeja mantra of Agni tattva is:

रं

It is noteworthy that vaidikas advocated Agni-upasana and Surya-upasana for purification. So also, Vayu and Jala were considered for purification, consecration and sanctity. Now, let us consider the fourth element.

VAYU IN PHYSICALITY AND MINDALITY

How is this Vayu? It has no shape or form of itself, but is a shaper and builder of other things. It is similar to Agni and Aap in one respect: it can take different shapes. The Hindu mindset may recall Sri Hanuman and Balabhima as Vayu-Putras who were the personifications of power, strength and valor. They had exceptional and awesome strength and prowess.

Ayurvedic physicians cannot forget Vayu vikara in the form of very painful body-conditions and disfigurations of body. The victims of Vayu-vikara are greatly petrified by it. Vayu has positive-negative and element-induced manifestations such as:

Pinstripe body
Infirm body
Fugitive-restless body
Arthritic body
Disfigured body
Paralysed body
Speedy-athletic body
Strong body
Morbid body
A body suffering from Parkinson's and a
Mercurial body.

On the plane of mind, there are similar conditions such as:

Mercurial mind
Speedy mind
Fugitive mind
Dynamic mind
Controversial personality etc.

Vayu vikara in body can result into either morbidity in noble or inert body conditions or even paralysed or pain stricken body conditions. The defect, on the other hand, can manifest into a body with tremors or Parkinson's syndrome or restless, mercurial body.

One kind of manifestation can work to make someone an exceptional and distinguished athlete and gymnast. Vayu can similarly constitute the mind-set. It can either be an exceptionally strong, resolute mind of Sri Hanuman, an exalted steady mind or a shifty mind. Yog practitioners can easily understand the role of vayu, shvasa, shvasayama and pranayama.

Needless to say, the current topic of Pranayama-shvasayama deals with breath, air and Vayu.

We need to have mind regulator in its speed aspect such as:

Slow speed mind (to be thoughtful)
Fast speed mind (to be enterprising).

It is not proper to hasten where we should be creeping and creeping where we should be quick and fast. Thus we can understand the importance of Vayu management within us. The theorem of *Hathayoga Pradipika* can be recalled here:

"If vayu is restless,
the chitta is restless;
If vayu is at rest
the chitta is at rest."

So also another theorem which comes in several texts including *Maha Upanishad* which says,

"Breath (vayu) is the master of the mind."

Thus, vayu management is paramount. Again in pranayama it takes place by inhalation, exhalation, retentions, puraka, rechaka, kumbhaka, uddiyana, mulabandha, Jalandara kriyas and mudras, Agnisara, Kapalabhati kriyas in

Vayu-prana kriyas
and
Vayu-tattva kriyas.

The letters of vayu prana kriya are as follows:
य या यी यू ये यै यो यौ यः ॥१९॥
The letters of vayu tattva kriyas are as:
यं यां यीं यूं यें यैं यों यौं यं: ॥२३०॥
The beeja mantra of Vayu tattva is:
यं

Just as Prithvi becomes a devata for a yogi to make anusthana in Ashtanga yog for its compassion, magnamity, generosity, aap also similarly becomes a devata for its noble qualities such as purity, piety, transparency and life-giving vitality.

Tej also becomes Agni devata which again is an exalted shakti and again a purifier, transformer etc. The vayu too is such a devata: an excellent purifier, energy-form, a life-giving element a yogi can perform anusthana with by pranayama. Vayu is a unique purifier and transporter. It flows away the dirt and dirty smells while it brings in purity and odour from distant quarters. Finally we come to Akash.

AKASH IN PHYSICALITY AND MINDALITY:

Akash is not one of the five elements but the first one and the source of the rest of the four elements. According to Metaphysics, these are not five elements but five generations. They are Akash → Vayu → Tej → Aap → Prithvi generations. Thus Akash is in all the rest. Moreover, Akash is an all-pervasive element or principle or matter. It is not only a parental element but physically all-pervasive. Every part of the universe is spacial. Although the anatomy-physiology of the human body says that the body contains 80% water, metaphysics says that our body has 99.999999999 % space.

According to nuclear or particle physics, a nucleus has

three sub-atomic particles. These are protons, neutrons and electrons.

Neutron and electron orbit around the proton at the velocity of light. If each particle is enlarged to the size of a lemon, each one is some million lemons apart from each other. This tells us about the space that lies in an atom.

The point is that space is all-pervasive; moreover, spotless and taintless.

When this management is improper, we are not present where we should be present! We are unaffected where we must be influenced, and influenced where we should be taintless like space.

Etymologically, the word *Akash* means that which gives space for anything and everything and finds its space everywhere around everything and inside everything. Every element comes from space and every element has space subserving it.

Any phenomenon, action, reaction, act, response and consequence needs space and all these are metaphysically constituted by space. Thus Akash kriya is integral, basic and foundational to all kriyas.

A little thought will reveal how space has a role in our physicality. Body needs space and body has space very prominently. All the internal organs in our body have their space. Even the mind, for its thoughts, needs space. Thought depends upon space.

What happens to thought with dearth of space and sufficient space can easily be imagined; space is paramount for a proper thought process.

Is there anything in the universe that can do away with any space? Does any thing have even an existence without space? The mind similarly works in space.

Thoughtfulness is plenitude of space and
Thoughtlessness is dearth of space.

In the management of Tattvas, all those are combined with management of Akash. Pranayama carries out with modes and instrumentation mentioned on an earlier occasion such as inhalation, etc, Puraka etc, kriya-mudra etc, mulabandha mudra etc. There are again two kriyas here, namely,
1) Akash prana kriya
2) Akash tattva kriya.

The Akash–prana kriyas is based on the following nine sound forms:

ह हा ही हू हे है हो हौ ह: ॥९॥

Akash tattva kriya is based on the following nine sound forms:

हं हां हीं हूं हें हैं हों हौं हं: ॥९॥

And the beeja mantra is:

हं

Sharirakopanishad has the following to convey:
Element of Prithvi: bones, dermis, nadis, hair, flesh, etc.
Element of Aap: urine, phlegm, blood, sweat, body chemicals (secretions),
Element of Tej: thirst, hunger, laziness, languor, delusion, sex act,
Element of Vayu: to lay, to stand, sit, run, walk, etc.
Element of Akash: Kama, krodha, lobha, Moha, matsarya etc.

It clearly shows how the mind is constituted by space or Akash.

The following information will be informative as well as interesting and even amusing.

Just as the body and mind have intakes, ingestion, nourishment and ejections, emissions, dispensation for sustenance, the five elements can be traced in each of these cases.

Prithvi can be seen in our solid consumption and solid excretions.
Aap too comes in the form of fluid intakes and fluid emissions.
Heat or Tej comes in the form of hot intakes as well as substantially heaty things are such as ginger and turmeric or saffron etc. There is heat emissions in our breath and in our excretions. Even when we sit for some time, we end up heating the seat.
Vayu comes in by breath and breathing (inhalation), gaseous emissions are there in sneezing, belching farting etc. In yawning, there are both kinds (inhalative and exhalative).

Akash comes in chanting mantras, mantra sadhana, mantra-uchchar, shravana sadhana (listening). The akash emission is a philosophical and sublime thought process.

Anyway, let it be as it may. So far in Tattva kriya, we are referring to Pranakriya. It was also repeatedly occurring while dealing with Pranayama kosha. There was a reference to silent speech each time. Let us consider that now.

Chapter : 31

SILENT SPEECH AND THOUGHTS

There was so far a very frequent mention of silent speech. This is called "Madhyama Vani" in Adhyatma. There are essentially four kinds of speech:

Paraa
Pashyanti
Madhyamaa
Vaikhari.

The last one called Vaikhari is our express oration through vocal cords and mouth which is an oral organ. Indian philosophies and Vyakarana shastra deal with four speeches. No other culture in the world has so far dealt with all these. It has earlier been said repeatedly that Prana-kriya is by silent speech. Now the time has come for further delineation, exposure and clarification in this respect.

The four-fold speech is a subject matter that comes in Panini's treatise as well as in Vedantic and adhyatmic subjects. It should be recalled that Patanjali was a grammarian. Thus he was well-versed in this four-fold vacha. So also yog, which deals with chitta-vritti and kaya-vachik-manasik karma deals with this four-fold vacha. According to adhyatma, the speech is four-fold.

The common man understands only two kinds of speech:
1) Express, oratory audible speech which turns out an auditory object to be heard by the ears, and

2) Speaking within the mind which is inaudible and akin to thought.

Therefore there is room for confusion between silent speech or speech within the mind and the thought process (a jumble of thoughts). A little deliberation will remove such confusion. There is a distinguishing factor between the two. It is very evident that 'our' so-called 'mind' is absolutely not in our control. Our helplessness, haplessness and hopelessness knows no bounds when it comes to our own mind. One faces great miseries with respect to our own mind. We really have almost no control over our own thoughts. We often become helpless spectators of our own mind. What thought should or should not come in our mind is really not in our hands.

"We are conquests of our own mind."

Nothing is as vexing and harassing as much as our own mind. Control over one's own mind is the sign of being spiritually on a very much evolved plane.

Swami Ramdas has a beautiful sermon for our mind. Only a saint like him qualifies to give advice.

But this is not the case of silent speech. It is in our control as much as the express speech is in our hands. We are not as miserable, helpless, hapless, hopeless in silent speech as much as we are in our thought process. There can be an agenda, plan and scheme for silent speech. The operative rights are with us. Thus, the evolvement process greatly lies with this silent speech which is Vachika Karma.

Moreover, when the silent speech is on, the mind has an indirect control exercised over it. The express speech (Vaikhari) or 'impress' speech (Madhyama) exercises a partial control over our naughty mind.

Now, one should understand the difference between these semantics

"I am thinking"
and
"Thoughts are coming to my mind."

The former is actually silent speech or Madhyama vani, which has voluntary operations. The latter is an involuntary operation and not at all in our control. In simple words, voluntary thought processes which are voluntary actually operate through silent speech discovered by Adhyatma, Yog and *vyakarna darshana*. It is not "thought" but "thinking" – usually a serious thought-process. This orientation should at least create a thin dividing line between

vichar of mind
and
madhyama vani.

Madhyama vani is, in a way, an

'AUTO-IN-LOGUE'
or
'AUTO-MONO-LOGUE'.

What is required in Prana kriya and Pranayama is to silently utter svara, varna, vyanjana, shabda, naama or mantra and beeja mantra. It is not thinking those but uttering those without using vocal cords for acoustics and sound; or by taking a bypass cutting out the organ of speech. Vaikhari express and oratory speech needs an exhalative act. Without exhaling or restraining exhalation, we cannot at all produce a vocal sound. Speech is always preceded by inhalation and speech is invariably an exhalative act.

"But silent speech can
even can take place in
inhalation."

Thus, the prana kriya is possible inhalatively, exhalatively or even retentively. Silent speech does not depend upon the instrumentality of oration which are

Expirating lungs,
Vocal cords,
Teeth,
Lips,
Tongue,
Palette,
nose

Voice is immaterial for Madhyama Vani;

silent speech or Madhyama is an
Indispensable organ of pranayama.

Pranayama without exception has to take place through and by prana kriya. This prana kriya takes place by

shvasayama with swara, Varna,
Vyakarana, nama, beeja mantra
Or mantra by madhyama.

This is implied definition of Pranayama of which quacks are absolutely unaware. Shabda-brahma, naada and mantras are a means of pranakriya along with breathing (inbreath, outbreath, pause/suspension/retention).

Let us understand an interesting
and fascinating aspect here.
A syntax or statement has meaning.
It is constituted by literal letters.
Each one of the letters has no meaning
as such, but their proper arrangements
explode with meaning.

Let us take an illustration here. The statement is,

"You are a stupid person."

This has an offending, insulting and intimidating meaning, emitting bitterness or hurt or anger and such negative states to the referred person. But if we break it into phonetic components or letters-components, it is a sound with no meaning at all, either positive or negative. The component will be as under:

Ya—uu—aa—re-- st—u—pa—ee—d
Pe—r—s—o—n.

This then is not at all an abusing statement. Thus one can say that it has no psycho-mental effect other than an auditory effect.

But when these are uttered in
Madhyama it can be basis for very
Vital and significant prana kriya
For chakra, tattva, naada—laya and
Dhyana etc. effect which are launch pads for
SUPRA CONSCIOUS STATE.

Beeja mantras and Dhyanamantra are but a constitution of sound forms.

Pranic physiology truly is a magnificent
Discovery of yog and adhyatma.

Finally a theorem that

Madhyama Vani and Pranakriya are a great
combination for chitta-Parinama and
evolvement of human consciousness.

Chapter : 32

COMMENCEMENT OF PRANA KRIYA

The whole universal creation has commenced with what is called

Primordial sound
Or
Adi-nada (adya naada)

Pranava is the source of creation and of all forms and sounds according to mysticism. There is a traditional verse which is thus:

नादरूपो स्मृतो ब्रह्मा नादरूपो जनार्दन: ।
नादरूपा पराशक्ति: तस्मान्नादात्मकं जगत् ॥

It means the trinity is of the nature of naad. The primordial shakti too is of the nature of naada. Therefore, the whole universe is of the nature of naada.

Naada has an undoubted supreme position in Gnana Karma, Bhakti yog and upasana, so also in mantra, cosmology, ontology, philosophy and religion. It is the primordial sound. It is Adi shakti—Adi—nada, Adi-shabda, Adi mantra.

Its importance in mysticism is supreme and insurmountable. .

A—U—M has three mantras. A—U—M are the three matras. One can make the following experiment very safely with significant consequences and effects.

Expressly and orally utter the first
Matra 'A' (as in uncle);
do this like a siren until the voice disappears...
and still continue to utter it in
the mind. You will get abdominal
contractions.
Similarly utter the second matra
"OO" (as in fool),
the contractions will appear in the chest.

Do the same for the matra "MA" (as in gum). The contraction will occur in the brain.

In esoteric psycho-physiology, the abdominal pit is the passion zone, the chest region is the emotional zone and the brain region is the ego zone.

Thus, by exhalative utterances, there are contractions in three major zones:

Passion zone, Emotional zone and Ego zone.

This is a kind of vocal–oral therapy. In prana kriya, the utterances are silent and the whole range of 340 modes are used. These are single-lettered utterances. The student of pranayama should get used to carrying out these fascinating observations. But prior to this, one must be able to utter these swara-varnas (vowels and consonants) clearly, faultlessly and conspicuously. This is called

"Vaikhari Spashttochaarana"

The phonation must be clear and faultless. Then one must begin to carry out silent utterances which must be similarly clear and faultless. This table of letters has been given in an earlier chapter for perusal. There are 340 letters. In vernacular grammar these are referred to as

अ — Class   (अ वर्ग)
क — Class   (क वर्ग)

च — Class   (च वर्ग)
ट — Class   (ट वर्ग)
त — Class   (च वर्ग)
प — Class   (प वर्ग)
य — Class   (य वर्ग)
(See appendix I)
We get a set of joint letters such as:
Kya ehya lya ... Kra pra mra ... and so on
Kla pla mla ... Kva pva tva ... and so on
Ksha psha tvsha ... Ksa psa tsa ... and so on
Kha pha mha ...and so on
Single-lettered utterances form primary lessons in pranakriya. These become "Amantraka pranayama". Then, in samantraka pranayama one uses mantras, naama (Taraka mantra) and beeja mantra, Gayatri mantra, shadakshari mantra (Aum namo shivaya),
Ashakshari mantra (Aum namo narayanay),
Dvadashakshari mantra (Aum namo Bhagawate Vasuddevaya) etc. are some mantras used in pranayama. Bhagawan nama (Taraka mantra) also creates prana kriya.
There are also beeja mantras such as:

श्रीं ह्रीं क्लीं ॐ ...

These are all used in Pranayama.
"Mantra" etymologically means

मननात् त्रायते इति मंत्र: ।

In vedic rituals we come across the following usage –

"प्राणायामे विनियोग: ।"

implies pranayama before vedic ritual. The sankalpa for Karma entailed- pranayama. Let us understand purport of such pranayama in the following chapter.

Chapter : 33

PRANAYAMA VINIYOGAH

In Vedic ritualism, there is an important place for Pranayama in Sankalpa. It is commenced by uttering "Pranayama Viniyogah."

Today, we commoners make a mockery of it by touching the nose by the right-hand fingers and thumb (small finger, ring finger and the thumb). But there is a set process for it. Some sages like Vashistha, Vishvamitra and Yajnavalka displayed precise and superior functions here. It is thus.

Consider the kind, mode and nature
of karma and ascertain whether karma
entails Surya-nadi or Chandra-nadi
or sushumna nadi breathing

Then because of their expertise in karma-kanda, they would be meticulous about the fact whether the karma is under the influence of

Prithvi,	*Aap,*	*Tej,*
Vayu,	*Akash*	

and set right the breathing for karma. Pranayama had an important place in ritualism and there was a provision made for Pranayama in vedic notion of karma. Today, such nuances do not matter for us commoners and hence our mockery is justified.

The point is that in *vaidika karma kanda*, pranayama comes before the sankalpa. There is pranayama mantra, which is

Sapta Vyavruti Saha
Gayatri mantra.

One is supposed to sit straight, erect, firm and steady with the head down. The right hand needs to be taken in pranayama mudra. The index and middle fingers are folded in and the tips are brought under the root of the thumb. Small finger and ring finger are bent at the knuckles and tips are brought to face the tip of the bent thumb. The tips of the thumb and the two fingers are brought on the nasal membranes to be gently placed right under the nasal bone to be used on the two nostrils. The thumbs and fingers are used to open out properly or block the needed nostril. Block both the nostrils in the case of kumbhaka;

operate the required ida or pingala or shushamna nadi and also select the proper nadi out of the five elemental nadis and suitably manipulate the breathing.

The pranayama mantra is used in the following division.

Inhalation

ॐ भू: । ॐ भुव: । ॐ सुव: । ॐ मह:
ॐ जन: । ॐ तप: । ॐ सत्यम् ।

Retention

ॐ तत्सवितुर्वरेण्यं भर्गो देवस्य धीमहि
धियो यो न: प्रचोदयात् ।

Exhalation

ॐ आपो ज्योतिरस: अमृतं ब्रह्म भूर्भुव:स्वरोम् ॥

We do just one pranayama but the sages did as much as was required to set right the breathing and the corresponding mind to become transcendent. After accomplishing the pranayamic purpose, the left palm is brought on the left lap with the palm facing upwards. The right palm is placed over it facing downwards. The Sankalpa is then uttered.

The Sankalpa describes the region, place and the location where the karma is being performed. There are also time references such as the name of Kalpa-Manvanta-yog, Samvatsara-Ayana-season, month-pakoha-nakshatra-tithi-vara-yog and the resolution as to what karma and why is it being performed. Thus he takes the Anugraha for karma meaning injunction of karma from the Divinity. Thus one qualifies to perform the karma in subservience of the Almighty.

One gets the divya-kala and necessary transcendence. The karmas have their own characteristics. Success or fruitfulness of karma needs the right nadi out of

Solar (ida), Lunar (Pingala), Neutral (sushumna)

Thus some karmas are surya nadi karmas while some are Chandra nadi karmas while some are sun + moon or sun= moon or neutral which need the sushumna breathing. Thus that becomes the main classification. Then the next selection is of five tattvas, nadis or either of the sun or moon or combinations. Interested ones should look into some basic information in svara-vijnama of the treatise, "Shiva—svarodaya"

The breath has correspondence with not only karma but

Tithi—var—nakshatra.

The suitable breath depends upon the following factors
1) Nature of karma
2) On-going breathing at that point in time
3) Chronological and almanac position of ritual (Tithi-var-nakshatra-muhurta etc.)

Anyway, vaidik ritualism has a philosophic essence called *"Karma-yogic philosophy."*

Let us now consider pranayama in karma-yog in the following chapter.

Chapter : 34

KARMAYOGIC PRANAYAMA

In the previous chapter, we had a basic concept of pranayama in vaidik rituals, Sankalpa and proper state of mind for it and karma is important. Even if it is Kamya—karma by nature and intent, the mind must be sublimated for Sankalpa and ritual although there is a difference between such karma and Nittya or Nishkama karma. Here, we shall consider such karma-yogic karma. Now let us consider the following.

Inhalative breathing gives ascendance to pranashakti (apana scales upwards). This prana has roots in the Muladhara region at the base of the *merudanda* (spine) – the Adi-shakti in us (kundalini rests here). The micro-cosmic prana under the presidency of the kundalini is in the Muladhara. So also under the Antaryami called "Sarvantaratma". The *Brihadaranyaka Upanishad* says:

(3/4/1)

The Gita *says,*

**"I am the Atma supporting
all beings, by being in all beings. "**

(10/20)

He is the Antarayami. He is karmadhyaksha.

The *Shvetashvatara Upanishad* says:

One Divinity has mysterious presence in all the being. He is all-pervasive. He presides over all karmas. He is the withness, consciousurss only and Trausceudaut principle

Our karmas are caught in a tornado of vasanas, fate, luck, ill fate, destiny. Because of the vasanas, fate, luck, ill-fate, destiny and other mundane and material causes or carnality and cupidity, the "Karmadhyaksa"(Immanent Divinity) is kept aside. But a karma yogi is navigated by the radar of Divine will. The breath provides a hotline to the internal godly gravities. Breath, breathing and prana help the yogi to unite karma which in fact is an appointment of Divinity. He then sub-serves Divinity. His faith and conviction is

He is Bhagwad—Kinkara, thus the karma is Bhagwad Kainkaryam. Pranayama gives the yogi transcendence. The shadripus, kleshas and vasanas are evaporated. The philosophy of karmayoga fumigates the chitta, making it free from delimitations and defects. Pranayama wonderfully does this fumigation of the chitta.

Thus a yogi is bereft of shadripus, klesha vasana, Karma vasana, Kama, Ichcha, Apeksha, Kartutva-Abhimana, Phalapeksha etc.

Karmayogic principles of the *Gita* (2/48) come in Pranayama itself. Thus the psyche is exalted, sublimated and cosmicalised. Even the inhalation is received gracefully as if it is Divine grace. It is received humbly and gratefully. The exhalations come with a profound surrender to Antaryami, bringing an Arpana buddhi, Arpana-vritti and Arpana bhava. Pranayamic culture, philosophy, religion best teaches culture, philosophy and religion of karmayog.

Prana is a virgin, cosmic Divine principle which transmutes and transfigures a yogi and his consciousness. Now the question comes up as to which is this pranic principle.

Chapter : 35

PRANIC PRINCIPLE

Sankhya Shastra and Darshana speak of 24, 25, 26 principles but it does not count prana. Even the para-apara prakruti or Ashtadha prakruti does not speak of prana. Thus a question haunts a student of philosophy whether such a noble principle has been counted or not. Prana has been greatly extolled in yog but what dismays a student of yog is that it has not been counted in metaphysics or ontology as a principle or even as a cosmic principle. Even the cosmology does not bring it in. Patanjali's *Yog sutras* or even Sankhya does not count it in their metaphysics. This is truly a conundrum. Patanjali has postulated

Vishesha
Avishesha
Linga matra
Alinga

parvas of Prakriti. Where does the prana come from? It does not come at all. Even *Sankhya* elaborately counts 24 principles where prana does not get a berth. This is truly dismaying to students of philosophy. The *Sankhyas* have counted 24 or 25 or 26 principles. These are:

1)Purusha
2) Pradhana
3)Mahat
4)Ahankar

5 -9) *Five Tanmatras*
10-14) *Five Mahabhutas*
15-24) Ten organs
25) *Manas*
26) *Ishvara.*

But the million-dollar question is as to why is the Prana
not counted.

Those who are not well-versed in Vedantic studies are
not haunted by this question. In Sankhya parlance, the causal
phase is called Prakruti and effectual phase is called vikruti.

For instance, Pradhana is Prakruti and
Mahat or Buddhi which emanates from it
is called its vikruti. Then Mahat is Prakruti of Ahankar,
and Ahankar is its vikruti. Then, Ahankar becomes
prakruti of Tanmatra and Tanmatra becomes
its vikruti. At the top, the Pradhana is only prakruti
but not an effect of anything and thus it is not a vikruti
of anything. At the bottom of the cosmological table,
mahabhutas have no further metaphysical
generations to follow. Thus, they do not have
Vikruti.

But Prana is a unique principle. It is neither a vikruti of
pradhana nor does it have a vikruti.

Sankhya mysticism mentions that the union of Purusha +
Pradhana causes cosmological unfoldment. The first
generation is Buddhi (Mahat) and the cosmogonical unfolding
is as under:

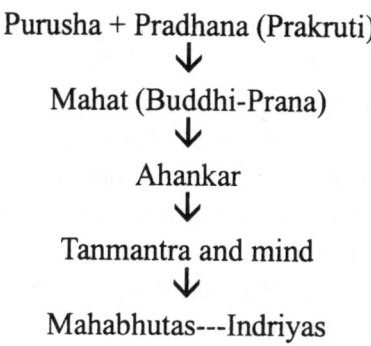

Purusha + Pradhana (Prakruti)
↓
Mahat (Buddhi-Prana)
↓
Ahankar
↓
Tanmantra and mind
↓
Mahabhutas---Indriyas

It can be seen here that prana has no progeny. Nor does it have prakruti meaning causal parentage. It should be understood that Tanmatra and Bhutas are not in one generation. The generations are:

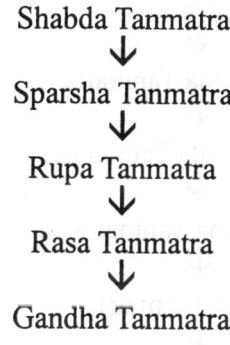

Shabda Tanmatra
↓
Sparsha Tanmatra
↓
Rupa Tanmatra
↓
Rasa Tanmatra
↓
Gandha Tanmatra

So is the case of Mahabutas. They are five generations and not one as is believed.

Akash
↓
Vayu
↓
Agni
↓
Aap
↓
Prithvi

The above delineation shows that prana is a co-generation of Mahat and could be called as a brother of Mahat, but having no progeny. But the progeny on the prakruti channel is because prana is a kind of offshoot of Mahat. Those who are well-versed in the Vedantic process, do not face any conundrum. The above process also gives us a revelation that Panchapranas and panchavayus should not create any confusion because there is a gap of nine generations between the two. The following table will divulge this:

1) Mula Prakruti
↓
2) Mahat -Prana
↓
3) Ahankar
↓
4) Shabda Tanmatra
↓
5) Sparsha Tanmatra
↓
6) Roopa Tanmatra
↓
7) Rasa Tanmatra
↓
8) Gandha Tanmatra
↓
9) Akash Tattva
↓
10) Vayu Tattva --- Pancha Vayus.

What is evident here is that Prana is of the second generation and Pancha vayus are of the 10th generation. Thus there is a yawning gap of eight generations and hence no room for confusion. A gap of eight generations is like an ocean of difference.

❖ ❖

Chapter : 36

ADHI-DAIVIK PERSPECTIVE OF PRANA

On an earlier occasion we have seen the inseperable relationship between Prana and Pranamaya kosha. While taking account of Pranamaya kosha, we saw that it is Dev or Devata kosha. It is the abode of 33 devatas and shakti facets such as Yaakini, Daakini etc.

It is also told us about Adhi–daivik constitution of our embodiment. One recalls the *Laghu Rudra* which has the following to say.

Brahma resides in generative organ,

Vishnu in the feet, Hara in the palms,

Indra in the arms, Agni in the belly,

Shiva in the heart, Vasus in throat,

Saraswati in the speech organ,

Vayu in the nostrils, Aditya and Chandra in the pair of eyes,

Ashiva in the ears, Rudra in the eye brows (forehead),

Aditya in the Murdhana, Shiva in the crown of the head,

Vamadeva in the tuft,

Panaki in buttocks and shiva Shakti in the back,

Vayu all over and various other deities and demigods in their respective places;

prana in the heart, moon in the heart and mind, Dik-devata in the ears,

Jala-devata in semen, Prithvi in limbs, Aushadi-vanaspati in hair,

Indra in strength, Parjanya in murdhana, Ishana in anger...
and so on.

The *SubalaUpanishad* mentions 14
devatas in 14 senses.

Pranayama thus is a feast and party to Devatas.
It is like a festival offer.

The trinity is paramount in the Vedic pantheon. It is:

Brahma
Vishnu
Mahesh

The *Dhyanabindu Upanishad* points out that

Puraka is called Brahma
Vishnu is kumbhaka
And Rudra is rechaka.
These are the deities of Pranayama.

(Dh. Up/20)

By those three phases of pranayama, the three deities are
worshipped. Those are oblations into those deities. Even the
pancha maha bhutas do not remain Mahabhutas but become
devatas. In Vedism, the devatas are propitiated by yajna. And
even pranayama thus becomes a yajna. The *Gita* mentions
the following:

"Apana is an oblation into prana.
And prana is an oblation in Apana.
Thus is the yajna in Pranayama."
Some others being well-restrained in food intakes
offer prana in to prana.   *(Gita- 4129, 30)*

Pranayama is a kind of Atma-yajna. Bodhayana in his
Dharmashastra says:

Amongst all yajnis
Atmayaji is supreme.   *(21.7.112)*

It can be easily said that Pranayaji is the greatest *atmayaji*. All the aspects of yajnas or constituent of yajnas are prana in such yajna. The ninth chapter of the *Gita* says that all the aspects and factors or elements or constituents of yajna are Divinity. Bhagwan says:

I am kratuh
I am yajna
I am svadha
I am Aushedi
I am Mantra
I am Ajjya
I am Agni
I am hutam. (B.G. 9/16)

In Atma yajna they are subjectivistic and in Pranayajna, they are all pranas. And such Atma yaji is the greatest yaji as clearly stated by Bodhayana.

The Tantras describe the shat chakaras. There is a presiding deity to each of these chakras; chamunda etc. Shakti forms manifest here. Thus the Adi-daivik constitution in our body has locus in Pranamaya kosha. Not much can be said here since we are totally unfamiliar with yajna in the present era. Even until about 150 years ago, we were quite acquainted with Vedic ritualism. There were Ahitagnis who observed Agnihotra. But now it has slowly become extinct. Today we are totally unfamiliar with Agnitraya, namely,

Ahavaniya
Garhapattya
Dakshinagni.

Those interested should certainly look into a wonderful piece of literature penned by M. M. Gopinath Kaviraj. He has authored a book, 'Bharatiya Sanskruti Aur Sadhana,' in two volumes, which describes intriguing mysticism behind

Manta, Tantra, Yantra, Japa, Yog, Upasanas, Japa etc. While
mentioning pranayama, he says:

> *Garhapatya is the prana*
> *Of yajamana;*
> *Dakshinagni is apana*
> *And Ahavaniya is the meditativity of yog.*

Then Sabbhya and Avasyatha are respectively
Udana and Samana.

Thus Atmayajna or pranayajna does not require a physical
form of agni as the altar (or a yajna-kunda).

At this point, we must consider the *Adhyatmic Pranava
sadhana* in Pranayama. Pranayama therefore becomes a
Brahmavidya. Let us discover it in the following chapter.

Chapter : 37

PRANAYAMA – PRANAVA – BRAHMAVIDYA

Pranayama has its peak condition being a Brahmavidya. Brahmavidyas come in Upanishads which immediately bestow emancipation or Moksha. Some of the vidyas in the Upanishads become limbs of such vidyas. Incorporating pranava in pranayama can become a preliminary Brahmavidya. One easily recalls here the UDGITHA VIDYA which occurs in the very opening part of Chandogya Upanishad. It mentions this vidya with an Akhyana. The story goes thus.

As often was the case, there was a battle
between the devas and asuras. Devas and asuras
were the offsprings of Prajapati. He was their
preceptor too. In one of their battles,
the devas wanted to turn victorious. Thus,
they approached Prajapati Brahma for advice.
He advised UDGITHA (AUM) for success.

Devas did the upasana by the nose and nostril,
but lost the battle. Thus the nose supports
both, noble and ignoble objects.
The Pranavopasana by the nose was futile.

Then the devas took recourse to speech; the asuras defeated that upasana too.

So as much as the speech adheres to truth, it is also vulnerable to untruth.

> *Same was the fate of the upasana done with*
> *chakshu and even shrotra.*
> *Same was the fate of mind.*
> *So the helpless deities came back to Prajapati.*

He advised upasana by Prana and in Prana.

The asuras were totally devastated and the gods emerged victorious.

Thus the message that *Udgitha* by main Prana is supreme.

In Kaushitaki-Brahmana-upanishad there is Pratardana vidya. There, Brahma is synonymous with Prana. It postulates that

> *Brahma is Satya*
> *Satya is Indra*
> *Indra is Prajnatma*
> *And Prajna is prana.*

Pranayama in Brahmavidya becomes a run-up to gateways and further from gateway to sanctum sanctorum of Brahman. It is the means and even the end itself. Let us now look at what the *Mundakopanishad* says:

> *"All pervasive Divinity is prana in all beings.*
> *A yogi gets within himself by realising prana."*
> *(3/1/4)*

In the 36th chapter, we have dealt with Prana as a Tattva. We considered the distinction between prana and Vayu. It implied that Prana is not Bhuta vishesha while Vayu is. The Vedantic process has dealt with that topic. Those interested can turn to the *Brahmasutra* (Ch 2/pada 4). There occurs an adhikarana called Vayukriya-adhikarna. On an earlier occasion we saw the quotation from the Upanishads which said:

Prana is Shreshtha
Prana is Jyeshtha
Prana is Vashishtha.

Prana within us takes recourse to vayu as its vehicle. Vayu kriya is the carrier of the prana. Thus it amounts to equating the two. The Brihad-Aranyaka-Upanishad says:

"What is prana that is Vayu."　　*(3/1/5)*

The *Mundaka–Upanishad:*

"From Brahman comes Prana
From prana the Manas and
all the organs, senses (Indriyas)
and the five elements."

Even *Sankhya Karika* which is criticized for not counting Prana in the principles, is not true. *Sankhya Karika* in its 29th verse implies that Prana is distinct from Vayu and

Prana has Samanya Vyapar of
Manas buddhi and Ahankar
(Antahkarana)

Even Vyasa in his commentary (3/39) says:

समस्तेन्द्रियवृत्ति: प्राणादि लक्षणा:
जीवनं... ।

Thus prana is not just a breathing act but the whole animation which gives us life.

Now, we shall consider the relationship between prana and Pranava.

Pranayama, Pranava and Brahman are thickly interrelated; any of the Brahmavidya from the Upanishads is meditative upasana.

Sri Ramanuja in his philosophy has quite pedantically postulated that Upanishadic Brahmopasanas are all essentially Bhakti yog. And this Bhakti yog has lost its tradition today.

Bhakti and Bhakti yog are not one and the same. Bhakti and Bhakti yog must not be treated as one and the same. We still have Bhakti–parampara by way of Sharanagati, Prapatti and Bharannyasa etc. However, Bhakti yog parampara is no longer there. Of course, Bhakti yog must be taken to mean that it is that vidya which is initiated into a shishya that occurs in the Upanishads. Thus one should be twice-born etc. and Adhikari of Vedadhyayana. In short, all the upanishadic Brahmavidyas are meditative and thus one must be a proficient Dhyana yogi. Pranayama is the launch point of all the Dhyana-yogic dhyanas. Yogic-dhyanas have Pranava as an essential component.

Brahmavidya is upanishadic vidyas and Dhyana-yogic in nature and since Dhyana of yog has pranayama and Pranava as basic components, the intimate relationship between Pranava and pranayama and Brahman is absolutely inseparable.

Pranayama and pranava are inseperable and pranava and Brahman again are inseperable. Thus by deduction, pranayama and Brahman, too, are established. Therefore pranayama becomes Brahmavidya.

"SOHAM Sadhana" is an essential aspect of yog sadhna. "Soham" is naada sadhana. Generally, every spiritual seeker knows that "SOHAM" is breath-related sadhna. It is yog sadhna as well as naada sadhana.

There are four letters here, which are

"Sa", "O", "ha" & "M".

Out of these four, the sound (naada) of inhalation is said to be "sa"and the sound of exhalation is said to be "ha". There are four parts in the breath viz

1) Inhalation (Sa)

2) terminal / roll over (o)

3) exhalation (ha)

4) terminal / roll over (m)

When a yogi is in supra-conscious state or kevala kumbhaka, "s" and "h" are obliterated; thus what remains is O-M, meaning A - U - M (our essential from the mystic state of "That Thou Art"). From the above four letters, if 'sa' and 'ha' are effaced, what remains is "OM" which is the mystic state.

OM (AUM) is the denoter of Brahman. Pranava also means to be keval kumbhaka or its naada. This kumbhaka is neither internal nor external but kevala. This is also called Pranavana sadhana or "Ajapa-japa" in Adhyatma.

Now let us see as to how it is Ajapa-japa.

Just as butter is kept in water, where it is untouched by water, the immanent Divinity in us called Antaryami is in AUM, as if that is its atmosphere. There is said to be an incessant resounding of AUM. That is called Anahata naada or Anahata AUM in us.

According to mysticism this goes on incessantly in our mystic heart.

The yogi takes recourse to a Madhyama vani and meditative Japa of Aum. Therefore, there are now two Aums, namely, Ahata and Anahata. Ahata is operated and Anahata is incessant.

According to naada shastra, there is what is called sympathetic consonance and Resonance.

A musician intending to use two Tanpuras first tunes one

to the required pitch and tune. Then he
lays it on the floor and starts tuning the
other one to the same pitch and tune.
When the second Tanpura
matches the first one (laid down),
it starts vibrating in resonance.
One is being plucked and the other
one is sympathetically matching.

Similarly when a yogi is having AUM
as a meditative japa and when the mind is so
cosmicalised, the yogi's meditative AUM starts
resonating to the mystic Aum within the spiritual
heart. Thus his japa fades out and merges with
the mystic japa. Thus it is called Japa without
Japa (Ajapa-japa).

On such an event the yogi is in supra-conscious
State or SOHAM becomes merely "OM"
(AUM). Is that not a Brahmopasana or culminative
Pranava-based pranayama?

Thus far we had a long delineation with a cluster of various
and numerous chapters to decipher a sutra on pranayama:

Now let us go for analyzing and ascertaining the implied
purport of the next sutra which is

बाह्याभ्यन्तर स्तम्भवृत्ति देशकाल संख्याभि:
परिदृष्ट दीर्घसूक्ष्म: ।

Let us proceed word by word in the following chapters.

Chapter : 38

BAHYA VRITTI, ABHYANTARA VRITTI AND STHAMBHA VRITTI

Merely conditioning and regulating the breath is not Pranayama as is the popular notion. Nor is the voluntary, devised and customized retention, Pranayama, as is the popular belief.

Pranayama takes place by Puraka
(not an inhalation) or by rechaka
(again not an exhalation) or by kumbhaka
(not a retention).

We had an orientation of the characteristics of Puraka, Rechaka and Kumbhaka in an earlier chapter. But closer attention is drawn to Patanjali's expression here:

"In Pranayama, the inhalative breath becomes
Internal manifestation and the exhalation
an external manifestation while the retention
becomes frozen manifestation."

It should be understood here that inhalation more so in a conditioned way is a kriya. While in Pranayama, puraka is 'vritti' and not a kriya. So also in the case of exhalations and retentions. All the three are vrittis and not kriyas.

Now it should be understood that
Behind vrittis there is thought,

*culture, sanskara and even philosophy
and religion.*

*Thus in pranayamic in-breath, out-breath
and retentions there is not merely a
technique-profused process and regulation
but Vritti, Vichar, Sanskruti, Sanskar,
attitude, philosophy and religion.*

*Thus Puraka, Rechaka and Kumbhaka
have philosophies, culture, attitude and
religious fabric.*

*Pranayama has more of culture, attitude
philosophy and religion than technical
profusion or technical modalities.*

Bahya-vritti Pranayama is thus not merely technique-studded exhalation. It is not only Uchvasa or Prashvasa or an expulsive or expiratory act with conditioning merely in volume, velocity, density or a technical modality. So also is the Abhyantara vritti which is not such an inhalation, nor is the case of Stambha vritti which is not merely retention with technical modality but all those are:

> *Vritti*
> *Pravritti*
> *Vichar*
> *Sanskruti*
> *Sanskar*
> *Dharma vritti*
> *Jnana dharma*
> *Tattva jnana*

Or in short philosophy, religion, culture and a sort of metamorphosis.

All this seems just a hollow idealism for a minor who is not at all formally initiated into yog. Yog is a serious subject and what we have in our era is merely classes, workshops, camps, retreats, intensive courses offering consumeristic packages. This is really depreciating a philosophical subject which is the subject of mind-making and man-making. The result, therefore, is that there are no studies in respect of breath and prana.

Breath and prana are noble, cosmic
and very transcendent aspects within us.
Not really ours but for all that is deemed as
"we" and "ours".
They do not have delimiting factors such
As caste, class, creed, colour, race, ethnicity
and karmic, genealogical backgrounds.
They (breath and prana) have great
worship-worthiness and veneration.

Pranayama is cosmic poetry and sermon on eternal philosophy. It has a rich ethos and theos. Pedantic study of yog shastras, yog darshana and yog-dharma soak one in its ethos.

Pranayama is Devopasana, Ishvaropasana
Antarayami upasana.
Thus it has very rich religiosity
and framework of Anushthana as the rest of
the aspects of yog. Pranayama is for Pranamaya
Kosh which is the abode of deities within us. These
Gods huddle around the Immanent
Divinity whom they
Sub-serve.

Thus in pranayama one needs to become godly
To worship gods who worship "GOD".

These will give some idea of "vritti" in Bahya antara and stambha aspects of vritti. The puraka is nourishment and replenishment to Pranamaya kosh and Rechaka is emission from Pranamaya kosh. The two are not merely biological entities in us.

They are not Puraka-Rechaka
for us and "we" but for the gods
within us.

Chapter : 39

DESHA, KALA, SANKHYA

The conditioning or regulating of breath or Prana is no doubt by:

Inhalation/Puraka And
Exhalation/Rechaka
Retention/Kumbhaka.

But conditioning or regulation becomes widely versatile and/or multi-faceted by these conditions:

Desha (region)
Kala (length or time or duration)
Sankhya (number of cycles)

Basically the pranic or breathing condition is by volume, velocity, density, length, duration, confinement, deployment, function, role, mode, process, deployment, allocation etc.
This is short-listed quite inclusively by:

Desha-Paridrushta
Kala-Paridrushta
Sankhya-Paridrushta,

which is a comprehensive scheme of regulating the breath or prana. It is, therefore, that pranayama or shvasayama is more an irrigation than supply. One needs to understand the concepts such as:

Pranic supply
Breath supply

Irrigation of/by Prana
Irrigation of/by breath

Pranayama and shvasayama are more irrigative schemes rather than supply schemes. Regulated conditions here are more of irrigation than supplies. Supplies stand logical only in respect of in-breath but not out-breath or even either of the retentions.

In the earlier chapter we considered regulation or conditioning by:

Volume
Velocity
Confinement
Graphic mode
Design mode

while dealing with Shvasayama. By implication there were aerodynamics, roles, functions of breath.

Patanjali is precise and to the point in his characterization of the regulation of prana and breath in saying,

बाह्याभ्यन्तरस्तम्भवृत्ति देशकाल संख्याभिः परिदृशः दीर्घसूक्ष्मः ।

Let us consider each one of the three and the composite conditioning.

1) Regulated by region: This is a regulation where the region in body is cordoned out and the breath is given a confinement. Following are the confinements in body:
   1) Perinium region
   2) Pelvic region
   3) Umbilical region
   4) Abdominal region
   5) Diaphragmatic region
   6) Thoracic region
   7) Vocal, throat region

8) Facial region
9) Coccygeal region
10) Lumbar region
11) Dorsal region
12) Muladhara region (apana)
13) Svadhisthana region (apana)
14) Manipuraka region (samana)
15) Anahata region (prana)
16) Vishuddhi region (udana)
17) Agnya region (udana)

The mode, function and role of breathing change from confinement to confinement. As our acts, actions and conduct also depend upon where we are and what we do at home, work place, gym, swimming pool, shopping complex, garden or any other place, the breath confinement too works in variegated ways. The above list towards the end mentions prana, apana etc. – the vayus and pranas. We have seen that they have different functions because of their confinement. Thus it can be easily understood as to how the breathing would change because of change in role and functions because of confinement. Thus by mentioning

conditioning or regulating by confinement called Desha-Paridrishta, Patanjali implies a cluster of regulating and conditioning acts.

Thus there will be such Desha-Paridrushta for inhalation/exhalation or puraka/rechaka/ kumbhaka. One can easily imagine as to what teachers must teach the students in formal and classical training programs. But quacks hasten to teach

Ujjayi
Viloma
Anuloma/pratiloma
Suryabhedana
Nadishodhana
Bhramari
Bhasrika etc. which is absurd and ridiculous.

There are two aspects or even classes of Desha-Paridrushta

1) External Desha /region
2) Internal Desha /region

What is described above is called internal regions. But what is the meaning of external region? This is to circumscribe the velocity of breathing in the cluster of conditionings mentioned above.

Suppose, the in-breath is very thin rarified
and gentle. The breath is drawn from
proximal regions of the nose. But if the
breath is sharp, then it is drawn from distant regions.
Similarly with exhalation. When it is very thin
and gentle or tender, it gets immersed in
proximal atmosphere, but if sharper, it goes
to distant atmospheres to get immersed.

Shastras describe it thus. Hold a thin cotton fiber close to your nose. The fibres will sway in and out by inhalation and exhalation respectively. If it sways softly and slightly, the breathing is soft, tender and thin and of low velocity. On the other hand, if it sways heavily and strongly the breathing is sharp, thick and of high velocity.

Thus is the description of "Desha Paridrushta" in pranayamic breathing.

KALA-PARIDRUSTHA

This is regulation by time or duration. There are again two aspects here:

1) Time and duration of the in breath, out-breath and retention by which the modality, function and role change.

2) About interproportions between the in-breath, out-breath and retention or puraka-rechaka-kumbhaka, the shastra mentions

Samavritti Pranayama
and
Vishamavritti pranayama.
These are proportions such as
1 : 1 : 1 : 1
or
1 : 2 : 1 : 2
or
2 : 1 : 2 : 1 and so on.
Let us now delineate this. Duration of the in-breath or out-breath or puraka, rechaka depends upon two factors.
1) Velocity
2) Volume
Low velocity takes a longer time or a greater volume of breath takes a longer duration. High-velocity, sharper breath would take relatively less time or lesser volume would take similarly shorter duration.

Regulation by velocity and by volume modulation are different kinds of regulation. Both are regulative acts. And they can work in combination as well.

Teachers need to train students in both these modulations, their processes and their effects.

One has to carry out prayoga with respect to trials, as well as experiments and learn the applications and addressals.

Effect of Kala-paridrushtata in respect of volume and velocity are different in breath, drive, skill in various locations mentioned in Desha-Paridrushta. Thus it is important to learn this combination of regulation by region and time. These are different prayogas (usages, applications, addressals and experiments).

A reminder here: there is a dual aspect as touched upon in initial chapters.
1) regulation of breath/prana
2) regulation by breath/prana

This is also implied in Desha-Paridrushtata considered earlier and Sankhya-paridrushtata, yet to be considered.

The second aspect is in respect of mutal proportions between in-breath and out-breath cycle or puraka-rechaka cycle (for the time being, we are setting aside the retentions/kumbhakas). The proportion between the in-breath and the out-breath or vice-versa can be such as:

$$1 : 1$$
$$1 : 2$$
$$2 : 1$$
$$1 : 3$$
$$3 : 1 \text{ etc.}$$

by velocity handling or volume handling or handling in different combinations. These proportions are in respect with time i.e. seconds. Let us illustrate this:

IN-BREATH PURAKA	OUT-BREATH RECHAKA
10 seconds (or counts)	10 seconds (counts)
10 seconds (or counts)	20 seconds (counts)
20 seconds (or counts)	10 seconds (counts)
10 seconds (or counts)	30 seconds (counts)
30 seconds (or counts)	10 seconds (counts)

The modulations or proportions can be effected by velocity-handling or volume-handling or combinations thereof.

Effect–wise, conditioning wise, these aspects would make a significant effect, changes and transformations.

SANKHYAA PARIDRUSHTATA

These are the regulative acts by a cluster of cycles in replicated conditionings. Pranayama essentially does not take place by one or two or few cycles but sufficient number of cycles in a round. This is a very important fact to be noted. Conditioning of pattern and mode needs to be persisted with consistently and constantly for multiple cycles.

One deep and conditioned inhalation or exhalation is not a precept of pranayama.

But the fact remains that this is not at all easy. The practice package for a novice or a neophyte is as follows:

Have the in-breath or out-breath with decided and preset conditioning in one cycle and give a lap-time of 2-3 normal cycles; repeat the proto, pre-decided conditioning and have 8-10 rounds of such cycles comprising a final total of 20-30 cycles of conditioned + relaxed-conditioned cycles.

Replicated, breathing cycles is the major precept here; effectively, it is a creativity exercise.

Can there be fasting for one moment or one second or one minute or one hour?

If so, then we are under eternal restraint. Similarly, pranayama as conditioning or regulating is never of one cycle.

One deep breath or a couple of deep breaths does not become Pranayamic, as it is believed today. Deep breathing cannot become Pranayama.

If classical pranayama is described as naada-sadhana in ancient wisdom, it must have

Sur, Swara
Laya
Meter etc.

Anyway, one of the lessons for such classical pranayama is to define dimensions and definitions of natural, spontaneous, normal mechanical and unconditional breathing and to render it as conditional, normal breathing. And repeat-replicate it for multiple cycles without modulations and modifications. The parity between

Unconditioned, normal breathing
and
Conditioned, normal breathing must be overcome.

This is quite an exercise and skill-attaining education. One needs to develop sensitivity for dimensions and qualification for it as well as qualification of such breathing and turn out such cycles voluntarily without either

Over-shooting
Or
Under-shooting those definitions and dimensions.

In quack teaching, without such a comprehensive training or education, one is inducted to 'breathing gymnastics'.

Anyway, the formal education in classical pranayama is to carry out prayogas in
1) Desha Paridrushtata
2) Kala Paridrushtata
3) Sankhyaa Paridrushtata
4) Desh + Kala (paridrushtata)
5) Kala + Sankhyaa (paridrushtata)
6) Desh + Sankhyaa (paridrushtata)
7) Desh + kala + Sankhyaa (paridrushtata)

There are initially exercises and then one learns usages, applications and addressals. Then one evolves skill and ease as well as efficacies. These must be attempted in rounds of multiple cycles and then such multiple rounds consequently.

It must be understood that one such round of any such exercise or even a pranayama is just a mockery unless one is a master and has mastery in Pranayama, because the first round or few rounds do not take one beyond orientation. A student cannot be stuck in orientation and needs to go well past it and go a long way in getting educated and then evolve qualifications for practice. However, there can be intermittent, short breaks, so that the capacities are replenished.

When the above conditions are attained then pranayama can become Deergha and Sukshma as stated by Patanjali.

What is this

Deerghata
and
Sukshmatva?

Let us address them in the next chapter.

Chapter : 40

DEERGHA – SUKSHMA

A naïve commoner would take the predicate "Deergha" to mean:-

an extraordinary long, long, long inhalation

or an extraordinary long, long, long exhalation

or an unduly long, long retention after inhalation or after exhalation.

But classical pranayama is not at all breathing gymnastics or performing such feats as is generally believed. More often, such people do these breath feats as street performers or as performative acts.

Pranayama is more a spiritual culture or Parmarthik sanskruti. It is a spiritual-culture inculcation than the Maya of a "breath-gym work-out."

When one goes through Pranayamic training, what such a yogi develops is not just a very mean capacity for an extraordinarily long inhalation, exhalation and retention.

That is not this deerghata; it is not a gymnastic ability to breathe very subtly. The predicates in the sutras have mysterious meanings. Let us understand them. These are not the effects of capacity but are the results of a rich, sublime,

cosmic, divinised culture in chitta. Such a person is a personification

of an accomplished yogi. The meaning of these predicates (which will now be given) might seem like a fantasy and quite incredible.

These might seem wild imaginations or even very abstruse, imaginative notions; but the meaning is as they appear in pedantic studies.

Actually long, long, long pranayama comes to state that pranayama is on for a long, long time and not for a short duration of 10-20 mins or 1-2 hours, or 7-8 hours or 12-15 hours or 30-40 hours. It is for a very long time.

Pranayama lasts for many, many days, weeks, months, years, decades and even centuries and millennia. This is the pedantic interpretation of the sutra which uses the predicate "deergha."

We, the temporal people, will consider this as fantasy. But a yogi's world is altogether different, perhaps transcending temporal concepts of space and time.

Without doubt such a yogi is in Samadhi. This is the pranayama while a yogi is in Samadhi. It should be noted that Samadhi time-scales are not in seconds, minutes and hours but in weeks, months, years, decades and eons.

For instance, if one cycle of a yogi's breath takes one minute hypothetically, the state of Samadhi will have to last 12 x 12 x 12 x12 minutes (20,736 mins.) that is nearly 14.4 days. This is the minimum span of time mandated to be considered a state of Absorption (Samadhi), and anything less than that disqualifies to be called Samadhi.

It means that pranayama would persist without variation or alteration for such a period as 14.4 days! But if pranayama also becomes subtle, the breath should become extraordinarily different. If such a breathing cycle takes place for 10 minutes rather than for a minute as in the above assumption, then Pranayama would last for 140 days. It is believed that yogis transcend time and space and thus remain in Samadhi for centuries and millennia easily.

The second predicate here is 'subtle' (sukshma). The breath and breathing become so subtle that the breath rate goes down to an astonishing extent such as one cycle might take centuries. Such yogis may be declared dead clinically. This has even been testified by modern physicians; many yogis have stopped even the electrical beats of the heart. The breath becomes so subtle and fine that even for modern machines the breathing is almost not there or not at all there.

Just as there is paridrushtata (regulation) by Desha, kala, sankhya for breathing, the same is the case with kumbhaka. Suppose a yogi is having a kumbhaka for 10 to 15 years, what shall we conclude?

Chapter : 41

KUMBHAKA PARIDRUSHTATA

As seen towards the end of the last chapter, there are Desha, Kala, Sankhya paridrushtata/s for kumbhaka as well. There are two Kumbhakas, namely,
1) Bahya Kumbhaka
2) Antara Kumbhaka
Bahya kumbhaka is the one which comes after rechaka pranayama and antara kumbhaka is the one which comes after Puraka pranayama. Of course the fourth pranayama or third kumbahaka is that which is called Kevala Kumbhaka. We shall consider this in the following chapter, and not deal with it here.

The kumbhakas can take place in various internal locations such as thoracic, abdominal, pelvic, and so on. This is the Desha-paridrushtata. The Kala Paridrushtata is the duration of kumbhaka which can be multiplied –

$$(x) \ (x \ 2) \ (x \ 3) \ (x \ 4)$$

etc. Basics of retentions are taught in the form of pauses in pranayamas such as Viloma-1 (Inhalative), Viloma-2 (Exhalative) and Viloma-3 (both). We shall consider these in a later chapter. However, what can be said is that the concept of desha paridrushtata and kala paridrushtata will be introduced in the chapter of viloma pranayama. Then the Sankhya-paridrushtata means the pre-decided number of kumbhakas in one round (udghata). That is 8-10-12-15 kumbhakas in a round.

As an illustration, the triple conditioning
may be as follows:
Pelvic antara kumbhaka of (x) duration done
consecutively for 12 cycles of breathing or
Pranayama. Then with same confinement
the duration becoming (x2) and a round
of 8 retentions in consecutive cycles of breathing.

Thus there is mathematics involved in setting duration of kumbhaka and the number of kumbhakas in consecutive cycles of breathing in a round. If the retentive duration is shorter, there can be greater number of kumbhakas in a round called "Udghata". But if duration of retention increases, the number of kumbhakas may come down in a round (Udghata).

It is important to set the mathematics of capacity and effectivity. It is not justifiable to test capacity by keeping effectivity at stake.

ANTARA KUMBHAKA PROPORTION

As in quack teachings, here the kumbhaka is not done as long as possible. It is not a case of : take a "full inhalation and retain as long as possible."

But there is a set proportion such as:

Inhalation : Retention : exhalation

$(x) : (y) : (z)$

or

$(x2) : (y2) : (z2)$

or

$(x2) : (3y) : (z2)$

or

$(x) : (x - 2) : (x + 3)$

or

$(x + 2) : (x + 3) : (x + 4)$

These proportions need to be considered with ease of capacity and constant or progressive efficacies with a cluster of multiple cycles. Antara kumbhaka has to take place in a pre-set mode (confinement), with pre-set proportions and a pre-set number of cycles.

In other words, the proportions can be as follows:

1) (x)   :   (x)   :   (x)
2) (x)   :   (x 1)   :   (x)
3) (x 1) :   (x 2)   :   (x 3)
4) (x 1) :   (x 3)   :   (x 1) etc.

Thus there will be countless permutations and combinations. These will have a pre-set number of kumbhakas in rounds of consecutive cycles of breathing such as 8, 10, 12, 15 etc.

BAHYA KUMBHAKA PROPORTIONS

This is Inhalation → Exhalation → Retention.

The proportions are:

1) 1   :   2   :   3
2) 2   :   4   :   6
3) 1   :   1   :   1
4) 1   :   2   :   1 etc.

Again, there will be a pre-set confinement and a number of kumbhakas in a round which will come in consecutive bahya kumbhakas or outer retention such as 8 – 10 – 12 – 15 retentions or kumbhakas.

Both the kumbhakas imply Bandhatraya for an accomplished yogi and Mudra-traya for the rest of the practitioners. Thus in pranayama, all the three phases are metered. 'Moment' is the unit. For all practical purposes, *Kshana* or moment is ¼th of time taken for the flicker of an eye. Vachaspati Mishra in his *Tattva-Vaisharidi* says, "Matra is the time taken to snap the finger and thumb after taking the palm round the knees which are in Padmasan or Swastikasana position." The Shastras use the term "matras" as meter in Pranayama. Therefore, he defines it as accepted by ageless tradition. Markandeya says,

"Pranayama of 12 matras is inferior;
Of 24 matras, middling;
And of 36 matras, superior."

Vasishtha Samhita says,
"Puraka: 16 matras – Brahma dhyana,
Kumbhaka: 64 matras – Vishnu dhyana,
Rechaka: 32 Matras – Rudra dhyana."
There is also kumbhaka pranayama, which incorporates both kumbhakas. It is by
Puraka → Kumbhaka → rechaka → Kumbhaka.
It also must be noted that by Pranayama what is meant is

Puraka → Kumbhaka → Rechaka
Or
Rechaka → Puraka → kumbhaka

meaning an Antara kumbhaka. But there is also accepted traditional meaning that,
'Puraka, Rechaka and the two kumbhakas are three pranayamas which is accepted by Patanjali. Therefore he considers the Kevala Kumbhaka as the fourth pranayama.'
We shall deal with this in the following chapter.

Chapter : 42

KEVALA KUMBHAKA

The literal rendition of the sutra on kevala kumbhaka would mean:

"A rentention which is neither preceded nor followed by in-breath or out-breath is Kevala kumbhaka."

The sutra is:

बाह्याभ्यन्तर विषयाक्षेपि: चतुर्थ: ।

It means the kumbhaka which is neither Bahya Kumbhaka nor Antara kumbhaka is kevala kumbhaka or the fourth pranayama. It has the above implications. It is logical, possible, plausible and compatible that there can be a kumbhaka without being preceded or followed by an in-breath or an out-breath? Will any amount of brain-storming resolve the issue? It seems to be an insoluble problem. Many times it is deigned as a mystery, an enigmatic puzzle or a conundrum.

But this riddle is easily solved by taking recourse to a graphic method. If we try to graphically depict a pranayama which has all the four phases, that is,

In-breath (IB)
Inner retention (I-R)
Out-breath and (O-B)
Outer retention, (O-R)

the graphic depiction will be as follows:
THE GRAPH HERE...

IN BREATH, INNER-RETENTION, OUT-BREATH AND OUTER-RETENTION.

It is akin to a mountain range with plateaus near the mountain-tops and down the valleys. When the pranayama becomes smooth, it will lose the cuts and become serpentine, as shown below:

When pranayama becomes finer, it would be like this:

Here on the right hand side, it appears as merely a straight line

with no ups and downs. Now, what is the horizontal straight line here? It is kumbhaka. And what does the up or down – the "A" to "B" show? No in-breath or out-breath and thus, kevala kumbhaka.

It happens in Samadhi state and as said earlier, for quite a while with no in-breath and out-breath, thus no breathing.

It is an incredibly, exalted state of hibernated coditon in cellular metabolism. Such a possibility is there only in Samadhi.

Vyasa clearly states that there is

'Aati-abhava' in such a pranayama, and otherwise the pranayama is 'gati- vichheda.' There is a quotation in the Yog-tattva Upanishad:

'When kevala kumbhaka comes up, it is a condition bereft of in-breath and out-breath. Nothing is

impossible for such a yogi.' (Y. T. U.50)

Even **Hathayog Pradipika** mentions the total eradication of Puraka-rechaka in such a pranayama.

Now let us turn to fruition of pranayama or the culmination of pranayama which Patanjali mentions in the other two sutras pertaining to Pranayama.

Chapter : 43

PRANAYAMA PHALA

There are two sutras out of the four on Pranayama phala. We have so far considered the first two sutras in the preceding chapters. The two sutras here are:

ततः क्षीयते प्रकाशावरणम् । २।५३

धारणासु च योग्यता मनस । २।४

We are all capable of knowing what and how our breathing is. We can improve our breathing for biological purposes. We can have improved oxygenation and de-carbon dioxidation. This would benefit our body, cells, blood-cells, nerve-cells, etc. Even a common man armed with science and modern academics can understand what breathing of the respiratory system can do. One can know what the lungs and the breathing act of our respiratory system can do. But a student in yog is enlightened about what the organic or systemic breathing can do. (We have seen in the initial chapters what associated breathing can do.) Such breathing is prolific and a versatile, internal activity agency. It is an incredibly transcendent principle within us.

"It is not at all ours but keeps all ours affiliated to us;
Ours remain ours because of what is not at all ours."

It is a marvelous catalyst and *rasayan* in an associated condition. It is a grand transformer and transmuting agent for 'I', 'me' and 'mine' integral and inherent to us.

Anyway, improved respiratory breathing can exaltedly work on biological constituents such as body-cells, bloodcells, nerve-cells etc. By these being given exalted conditions, the relative mind will be benefited. Therefore the consumer package that is available today can provably work for health and vitality of the exoteric body-mind system. Pranayama of such a package can undoubtedly work for

> *Excellent physical, physiological, metabolic*
> *cellular, psycho-mental health. Thus also*
> *Excellent, mundane and materialistic*
> *health and well-being.*

That is why *Yogaaa* has a global market today.

> *However, classical Yog does not include*
> *Pranayama for such worldly purposes;*
> *It has a higher purpose and such worldly*
> *Benefits are only incidental.*

Health and well-being is an unintended by-product of Pranayama.

It is like using an expensive limousine or a Rolls-Royce car to transport coal.

Or using a multi-axle trailer truck to do your personal grocery shopping – a mere load of 8 to 10 kgs.

Doing, learning and dedicating oneself to pranayama for such worldly, mundane and mean purposes is the main thrust of today's Pranayama propagation. Patanjali does not indicate any fruit of pranayama with a consumerist's perspective. He mentions two kinds of fruits in Pranayama. These are Adhyatmic or Paramarthik fruits.

The sutras are:

ततः क्षीयते प्रकाशावरणम् । २/५३
धारणासुचयोग्यता मनसः । २/५४

It has been repeatedly said from the beginning that Pranayama is not merely breath control, or to have such biological health and breath-borne well-being. Pranayama works on a philosophical footing such as:

Chitta shuddhi
Vasana Kshaya
Klesha Kshaya
Evolving consciousness
Set-up apavarga (moksha sadhana)
Sub-serve Mumukshatva
Eradicate Bubhukshatva

Pranayama does not come for worldly, mundane, biological, psycho-mental well-being. Our chitta is engulfed and arrested in Anadi-maya, which insulates us from spiritual radiation and vibration. Thus we become worms in the world of objects. We become caterpillars of the world. This maya is in the form of vasana or precisely, klesha-vasanas. There is a forestation of it and it is pervaded by parasites of shadripus. To counter this formidable force, what is needed is pranayama amongst other things.

Shvasayama or merely breath control works like sticks and pebbles to counter the force of nuclear weapons.

Pranayama works for destroying or at least weakening the metapsychic, eternal, ageless defects called Klesha-vasana. Patanjali calls it Avarana-Kshaya. It is a cloud of kleshas around the psyche and consciousness. When this is cleared sufficiently The much cherished higher yog of meditation blooms in the chitta. What seemed fantasy or wild imagination blazes forth as reality now, just as the sun breaks through after the dark clouds are cleared in the sky.

Pranayama has such an exalted spiritual effect rather than a cosmetic treatment to psychological mind which is as fleeting as the mind itself.

Vyasa pens down the effect of pranayama in the following words; through these words, a wise person can easily understand the dynamics of pranayama which are:

Intent

Drive

Motive

Actions

Purpose

Modality

Constitution

Component

Culture

Process etc.

Vyasa says:

"The Karma of the yogi which covers up
the discriminative knowledge (means
of kaivalya) are destroyed as he practices
Pranayama. This is what is said by seers and sages."

By the magic panorama of desire, the essence which is luminious by nature, is obscured and covered up, and is directed towards vice.

This karma of the yogi which covers up
the light and blinds him to repeated births
becomes weak by the practice of pranayama.
Every moment it is then destroyed; is what is being said.

There is no purificatory action higher than pranayama
Purity is secured by that through
the destruction of impurity
and the light of knowledge shines.

Now, it can be argued that one really does not qualify to take up such pranayama practices since we are not at all vexed or harassed by the cycles of birth and death. Even if we are *astikas* and honestly believe that we are spiritual seekers, there is no basis where we can have the slightest vexation and harassment of the cycle of birth, death, birth, death etc. There is a credible basis that we cannot remember even our past lives and can imagine our next life. Hence there is no question of being harassed by the so-called

deadning cycle of birth and rebirth.

True that we shall never have a genuine urge for pranayama and such sadhanas. However, we can certainly begin the endeavour of carrying out pursuits. There is a lot to learn, inculcate and practice before the genuine and authentic cause of doing pranayama appears. Thus the above argument is easily set aside.

"Oh! even the Brahmopadesham takes place at a tender age of eight with pranayama and Gayatri. Such an early beginning can come even when one is hardly a seeker of Brahman."

THUS, PRANAYAMA CAN BE COMMENCED EVEN IF THE CAUSE IN THE FORM OF VEXATION BY KLESHAS MAY NOT BE IN PLACE. As a matter of fact, we may be relishing the kleshas as a delicacy in life, yet pranayama can be commenced.

Anyway, Pranakriya, Prana-sadhna and Pranayama will start working for conservation, house-keeping and the hospitality of our chitta for Paramartha. The Shastras mention the effects of pranayama as (also delineated by Vyasa),

"Pranayama Anushthana."

However, we are looking for commencing Pranayama, its adhyana and prayoga related to Adhyana meaning learning pranayama. Thus the above-mentioned argument loses its base.

The question is what pranayama does for us on our plane and our level. Of course there is a significant change in our attitude or vritti, pravritti, nivrutti and Sanskruti. Our hunger and thirst or even tendencies of flesh are set right and tuned for yog and Adhyatma Sadhana. Even if our pranayama does not work on kleshas, they can certainly work on klesha-vrittis such as Kama (lust), Krodha (anger), Lobha (avarice), moha (delusion), mada (self-conceit), Matsarya (Envy, jeolousy). This certainly helps reform our conduct of life. Moderation and temperence is turned out organically or at least facilitated. Ahara, Vihara, Achara, Vichara are set right and paramarthik tendencies are evolved or activated. Mind-management becomes astonishingly probable. Satsang–pravrittis, Sadhana-sang pravrittis and shastra-sang pravrittis are escalated. Basically, there is important education with literacy required for Adhyatma.

The buddhi can start grasping and inculcating adhyatmic instructions. The *Shastras* are better construed and seeped into memory and intellect (smruti and buddhi)

The *Shat sampattis* are harvested in chitta which are:

Shama (mental restraint)

Dama (sensory restraint)

Titiksha (tolerance)

Uparati (Satiation for worldly pleasures)

Jnana vairagya (jnana and thirstlessness)

Shanti-Samadhan (peace and contentment)

Of course, the by-products are rich too. These are:

Good physical-mental health and well-being,

Immunity to worldly torments and stresses.

Most importantly, one gets the literacy for esoteric body and esoteric mind. There is initiation into the basic but very fundamental questions,

"Who am I"

"Whence am I"

"What is this embodiment"... *etc.*

Even beginners' pranayama-dabbling provides incredible insights into his own mind and psyche. It introduces one to trans-empiricism.

Many of the Smrutis have repeatedly said that

"Pranayama burns the defects of the mind, psyche and consciousness.

Yajnavalkya received Veda-Samhita from the Sun in Ashva–mukha. He attained this great ability after purifying the mind through pranayama.

Vishnu Purana says:

Yajnavalkya and Maitreya had taken recourse to pranayama to attain their distinct positions in lore.
Yajnavalkya then attained the Vedas directly from the sun.

There are similar mentions in Skanda, Agni, Vayu Puranas and Yogi Yajnavalkya Smruti, Darshanopanishad, Trishikhi Brahmanopanishad, Amruta-nada-Upanishad.

Since pranayama purifies the mind, Vedic rituals admitted pranayama at the commencement of rituals. Bodhayana brought in pranayama as an atonement.

(Since choking (or gasping for breath) is great helplessness, the Smrutis mention retention of breath in penal code conditions. Although this is not pranayama, pranayamic aspect was modified as a form of punishment.)

Just as we draw water
with a rope from a well,
Pranayama draws the sublime, mineral
consciousness from the deep well within to the mind.

PRANAYAMA → MEDTATIVITY:

Patanjali mentions the fruit of pranayama as a lead-up to dharana (to Samadhi). Pranayama, according to him, is

Dharana–Yogyatva.

Pranayama is not only a gateway for dharana but has long follow through into Samadhi. As a matter of fact the procedural reality is that the uninterrupted process of Samadhi begins at Pranayama. The continuous and uninterrupted process of meditation in yog begins with pranayama. The launch-point of the Dhyana process is in the extensive process of pranayama which has a long corridor and a long follow-through.

Just as the Amazon river traverses an amazing 300 miles before it reaches the Atlantic ocean, Pranayama in its active condition takes the yogi into the field of dhyana. The process of Dhyana Sadhana in Ashtanga mode is thus:

AUM (Bhagwan-smarana) → Gross pranayama → to nirodha dharma (Antarmukhi on breath track) → Pranayama of heart-confinement → subtle, tender pranayama → support of AUM → Meditation AUM → Pratyahara → Deep Antarmukhi → Immersion of chitta in heart → psychomental confinement in the heart → meditativity → dream-like appearance of object of meditation → confinement in such support → Dharana → Absorption (Dhyana) → Transformation (Samadhi).

This is the voyage of a yogi to Samadhi. For those on a lower rung, they are absorbed in a meditative state. In the case of any interruption, even a yogi has to come to gross pranayama. In its culminative stages, Pranayama makes the body become a shrine of the Atma, Kshetra of Atma.

It is pranayama which makes the facal-mind-matter-freebody to become a temple.

It has Tantra, mantra to transform body, its tissues, cells, flesh and bones to become Kshetra.

It is the touch-stone of body.

Here, one recalls a theorem of Yog:

Master of senses is the mind,
Master of mind is the breath (vayu),
Master of breath is Naada,
And master of Naada is Laya.

(Varahopanishad; 2180)

Subtle and essential pranayama is naada-anusandhana. It should be recalled that Patanjali includes

Tattva kriya
Chakra kriya
Prana Kriya

All these have their centers in our nostrils, a marvellous organ. Further delineation on pranayama without elaborating on the role of the nose and nostrils will be a big blunder. Let us now begin the description.

Chapter : 44

NASAL PRANAYAMAS

It is almost a trademark of pranayama that pranayama mudra has invariable concomittance with pranayama. No doubt that there is a very close relationship between pranayama and pranayama mudra. The mudra is this:

Sit erect in padmasana. With the right hand
Finger-tips (small finger, ring finger and thumb),
Form a ring to be placed on the nostril with
the other two fingers folded in.
Keep the left hand on the left thigh or
Knee in Jnana-mudra
(that is index finger and thumb tip touching

And the other three fingers outstretched).

With quackery abounding, there is rampant and worsening mockery of this art and science. Modern quack teachers say

"If you want to block the right nostril, place the
forepart of the the thumb on the nostrils-heavily
press it (deviate even straighter septum. If left nostril
is to be blocked press 2—3 of the four fingers and deviate
the septum on the other side. And breathe with
deviated septum !"

The misguided and uninformed quack feels that the entire left nostril is Chandra naadi (Pingala) and the entire right nostril is surya (ida). Thus breathing by one of the nostrils is believed to be breathing by the respective nadis.

But the nadis do not have the
Entire diameter of the nostrils. Nadis
Are too subtle and thus esoteric.

The fact is that the left nostril has Chandra nadi and the right nostril has surya nadi. And to block a nadi, the whole nostril need not be closed. The point is that nasal pranayama is necessary to handle the very delicate aspect of breath and delicate mode of breath more delicately by instruments over it such as finger-tips, hand, awareness, mind advertence and attitude. The instruments are more delicate and emotional than being mechanical and machine-like.

NOSE – A MARVELLOUS MENTAL ORGAN

It might sound intriguing or exaggerating to call the nose and nostrils as mind organs. But the fact is that it really is a physiognomic organ.

The human face is almost a monitor of the mind.
Human facial muscles are remarkably flexible
for expression of the mind or as responders

to mind. Man makes a thousand and one faces besides having a thousand and one faces. Then there are countless invisible faces which go out of the realm of physiognomy.

There are innumerable human emotions and mental states such as anger to passion, love to aversion, fear to courage, reverence to agnosticism, faith to doubt. Many of these do not have physiognomy to be read by others. Therefore we have conjectures or presumptions. But according to psycho-mental and chaittic studies of yog there are premises such as

Every state of mind there is a corresponding
breathing mode and subtle changes in
face and eyes contribute for it.

The human face changes even if not visible, for every

state of mind from anger to love and dejection to enthusiasm of all degrees. The nose form changes either grossly or subtly and changes the breath-ways.

Imagine the face of disgust, anger, hatred,
Greed, love, affection, enmity, malice, fear,
Motivation, enthusiasm etc. The nose and
Nostrils are sufficiently modified or modulated to
modify the breath.
Therefore our breath is tempered by fugitive
and changeful state of mind.
If our mental vritti is in constant change,
the breath too becomes that fluctuating.

Thus yog advocates steady state of mind for consistent breathing.

Human face has subtle movements apart from grosser and visible changes like "actor's face" which are really many faces. The nose is easily influenced because of its situation and position as well as structure. The breathing that goes in the nostrils have incredibly sympathetic resonance to mind. Thus, the nose has a profile for every state of mind. So also, we have in our breathing repertoire every kind of breath mode for every state of mind.

Therefore it won't be an exaggeration or
meaningless or gibberish in saying that there is
Angry breathing
Passion breathing
Disgust breathing
Fondness breathing
Frightened breathing
Courage breathing
Doubting breathing
Confidence breathing
Diffidence breathing

Reverence breathing
Detest breathing etc...

Thus the nose is remarkably flexible but it is unacknowledged flexibility.

Anyway, it is only the science of yog that says that the two nostrils are almost mutually divergent such as 'sun' and 'moon'. Even the ultra-modern science of human anatomy has no clue of such things as

> *Solar nostril*
> *and*
> *Lunar nostril.*

The quacks in yog only believe in it. Thus they think they are for divergent functions. There are not only two nadis in two nostrils. The following facts will reveal much about it:

RIGHT NOSTRIL	LEFT NOSTRIL
1) Basic 350 odd pranas nadis but in fact by permutation-combination infinite nadis.	1) As said in the left-hand column.
2) Solar branches of Prithvi—aap—tej—Vayu Akash.	2) Lunar branches of Prithvi—aap—Tej—Vayu Akash.
3) Solar branches of shat chakra nadis	3) Lunar branches of shat chakra nadis.

Thus one can easily understand a very dense nadi-network in the nostril.

Isn't that a marvel? Isn't that uncrowned nadi junction?

The nose, which is just half a finger length, is a giant conditioner in pranayama.

Regulating breath and prana is a very delicate act. The

tips of fingers and tips of the thumbs should be delicately and dexterously used. The fingers should be like that on a musical instrument. The nostril is an instrument of music and pranayama too is swara-sadhana, naada sadhana etc.

In quack yog, which is nothing but mockery, for ida-pingla pranayama what is done is:

> *For ida pranayama, pingla is strangulated and vice-versa.*
> *If it is ida pranayama, the inhalation is a sniffing act and so is the case of pingla inhalation.*
> *For exhalation, the nostrils are made into a pneumatic device.*

It is a ridiculous thing allowed in neo-yog. In music, a novice, who does not know the basic seven notes, is never straight away made to delineate *Darbari Kanada*. But such things happen here. Quack teachers begin Pranayama right away with Anuloma, Pratiloma, Chandra-bhedana, Surya bhedana and nadi shodhana pranayama.

The fingers are used as if they are puckers. Anyway, let us keep this mockery aside and take a view of the classical model of digital (nasal) pranayamas. Basically it must be understood that nose and nostrils are very tender cells, tissues and fibres. Moreover, they deal with breath and in an endeavour such as pranayama the breath is exaltedly fine, subtle and tender. Thus, fingertips must become tender and sensitive as they become when handling an infant or a flower. Therefore one must not hasten to take up nasal pranayama. A traditionally rich teacher would teach nasal pranayama without fingers being used on nostrils. A great amount of sensitivity has to be developed and evolved. There is a great amount of education involved before one uses the finger on the nose.

Fingers are not to be merely used for blocking a nostril. In that case the finger should work as a clip. But as a matter of fact, they work like the fingers of a musical instrumentalist. Fingers are to be used for accessing the minute nadis and work for the tonal quality of breath.

In Pranayama, the breath is not blocked by fingers closing a nostril. Equating the blocking of the nostrils with locking or closing the doors of the body, is believing that when the doors and windows of the house are closed (or locked), no dust will gather inside and no insects and ants will enter. The breath or prana is blocked by retention or kumbhaka by the three mudras and/or the three bandhas and not by the fingertips or even the fingers.

This should be an important lesson for quacks who try to close a nostril or both by strongly pressing the fingers on the nose.

In mockery, one believes that by blocking the ida nostril and opening the pingla nostril by not blocking ida breathing takes place. This is either a laughable or an infuriating concept.

Basically nasal pranayama with fingers is like a post-graduate course. The student in classical approach is made to observe the nostrils by using ocean-like vast pranayama kriyas and a whole vista of figurations of the nostrils. Nostrils almost go into a kaleidoscope. There are nearly 350 forms which are all various graphic modes of breath.

Shivasvarodaya describes the five centres for the five tattvas. But a classical teacher makes the student get educated for those centres by merely using prana kriyas of:

"LUM" (prithvi)
"VUM"(aap)
"RUM"(tej)
"YUM"(vayu)
"HUM"(akash)

One can really feel these different spots and breath flows under these five tattvas. It is greatly fascinating and educative endeavour to monitor nose and nostrils in a wide range of prana kriyas. This will be nasal pranayama without using fingers on the nose. This is the way nasal pranayama starts traditionally and classically. Then there will be no room for senseless conventions, which have created a quagmire in yog. At the right point in time, after one has gone through the above process thoroughly, then there can be training for using fingertips on nostrils for breath. It might be said at this point in time that the nostril is a hi-tech and highly digitized organ. According to yogic precepts, the evolution of human consciousness depends upon breath and prana. Thus one must be exceptionally skillful in such an art of nasal pranayama. On a very primary plane of endeavor, in such a pranayama one must be able to use the fingers (ring, little and thumb) simultaneously in co-ordination and in mutual complementation. As said, no nostril is ever blocked or closed for either the in-breath or the out-breath. Unproficient ones may only close both the nostrils during retention only. But that is really not necessary as outer or inner retentions are by internal and organic process rather than at the gates. Additionally, there are the three mudras for retention.

Therefore as a matter of fact the palm rests on the right lap during retentions rather than blocking the nostrils by the clip of fingers and thumb.

Anyway, the right palm is to be used and the handling of velocity of the breath and pressure of fingertips must be learnt. In classical pranayama, fingers are to be used for both the purposes:
1) to open the nostril
2) and to close nostril simultaneously.
In the case of single-nostril breathing, the fingers are used for opening that nostril and closing the other nostril simultaneously. Therefore practically and most importantly 'finger tips on the left nostril are used not only for the left

nostril but in subserviency of the left nostril.

The thumb on the left nostril is not only
used on and for the left nostril, but also in
subserviency of the left nostril and
the two fingers there.
They (thumb, little and ring finger) play a role in
mutual co-ordination for each other mutually.
There is a concerted effort of fingers and thumb.

In the case of one nostril breathing, all the three play a double role simultaneously or in mutual co-ordination for:

Blocking one nostril properly and opening the other nostril properly.

This double role is a marvel. It must be noted here that it is a high tech pranayama. The roles here are not only

OPENING and closing but fine-tuning
The breath and thus CLOSING PROPERLY
And OPENING PROPERLY FOR OPTIMUM
EFFECT.

It must also be noted here that the breathing does not take place in the whole of the nostril but in a passage out of several passages. Nostrils are not like a water tap, in that from the entire diameter the breath will flow. A common man is not aware of this important fact. A quack tends to shut the entire nostril. This is ridiculous.

NOSTRILS ARE NOT BREATH TAPS, AKIN TO WATER TAPS.

Fingers and thumb in such pranayamas are not used to open or close the nostril but to OPEN and CLOSE the nadis through which the breath moves. As we commoners think that at times the

NOSTRILS ARE BLOCKED IS NOT TRUE
BUT THE NADIS ARE BLOCKED.

This is testified by the fact that during a bout of cold our nostrils seem blocked but the fact is that passage of breathing is blocked. Our fingers can be easily inserted even when the nostrils seems blocked!

THUS THE FACT IS THAT WE DO NOT BREATHE THROUGH THE WHOLE NOSTRIL, BUT A PASSAGE OUT OF SEVERAL PASSAGES.

Thus breath-passage sensing, and dealing with passages, is paramount in such pranayama.

The next crucial point is that the acting nostril needs pressure at its tips to manipulate and simultaneously provide counter-pressure to the opposite nostril. This pressure and counter-pressure is very important, otherwise the septum and the nose would be deviated and tilted. Let us now understand the role of thumb, ring finger and small finger.

1) The pressure of the tips should be such and so much that with minimum pressure the blocked nostril should be opened and the other opened. All the three tips play a double role as pointed out earlier.

2) To work as a team-work with mutual co-ordination This accomplishes the third function.

3) The double roles are of an opposite nature: opening and closing.

Pressurising and counter-pressurising play the counter and complementary role as well as the co-ordinating role simultaneously. To interact, to double act and to counter act. Thus, they play a major role for one side and a subordinate role for the opposite side.

The roles are too artistic to be described technically. Therefore such a venture is being set aside. However, the following guidelines may prove valuable for teachers, students and practitioners alike.

1) It might be any nasal pranayama, thumb, ring finger, and small finger must be used simultaneously on both the nostrils.

2) The finger tips are not be merely placed on nostrils but are to be placed on a specific location to either open one nostril and close the other nostril or open both the nostrils simultaneously or close one or both the nostrils.
3) Fingers and thumb are not to merely used for closing the nostrils.
4) The finger-tips need to be used both for opening or closing nostrils.
5) Although the thumb is placed on the right nostril and the ring and small finger on the left nostril, they play roles for both the nostrils.
6) They are always used in mutual co-ordinations and mutual considerations. The tips on the left nostril play a role for the left nostril as well as the right nostril and the thumb tip is placed on the right nostril for itself as well as the other nostril.
7) The double role in case of one nostril breathing is for opening one and closing the other nostril simultaneously in mutual co-ordination and consideration.
8) The pressure of the tips is for the two purposes simultaneously and have to be managed at one and the same time. It may be a pressure for opening one and closing the other simultaneously. This skill is proceeded by good observation and experimentation.
9) Although generally the three tips have to be placed at one location i.e. immediately below the nasal bone the subtle positioning constantly changes. These changes are because of a condition of – a) nostrils such as fully opened or semi-opened or semi-closed or fully closed, b) state of nostrils such as dry or damp or ideal. These can be temporary conditions or chronic conditions.
10) A beginner should not work on pre-decided pranayama such as inhaling on the right or left or exhaling on the right or left. Initial attempts do not pertain to opening a

closed nostril but to deal with a nostril which is already opened and not blocked.

11) There are possibilities that a nostril may be opened for inhalation but not for exhalation and vice-versa.

12) Finger tips directly pressurize their side and indirectly pressurize the other. That is, they simultaneously provide pressure and counter pressure.

13) Pressures have greater corresponding with velocity of breath. When the velocity is higher the pressure is less and when the velocity is less, the pressure is more.

14) Beginners attempt to use tips on both sides and deal with the nostril which is superiorly open.

15) Manipulations of finger tips and thumb tips is a constant process even in one breath since velocities change from the beginning of breath to the end of breath.

16) In no case the tips are disconnected in nasal pranayama or ornamentally used on nostrils.

17) Most importantly, the nostril should not be blown and cleansed immediately before such pranayamas but well before such pranayama. Because blowing may clear the nostril of mucus but irritates the membranes and septum carpets.

18) Ideally, nostrils should not be dry but optimally damp.

19) All nasal-digital pranayama imply constant manipulation and repositioning stage by stage in breath. Due to lack of skill it may seem to be a complicated process. But it does not at all justify simplification brought by modern trends such as
"Use the fingers or thumb to merely
block and close the nostrils."

Such simplicities mock the depth of this subject. In the feverish race to propagate and popularize yog and to make it globally acceptable so that any Tom, Dick and Harry can take it up, yog is simplified and taught at (weekend) workshops, shibirs of a week or two; then diplomas and certificates are distributed and/or young ones are seduced to take it as a career, profession or vocation and make a fast buck; to succeed quickly and gain name, fame and recognition, the subject has been ridiculously simplified.

And it is here that Pranayama becomes a method to:

*Block the right and breathe with the left
or vice versa, and give a precept that
The entire right nostril is surya nadi
And left is chandra nadi and make a mockery
Of Chandra-bhedan, surya bhedan pranayamas
and even nadi shodhana, Anuloma-Pratiloma.*

This noble subject of yog is not merely something for shibirs, workshops and retreats of 3, 4, 5 or 10 days.

*"Man making and mind making
have become that simple and also
exceedingly attractive and goody-goody."*

Perhaps Lord Yogeshvara Shri Krishna had no clue to such simple and goody-goody Yog! That is why he endorses the fact presented by Arjuna and says,

*"No doubt the means of yog
(abhyasa and vairagya)
are extremely difficult."*

In the modern era, we have genius yogis who are way ahead in generations than Krishna, Patanjali, Vyasa, Yajnavalkya and all seers, sages and the *Purana*-Purushas. Anyway, let us stop this sarcasm and proceed further.

It was said earlier in this chapter that nasal pranayama in a classical way is very complicated. One of the most important reasons for something being too complicated is that not every such thing is inherently and intrinsically complicated, but because inadequate preperatories, insufficient and orientations and dispositions and incorrect attitudes, the things become complicated. Another reason is opting for shortcuts in the run-up to such attempts.

In order that nasal pranayama does not become complicated on the classical tract, there is an extensive, deep and broad–based preparatory. The courses and instructions are not given prematurely but at the right point of time. The following process of nasal pranayama may appear a little strange and funny for neo-yogacharyas.

1) A long, long supine-positioned pranayama-shvasayama to be attempted. And evolve preperatories of various lower hierarchies.

2) Several pranayamic exercises to be carried out, which are sharirayama, manayama and shvasayama in the beginning.

3) Reach a level of *chitta prasadana* by those in supine position.

4) Reach up to pranakriya, chakra kriya, tattva kriya, laya kriya and dhyana kriya in the supine position.

5) Evolve the above stages even in the sitting position

6) Learn the finger usages, not in the seated position but in shavasana position. Learn the hasta mudra and the usages and skills of finger-tips in shavasana;

7) Unless one is well-versed in the seating position for pranayama and meditation and can easily maintain that position for 20-30 minutes, one should not attempt seating nasal pranayama;

8) Do the hasta mudra more easily now and learn usages on exhalation in supine positions in one cycle, then with 3 to 4 cycles with palms resting on chest or on the sides.

9) Beginners should not attempt multiple cycles in one go.

10) Learn to use tips skillfully, tenderly and dexterously. Palm should be akin to an aesthetic ornament on the nostril and not as a tool or an instrument.

11) One should learn the precise postions and master the positioning of the finger-tips and then work on improving the tonal quality of the breath.

12) Since finger-tips are to be used, nails must be cut (until they are below the tips); this is not for beauty alone. There is no provision for using the forepart of the top of the fingers and the thumb.

13) Wrist, back of palm and fingers should be well rounded. The knuckles should be bent for rounding and not be kept with straightness.

14) Initial attempts are in exhalation and not in inhalations.

15) Single-nostril exhalation should be strictly avoided in the beginning.

16) After taking a voluntary deeper inhalation with open nostrils, towards the end of it, hasta-mudra should be taken and be placed on nostril at a fixed spot just below the nasal bonc before exhalation.

17) Exhalations should be done by partially blocking both the nostrils and thus exhalations be attempted in both the nostrils and work on varied apertures of the nostril.

18) This exhalation must be slower, thinner and longer ideally done in stages rather than continuous .

19) Usage of tips should be used for naada parinama which will be/should be sonorous.

20) Initially, the aperture of the nostrils be reduced to effect a condition such as 30 to 40 percent closed and 60 to 70 percent open.

21) As the skill appears, the above proportions may be reversed.

22) Rather than attempting Pranayama (precisely shvasyama), one must carry out prayogas (experiments) in respect of:
   a) velocity of exhalation
   b) pressure management for aperture.
   c) pressure management for naada.

d) velocity and naada relationship.

e) velocity-pressure naada management.

23) After one such exhalation, the mudra should be relaxed for 3 to 4 cycles and redone for the next nasal exhalation.

24) Some prayogas are important in respect of micro-positioning for reaching breath passage. This literacy is paramount. There is a search mechanism and search process in place. Precise positioning will have ideal naada parinama. It is important to trace exhalative spot.

25) It must be noted that velocity and pressure units have reverse proportions that is higher velocity lower pressure and lower velocity higher pressure.

26) If the spotting of the passage is perfect–pressure is minimised. If imprecise, then the pressure is greater.

27) Velocity and pressure both are under voluntary control.

28) Usually both the nostrils are unevenly opened . This is an important consideration. One must be able to ascertain this disparity. It is a case of superior nostril and an inferior nostril.

29) On arriving at such disparity, one may deal with superior nostril for single-nostril exhalation than predecided nostril.

30) Initially avoid working on the inferior nostril but work on superior nostril to improve the naada parinama. The inferior should be closed and improve tuning of superior nostril.

31) Get convinced that by full nostril open without tips being used is not shvasayama or pranayama. And that skillful usage of tips for closing and opening the nostril is important and imperative.

32) Interactive role of tips on either side is important.

33) In nasal pranayamas, naada is important and not breathing in one nostril.

34) After sufficient prayog on exhalative breath, inhalation may be tried again in both the nostrils and not block any of the two.

35) Realize that role, placement, micro-placements are different between inhalations and exhalations.
36) Naada-parinama of in-breath and out-breath are different.
37) Naada parinama is more important than volume and length or duration.
38) Become familiar with differences in the usage of tips, their role, their skills for in-breath and out-breath.
39) As the breathing is supposed to be thin, rarified and fine thus be done in steps, not to loose breath while fingers are being manipulations is on. Suspend the breath for a while.
40) In case of loss of tonal quality of breath, suspend breath immediately and work on repositioning of finger tips and thumb tips.
41) In higher velocity, the tonal quality of breath is inferior, and in low velocity, it is superior.
42) Do not consider the role of the little or small finger less important; it is a fine-tuning tip.

If one feels that attempting nasal pranayama or shvasayama is complicated, suspend these practices and postpone it to a future point and go for preparatories once again.
Trying and simplifying it is not justifiable.

Finally, do not ever succumb to mockery such as:
1) Inhale from left, exhale from open
2) Exhale from left, inhale from open
3) Inhale from left, exhale from right.
4) Exhale from left and inhale from right etc.

and even incorporate either inner retention or outer retention.

Anyway, before heading for pranayama or naada parinama, there is much to learn and inculcate as described in the earlier chapters, it is wise not to hasten for nasal pranayama. There is a lot for

1) Literacy in shavasayama and pranayama,

2) Lot to observe and learn application, usages and addressed of/on/by breath,

Now comes the final statement in the chapter which is thus:

In nasal pranayama, the breathing is not in
one or both nostrils or exhalation or inhalation
Or both in one nostril; or two nostrils
but the breathing takes place in one naadi
of one nostril or one or two naadis of two nostrils.
As generally believed, the breathing is not
In one nostril but the nadi in one nostril;
Thus this pranayama is in nadi, of nadi and
by nadi, but not of, for, by or in cavities.
There are thousands of nadis in the right nostril

And one of them is the Surya nadi. So also, there are thousands of nadis in the left nostril and one of them is the Chandra nadi. Therefore by keeping the right nostril open, the chance of getting surya nadi pranayama has a 0.100000% chance.

So in the case of Chandra nadi pranayama in
The left nostril. Of course not to equate the
Suryanadi breathing with suryanadi pranayama.
And so also Chandra nadi breathing with
Chandra nadi pranayama.

In any case and any of the nasal (digital) pranayama, it is vitally important to develop the 'fingering' of nostrils like instrumental musicians need to develop exalted skill, sensitivity, tenderness and dexterity. In such pranayamas there is

Svara sadhana
Naada sadhana and
Prana sadhana.

Let us deal with such exercises in another chapter.

❖ ❖

THE ART OF FINGER-TIP SKILL

We have seen in an earlier chapter that nasal pranayama is initiated to a child of eight years in Brahmopadesham for the twice-born. The hasta mudra is taught then. This mudra is common to all the twice-born.

But it is highly astonishing as to who started 'the mockery-mudra', which has no validity, yet it is widely practiced in the yog community today.
The classical mudra has remained in Vedic rituals but nowhere else.
The current practices of pranayama mudra must be set aside.
Anyway, let us see the description of this pranayama mudra.

It must be understood that the right hand fingers should not be kept anywhere or in anyway on the nose. There are specific fingers generally to be used in a specific way as well as in a specific place but there is no specific spot and way to use them on the nose. Perhaps it is each of the cycles of breathing in search of the point of placement changes. Even during an exhalation or inhalation, it will be with constant manipulation. There is a hasta-mudra for all such pranayamas for all those who do it and at all times and in any case. Following are the invariable factors:

1) Right hand only must be used,

2) In no case, the middle finger and the right index finger are to be used; thus they are folded in to settle at the base of the thumb; the tips of these fingers are bent at the knuckles.

3) The thumb should be brought as an opponent to touch the tips of the ring finger and small finger which are joined together. This is called hasta-mudra for Pranayama.

4) The two fingers and the thumb must be bent to form a ring-shape rather than a clip-shape. In nasal pranayamas, the tips or fingers do not come as a clip on the nostrils but as tuners and adjusters for tonal quality of breath.

5) The right hand (in mudra position) should be taken up by bending the elbow joint. Then slightly open the contact between the thumb and two fingers and place it immediately below the nasal bone and not too far down on the nostrils.

6) The back or the wrist of the right hand is slightly bent for convexity on the posterior side. This is just a slight curve of the wrist.

7) The tips of the fingers (ring, small and thumb) are to be gently placed; they should touch the membrane as if the nose is as gentle as a flower.

8) Skin of the fingers and thumb tips should be as gentle as the skin of the nose.

9) What these tips are going to handle is again very tender and infant-like. Thus one must be aware of the handling culture, The hand work, finger work, arm work etc.

10) Finger work is almost like finger work for "touch screen" mode.

11) The finger tips are placed for sensing naada parinama

of pranayamic breath and does not deal with pneumatic ˉ breathing.

12) Tips or even fingers are not to be used for physically closing the nostrils. By such an act of the fingers, it is ridiculous to think that the nostrils become air tight. Only breath passage is to be blocked. When it is a question of blocking, nostrils are not a passage for breathing.

13) One must be aware of the breath passages grossly. These are described as under:

Base of nostrils is that part when we have a running nose and to avoid embarrassment, we clean the nasal water from that location. Then inserting the index finger straight into the nostril which is facing you, that part of the nose it touches is "the carpet of the floor of the nostrils." When the index finger is inserted in the right nostril while it is facing the left side, it is the carpet of the septum of the nostril. When the same finger is turned to the right side and inserted, the part that it touches is called the carpet of the membrane and where the tip of the index finger touches is called the roof of the nostril. These parts can similarly be indentified in the left nostril as well. Thus the parts are:

1) Base/gates of the nostrils,
2) Carpet of the septum (divider wall),
3) Carpet of the membrane,
4) Roof of the nostrils,
5) Carpet of the floor of the nostril.

Thus, these are five parts (grossly) of the nostrils of which one should be sensitive in breathing. Then one must be able to inhale or exhale in these five parts; or bracing these five parts. This is one of the preliminaries for nasal pranayama. Now let us continue the list.

14) Then one must be aware of the subtle parts of the nostrils which are again five. And these are initially to be taught by teachers to students.

The description is as under:
Identify the prithvi kendra or spot of breath under prithvi tattva. This is done by inhaling voluntarily and sensitively by silently uttering 'Lum', which is prana kriya. This will help ascertain the spot location by breathing under the presiding element of earth.

Then silently utter the letter 'Vum', while inhaling and exhaling similarly voluntarily, sensitively and deeper. This will help us to identify the spot location of the breath by the presiding element of water.

Then do a similar breathing by silently uttering the letter 'Rum', which will help indentify the spot location of breath by fire element.

Similarly breathe sensitively, voluntarily and deeply by using the letter 'Yum' to indentify the spot location of breath by the element of air (vayu Tattva).

Then finally use the sound form of the letter 'Hum', silently uttered for breathing by the spot location of the element of Aakash Tattva. These are the spot locations of breathing by the five elements. This is the precept of scientific yog (*Shiva-Svarodaya*) and a fact that we breathe cyclically under these five elements by rotation and it is a cycle of 60 minutes. Thus we come back to the same breathing after every 60 minutes. Before taking up nasal pranayama one must be literate about it. The postulations of Shivasvarodaya can be experienced and testified by any one who is an ardent seeker of yog. Without the usage of fingers, these must be practiced (and sensitized). Now let us again move towards the list.

15) One must have sufficient training, sensitivity and literacy of the pressure of finger tips and aspects and factors concerning it. There has been a detailed delineation of it to describe velocity, tone and pressure consideration. There is a spot to pressurize and counter-pressurize and a way to pressurize and gauge the amount of pressure in practical aspects.

Here is a description of this. The pressurization and counter-pressurizing or even depressurization and counter-depressurizations are important considerations. They correspond to velocity of the breath, exact spot location of breath and tonal quality or naada-parinama of breath.

We have already seen that there is a concerted effort of thumb-tip pressure, ring-small finger-tip pressure in mutual co-ordination. Then velocity management should be considered. Right pressure must be exercised by the tips. The other conditions are also to be considered such as:

a) Whether the nostrils are dry or damp or average

b) Whether the nostrils are blocked or open.

In such cases, the way to pressurize is important to be considered. This can help mitigate or overcome a negative condition and even improve the positive condition and improve nada parinama and get a superior condition. The way to pressurize are basically in four directions and then eight figuratively called dasha-disha meaning the 10 directions. Directions are the same as in navigation endeavors. These directions are:

1) upwards (north)

2) downwards (south)

3) towards the face (west)

4) away from the face (east)

One must attempt these apart from the amount of pressure. If proper direction is taken, then pressure will become tender and in case of imprecise selection the pressure will be heavier

for tonal quality. Once the above four directions are identified, then there will be identification of other four sub-directions such as:
1) Agneya (south-east)
2) Nairuttyya (south-west)
3) Vayavya (north-west)
4) Ishannya (north–east).
These are the directions for pressurizing. These are parts on which the tips and the use of directions are placed. The cases of membranes moved in those directions are always of pressurizing. Even if one attains some proficiency and fluency in indentifying hundreds or thousands of nadis we are not in a position to know which nadis are those functionally. However Jnaneshvars, Vyasas, Vasishthas and Yagnavalkyas etc can certainly identify those hundreds of nadis functionally. So also they can modify the breathing and attain suitable breathing.

Thus in Vaidika karmas, these veteran
sages know the kind of karma in terms of energy,
so also time in terms of chronology by
Graha, nakshatra, etc. panchanga aspect
and select suitable breath for clemency
in karma. The karmas are the influence
of one of the five
Elements or devatas. They have corresponding
Nadis and energies. Thus they can select suitable
breathing pranayama before karma
in the sankalpa or intension.

We can mock such practices but they are served by vital purpose in pranayama. Thus their karmas and karma *anushthana* is exclusive.

The interested ones may study the treatise of Shivasvarodaya which tells us of Tattva influence of karma, karmakala, grahas (planets) and constellations (nakshatra) as well as Tithi-vaar etc. Yogis and sages can set right their energies to suit the karma and make it exaltedly successful. They set right their energies by Pranayamas.

Anyway, now let us consider some sundry aspecsts or miscellaneous aspects. In such nasal pranayamas, only right hand (its mudra) is used. Even left-handers have no option. The use of middle finger and index finger is strictly prohibited. The applied fingers and thumb should not at all be erect but bent at the knuckles. Never use the foreparts of the digits. Do not make a clip or clamp of the fingers and thumb. The hasta-mudra apart from being skilful and functional should have ornament-like beauty and tenderness. The right-hand wrist should not be raised but must be running down. In any case in any such pranayamas the nostrils are never disconnected from the tips or vice versa. Ideally, the aperture should be minimum for fine, super-fine and precise breathing. This is attained by minimum pressure and by precise positioning and pressurizing. This will ensure sonorous nada-parinama. The opening session of such pranayamas should start with exhalations rather than inhalations. Such prayog should go on for a long time before the inhalative process is attempted. Most of the control skills are to be learnt in exhalative process. Using minimum but precise pressure must be the goal.

Now, let us analytically arrive at reasons why pressure points and pressure modes change for the tips. This will be helpful for studious practitioners. The following factors have to be considered for finger-tip pressure and dynamics or skills.

1) Right nostril to be closed and left to be opened for breathing.
2) Left to be closed and right to be opened for breathing.
3) Breathing to be done in both the nostrils.
4) To be inhaling in right and exhaling in left.
5) To be exhaling in right and inhaling in left.

6) To be inhaling in right and exhaling in the left.
7) To be exhaling in right and inhaling in left.
8) To be inhaling through the right when the right is clear.
9) To be inhaling through the right when the right is not clearly opened.
10) To be inhaling through the right when the right is blocked.
11) To be exhaling through the right when it is very clearly opened.
12) To be exhaling through the right when it is not fully clear and open.
13) To be exhaling through the right when it is blocked.
14) To be inhaling through the left when the left is clear and open.
15) To be inhaling through the left when the left is not fully clear.
16) To be inhaling through the left when the left is blocked.
17) To be exhaling through the left when it is fully clear.
18) To be exhaling through the left when the left is partially opened and partially closed.
19) To be exhaling through the left when the left is blocked.
20) To be exhaling through both the nostrils when one is superior and ideal while the other one has semi-good or bad condition.
21) To be inhaling through both the nostrils when one is fine and the other one not so fine or very bad
22) Pressure on a good nostril while counter pressure is ideal /not ideal/inferior, for inhalation/exhalation/ both
23) While the *ida* is operative, ida inhalation/exhalation/ both to be done.

24) Open the *ida* and exhale/inhale/both through that nostril

25) When pingala is operative and inhalation/exhalation/both to be done.

26) When the pingala has to be activated and be used for inhalation/ exhalation/both.

27) When sushumna is operative, inhalation/ exhalation or both to be done.

28) While sushumna is operative, inhalation by one and exhalation by both.

29) While sushumna is operative, exhalation by one and inhalation by both.

30) Transfer from Ida breathing to pingala/sushumna.

31) Transfer from pingla breathing to ida/sushumna breathing.

32) Transfer from sushumna to ida/pingla breathing.

33) Prithvi inhalation in right/left/both in suitable/ unsuitable conditions.

34) Prithvi exhalation in right/left/both in suitable/ unsuitable conditions.

35) Aap inhalation in right/left/both in suitable/ unsuitable conditions.

36) Aap exhalation in right/left/both in suitable/ unsuitable conditions.

37) Tej inhalation in right/left/both suitable/unsuitable conditions.

38) Tej exhalation in right/left/both in suitable/unsuitable conditions.

39) Vayu exhalation in right/left/both in suitable/ unsuitable conditions.

40) Vayu inhalation in right/left/both in suitable/ unsuitable conditions.

41) Akash exhalation in right/left/both in suitable/ unsuitable conditions.

42) Akash inhalation in right/left/both in suitable/ unsuitable conditions.

(In case of these pancha tattvas there will be pranakriyas of Lum, Vum, Rum, Yum, Hum for the five elements which are invoked by silent utterances in *madhyama vani* or speech.)

43) Muladhara kriya pranayama (Bahhya-Abhyantara/ sthambha vritti)
44) Svadhishthana kriya pranayama (Bahhya-Abhyantara/sthambha vritti)
45) Manipuraka kriya pranayama. (Bahhya-Abhyantara/ sthambha vritti)
46) Anahata kriya pranayama (Bahhya-Abhyantara/ sthambha vritti)
47) Vishudhi kriya pranayama (Bahhya-Abhyantara/ sthambha vritti)
48) Ajna kriya pranayama (Bahhya-Abhyantara/ sthambha vritti)

In both kumbhakas, the hasta-mudra is relaxed and the palm rested on the lap; this is because kumbhakas are by mudra-traya or bandha-traya.

Then, the amount of pressure depends upon certain factors such as:

1) What is the role of these tips as sahayogi And Pratiyogi meaning complimentary pressure and counter pressure.
2) If the pressure spot is imprecisely selected, the pressures are more and if selected properly, the pressure is normal.
3) Whether the proponent has selected proper spot or not.
4) The condition of the nostril on 'as is basis' such as dry, damp, idcally opened, closed etc.
5) Whether the nada parinama is proper or not.

6) Velocity pattern of the breath, i.e. higher velocity-lower pressure or lower velocity-higher pressure.
7) Whether pressure is for inhalation of its side or opposite side.
8) Whether the pressure is for exhalation of its side or opposite side.
9) Whether it is pressure or counter pressure or both.
10) Velocity tapering for exhalation/inhalation or both.
11) Whether the breath is of ida/pingala/sushumna and prithvi/aap/tej/vayu/akash.
12) Whether the nadis are to be altered or nadis of tattvas to be altered.
13) Examining/altering nadis of ida, pingala, sushumna or the five tattvas.
14) Whether the present nadi is vata, pitta or kapha.

An unprepared, unqualified and immature practitioner may faint at the above details. One can understand as to why it is called digital pranayama here. In neo-yog, however, there is whole-sale mockery and nasal pranayamas are taught even in one-week camps.

Coming to some miscellaneous aspects here, it may be said that there is vata, pitta, kapha chakra in 24 hours. They do become affecting factors in nasal pranayamas. Morning time is kapha period; after sunrise to day time pitta time, and night (sleeping hours) are vata influences, again leading to kapha is Brahma-muhurta (morning). These cycles do impact breath centers, breath nodes, breath functions, and breath chemistry. Therefore at the time of pranayama, these have a major influence. The seasons again contribute to the above factors. Vasanta, Grishma, Varsha, Sharad, Hemanta, Shishir are the *rutus* (seasons). So also subjective pathology (dhatu, rasa, mala, dosha, vaishamya etc.) again influence the outcome.

Therefore the nostrils are the keyboard of the synthesizer. Nostrils have countless control points and switches. The student's Pranayama package has many such considerations, while, pop-yog simplifies it this to

'*Inhale on right*
and Exhale on left, etc.

The nose and nostrils are like "Prana-vaddya" for a yogi. Just as a musician holds the instrument above the heart, this is the prana instrument for yog; thus dearer than heart. In neo-yog, nostrils are ridiculously belittled. This is a heart-breaking travesty. Pranayama is *naada sadhana*. Just as sangeet (music) has sapta svaras (seven notes) and 22 strutis, there are svaras in pranayama too such as:

Ida svara
Pingala svara
Sushumna svara
Prithvi svara
Aap svara
Teja svara
Vayu svara
Akasha svara

and infinite prana-svaras, nadi svaras, chakra svaras etc. Our nostrils are like a Pranic harp.

❖ ❖

Chapter : 46

NOSTRILS – A MARVEL

The nose works as a dual organ; one as a breathing organ and the other as an olfactory one, i.e. an organ of smell sensation. Even if the mouth is a food organ, the food to be ingested is examined by the eyes, nose, and tongue for the NOC (no objection certificate) of visual, olfactory and gustatory organs. Thus the nose is a major organ of ingestion. Before the food goes to the tongue, visual and olfactory organs have to give an NOC. Moreover, for some fragrances and smell, we need to inhale to smell an object.

Now, coming to the most vital act of the nostrils, it is to take a breath duly examined and processed. There are 21,600 cycles per day or an in-breath every four seconds. Within four seconds it examines and processes the breath, filters the breath, conditions the breath, homogenizes the breath for all cycles. It has 24 x 7 duty for 365 days from birth to death. Within four seconds, the temperature of the breath is brought to 98° degrees F., even if the external temperature may be -15 degrees to +55 degrees C. Every breath is thoroughly tested, examined, moderated. In no time, it makes the breath 98 degrees F; this is an unquestionable and incredible marvel, not duly acknowledged by the intelligent but ungrateful man.

Breathing is an absolutely incessant act
Going at an incredible rate such as more
Than 15 cycles per minute. It goes on
Incessantly 24 x 7 x 365 ´ years of life.

Here, the deity presiding over the organ is Ashvinikumars, the celestial physicians. Ashva meaning horse is again known as a tireless animal. Within a short time such as four seconds and that too every four seconds thse nose does several acts such as:

Sorting out Filtering Sterilization
Regulating the temperature
Making it lung worthy.

There is no such karmayogi ever who does the duty without any expectation and fruits. Can one imagine if we got a bill for breathing every day?

A noble person with spiritual and religious consciousness knows the worth of this bounty. Thus yogic pranayama is eulogy to the Almighty. Pranayama can be called cosmic poetry. The greatness of the nose does not stop here. It is also a voice organ. It contributes for voice and even vocalists are not aware of it. They attribute the voice to the throat. They need to be educated here that the nose and nostrils make a great contribution to our voice.

Why does our voice change during common cold and when we close one or both the nostrils?

Finally, it can be said that in our

Nose, nostrils, breath and prana lies the greatest of mind
and chitta conditions to evolve than to achieve any
Pranayama. We know the nose as an organ
of breathing and our biological existence.
Although it is one of the most vital organs, its
role as a breath organ is one of the most insignificant
functions if we consider its functions in their entirety.
The most unwieldy mind can becomes a puppet through it.

In the next chapter let us consider how we can carry out Pancha Tattva prayogas at our hierarchy.

❖ ❖

Chapter : 47

A FASCINATING EXPERIMENT

Take up a steady, restful passivating shavasana-position. Go for yogic and pranayamic preparatories with good amount of prominence. Evolve insulations to all the anxiety currents become transcendent , neutral, insulated in mind by breath associations and breath sensitivity culture.

Become nose aware, nostril aware, and breath aware. Evolve close awareness to breath and its movements, its seepage in and around the nose and nostrils. Keep neutrally watching the face and facial expressions as if those are of a distinguished actor. Soon you will see various expressions of physiognomy.

commence soft, subtle, tender, gentle, thin and rarified but little slower and creeping breath. Then commence the pranakriya as described in an earlier chapter. Silently utter लं- - लं- - लं- - लं which is Beeja mantra for Prithvi. Imagine and consider the breath as a river and indentify source → course → mounth. Watch the in breath river and the in breath terminal as well as the out breath river and its terminal.

Keep watching your facial awareness despite the eyes closed. After a few cycles start the pranayama of aap which is वं... वं... वं..., etc. This will be another river originating in nose and nostrils. Keep watching the face by sensitivity. Then comes the prana kriya by agni which is रं... रं... रं, etc and then

Vayu pranakriya of यं... यं... यं..., etc. And akash by हं... हं... हं..., etc. So also the pranakriya of prithvi Taltva which is LA, LAA, LEE, LOO, etc. It will be a fascinating physiognomic study . These are the five major river s of the prana kriya of Tattvas They have tributary rivers by vowelisation as mentioned below.

and its terminal. Keep watching your facial awareness despite the eyes closed. After a few cycles start the pranayama of aap which is वं-- वं-- वं-- वं. This will be another river originating in nose and nostrils. Keep watching the face by sensitivity. Then comes the pranakriya by agni which is रं-- रं-- रं-- रं and then Vayupranakriya of यं-- यं-- यं-- यं. And akash by हं-- हं-- हं-- हं It will be a fascinating physiognomic study.

These are the five major rivers of the pranakriya of Tattvas They have tributary rivers by vowelisations as mentioned below.

ल ला ली लू ले लै लो लौ लं ल: ।
व वा वी वू वे वै वो वौ वं व: ।
र रा री रू रे रै रो रौ रं र: ।
य या यी यू ये यै यो यौ यं य: ।
ह हा ही हू हे है हो हौ हं ह: ।

We will be introduced to so many physiognomic conditions with rich pranic irrigative schemes. Then by using svara---varna---vyanjan we can have
10 + 40 +250 = 300 rivers in nostrils. The nostrils will be a KALEIDOSCOPE. The breathified face will be like a proficient actor making several faces for one expression of

Quietude, placidity , passivity, neutrality
Virginity, purity, piety, sanctity, nobility
Sublimity etc..

The following experiment may be attempted by those who are well settled in nasal pranayama.

The ida is the nadi in the left nostril
Which is lunar and of shakti,
While the pingala is in the right nostril
Which is solar and of shiva.

Now looking at the following table, attempt ida—pingala, shiva—shakti, Chandra—surya,, pranayamas by silently uttering the beeja mantra of Tattva and breathing in well-tuned nostrils.

LEFT / SHAKTI IDA MOON	RIGHT / SHIVA PINGALA SUN
लं Round	लं Round
वं Round	वं Round
रं Round	रं Round
यं Round	यं Round
हं Round	हं Round

The point is that there is solar manifestation of five elements as well as lunar manifestations of five elements. Just as the sun has many manifestations from dawn to dusk and from chaitra to phalgun, there are such here.

Just as the moon has several manifestations from new moon to new moon or full moon to full moon of chaitra to phalgun there are several ida-pinglas manifestations. These are all to culture the chitta.

Again it is suggested here that one can study Shivasvarodaya.

Chapter : 48

REPERTOIR OF KUMBHAKA

We have considered the aspect of kumbhaka in our earlier chapter. We had considered Bahya Kumbhaka and Antarakumbhaka and the subject of:-

Prana kriya
Tattva kriya
Chakara kriya,

so also by extrapolation Ida—pingala---sushumna nadi kumbhakas. Thus there are countless kinds of kumbhakas and it can be a mega—project to make an exploration. We might easily get lost in making such an endeavour. However, in pedantic approach we cannot get lost in this forest. The shastras have given precise classification
Basically there are two classes called
   1) Sahita and
   2) Kevala
apart from
   1) Bahya and
   2) Abhyantara
The Sahita kumbhaka is conditioned by Desha—kala—sankhya as laid down by Patanjali. Thus there are either post-exhalative or post-inhalative meaning bahya or abhyantara. While Kevala kumbhaka is neither bahya or abhyantara (this is discussed in a separate chapter too.)
   Sahita kumbhaka is again Sagarbha or Nigarbha. Sagarbha means with the support of the beeja mantras such as :-

लंवंरंयंहं
श्रीं हीं क्लीम् ॐ

Nigarbha means the ones based on svara, varna,vyanjanas
excluding " UM" form such as:-

कं खं गं ect
चं छं जं ect
टं ठं डं ect
तं थं दं ect
पं फं बं ect
यं रं लं ect

Gheranda samhita gives the following classes:-
    1) Surya bheda (Chandra bheda implied)
    2) Ujjayi
    3) Sheetali
    4) Bhasrika
    5)Bhramari
    6)Murchha
    7) Sahita
    8) Kevala

By basic pranayamas using single lettered breathing there are
nearly 350 kinds. Neophytes can have another set to go through
orientation for profundity which

Bahya—abhyantara kumbhaka
Of the muladhara chakra.
    Svadhisthana chakra
    Manipuraka chakra.
    Anahata chakra
    Vishuddhi chakra
    Ajna chakra
These are preceded by
    Pancha Vayu Bahya Abhyantara kumbhakas
    Pancha Pranas kumbhakas
    Mulabandha mudra kumbhakas

Uddiyana mudra kumbhakas
Jalandara mudra kumbhakas.

Secondly pranayamas in the classical mode are by proportions as seen earlier as samavritti pranayama and Vishama vritti pranayama. Shastras have said:-

Superior Pranayama is of
16: 64 : 32

Middle pranayama is of
8 : 32 : 16

and Inferior Pranayama is of
4 : 16 :8

mantras.

Neophyte should try this proportion aspect by mental counting such as one, two, three, four, five ---ten. These may be mental seconds and proportions can be attempted such as:-

1)	5	:	2	:	10
2)	5	:	3	:	10
3)	5	:	4	:	10
4)	5	:	5	:	10
5)	5	:	6	:	10
6)	5	:	7	:	10
			OR		
7)	6	:	4	:	10
8)	7	:	4	:	10
9)	8	:	4	:	10
			OR		
10)	5	:	5	:	5
11)	7	:	7	:	7
12)	8	:	8	:	8

Here middle unit is kumbhaka, the first and the third can be either in-breath or out-breath to result antara—Bahya kumbhakas. These kumbhakas can be attempted at a higher proportion of in-breath and evolve capacity. The proportions can be such as

Purak	:	Kumbhaka	:	Rechaka
Pu	<	Ku	<	Re
Pu	>	Ku	<	Re
Pu	>	Ku	>	Re
Pu	=	Ku	=	Re

Etc, etc,, etc.

Most importantly it must be borne in mind
That yogis would do kumbhakas
(with bandha Traya) and we
would be doing merely retentions
after inhalations or exhalations and
not puraka and rechaka.

Now let us have an over view of numerous kriyas in pranayama. This will be a separate chapter.

Chapter : 49

CLUSTER OF KRIYAS

This chapter comes as a facility to a student of yog and Pranayama in particular. Most of pranayama is ideally introduced, attained, practiced and is made profound in shavasana rather than seating position where the beginner has to struggle for mere seating position. The first and foremost kriyas is Prarambhana kriya. This has been dealt with in detail as preparatory of pranayama/ shvasayama. These following are kriyas of which some are to be attempted and many have to be merely known by a raw beginner. Some are to be tried, learnt, understood and perhaps some merely imagined !

However, this is not a sequential order:-

1) Prarambha kriya.
2) Shvasa kriya.
3) Prashvasa kriya.
4) Shvasa-Prashvasa kriya.
5) Antara sthamban kriya.
6) Bahir stambhana kriya.
7) Puraka kriya.
8) Rechaka kriya.
9) Antara kumbhaka kriya.
10) Bahya kumbhaka kriya.
11) Kevala khumbaka kriya.

Kriyas from seven to ten are not at all in the syllabus of neo-yogis !

11) Pancha vayu kriya.
12) Prana kriya.
13) Pancha prana kriya.
14) Uddiyana mudra kriya.
15) Mulabandha mudra kriya.
16) Jalandara mudra kriya
17) Agnisara kriya.
18) Kapalabhati kriya.
19) Prithvi prana kriya.
20) Prithvi tattva kriya.
21) Aap prana kriya.
22) Aap tattva kriya.
23) Tej prana kriya.
24) Tej tattva kriya.
25) Vayu prana kriya.
26) Vayu tattva kriya.
27) Akash prana kriya.
28) Akash tattva kriya.
29) Muladhar prana kriya.
30) Muladhara chakra kriya.
31) Svadhisthana pran kriya.
32) svadhisthana chakra kriya.
33) Manipuraka prana kriya.
34) Manipuraka chakra kriya.
35) Anhata prana kriya.
36) Anahata chakra kriya.
37) Ajna prana kriya.
38) Ajna chakra kriya.
39) Shat chakra prana kriya.
40) Shat chakra kriya.
41) Deshapardristha kriya.
42) Kala paridristha kriya.
43) Sankhya paridrishta kriya.
44) Ida nadi kriya

45) Pingla nadi kriya.
46) Sushumna/shunya nadi kriya.
47) Ujjai kriya.
48) Viloma (sarpita loma kriya.
49) Aakriti kriya (graphic modes).
50) Anuloma-pratiloma kriya.
51) Surya bhedan/Chandra bhaden kriya.
52) Nadishodhan kriya.
53) Sheetali/sheetakari kriya (with kaki mudra).
54) Bhramari kriya.
55) Matruka cycling kriya (matruka prayog kriya).
56) Pranava kriya.
57) Namaprayog kriya.
58) Pratyahar kriya.
59) Chitalaya kriya.
60) Karmayog sanskruti kriya.
61) Jayana yog sanskruti kriya.
62) Dhyanayog sanskruti kriya.
63) Aham tattva chyayana kriya.
64) Bhaktiyog sanskruti kriya.
65) Sthitavritti kriya (Gita chap 2)
66) Gunateetavritti kriya (Gita chap x 1v)
67) Yogavritti kriya (Gita chap x v111)
68) Bhakti vtitti kriya.(Gita chap (x11)
69) Pranayajna kriya (Gita chap v)
70) Dhyana transformation kriya.

This is an elaborate list of kriyas which occur in pranayama and various pranayamas. What follows is just one line description of these.

Arambha kriya or orientation and preparatory kriya has been elaborately described in an earlier chapter in the beginning. Students will be aware that exhalation has a paramount importance which becomes PRASHVASA KRIYA.

Then that is followed by in-breath as well which is SHVASA KRIYA. Pranayama comprises of several cycles'and there is never one cycle breathing pranayama. Quacks teach how to inhale and how to exhale but never consider the two "roll overs" These are in-breath to out-breath smooth roll over and exhalation to inhalation smooth roll over. The most important thing is neglected by quacks. Thus there is a kriya called SHVASA-PRSHVASA KRIYA. Then there is retention of two kinds which comes in pranayama. Thus there are BAHYYA KUMBHAKA AND ANTARA KUMBHAKA KRIYAS. In our case, they are Antara-bahya sthambhana kriyas and not kumbhaka kriyas. Thus there are also ANTARA STAMBANA and BAHYA STHAMBANA KRIYAS. Then there are Puraka and Rechaka kriyas. Kevala kumbhaka kriya similarly is of a yogi on supreme hierarchy. Then there are PANCHA VAYU KRIYAS. This is breathing by confinement such as:

Navel and below apana vayu kriya,
Heart to navel samana vayu kriya,
Heart to nooe prana-vayu kriya and .
Above heart is Udana vayu kriya
Vyana being all pervasive is common
Concomittant in all kriyas. So also peripheral
Actions are called Vyana vayu kriyas.

Then comes the prana kriya. It is by silent utterances with breathing. These utterances are of literal letters from अ to क्ष: which are nearly 350 sound forms. These are PRANA KRIYAS. Then comes the letters which correspond to five pranas. These are four kriyas in its subset. These are PANCHA-PRANA KRIYAS. These four kriyas are viz :-

1) Prana- Vyana
2) Apana -Vyana
3) Samana -Vyana
4) Udana -Vyana.

In Udana prana region there are Ajnya anf Vishuddhi chakras. The letters are as follows

ह Class
स Class

And अ आ ई ऊ ए ऐ ओ औ अं अः

Then in pranasthana there is Anahata chakra and letters are :-

क Class
ख Class
घ Class
च Class
छ Class
ज Class
झ Class
ट Class
ठ Class

Then comes the region of the samana. Manipuraka chakra comes in this region. The letters are:-

ड Class
ढ Class
ण Class
त Class
थ Class
द Class
न Class
प Class
फ Class

Then comes the region of apana where there are two chakras viz:- Svadishthana and muladhara chakra. The letters are :-

ब Class
म Class
म Class
य Class
र Class
व Class
श Class
ष Class
स Class

Pranayama breathing and retentions have Uddiyana kriya as an essential component. Thus there is UDDIYANA KRIYA or UDDIYANA MUDRA KRIYA. Then there are MULABANDHA MUDRA KRIYA and also JALANDARA MUDRA KRIYA and uddiyana Complementary AGNISARA KRIYA and KAPALABHATI KRIYA. Then there are PANCHATATTVA KRIYAS.

The subset is PRITHVI PRANA KRIYA
ल ला ली लू लै लै लो लौ ल: ।
There is PRITHVI TATTVA KRIYA
लं लां लीं लूं लें लौं लैं लौं ल: ।
Then there is AAP PRANA KRIYA वा वी वू वे वै वो वौं व:
AAP TTTVA KRIYA वं वां वूं वें वैं वां वौं वं: ।
Then there is TEJA PARNA KRIYA र रां रीं रूं रं रैं रों रौं रं ।
TEJA TATTVA KRIYA र रां री रें रैं रों रौं रं: ।
Then comes VAYU PRANA KRIYA
य या यी यू ये यै यो यौ य:।
Then VAYU TATTVA KRIYA यं यां यीं यूं यें यैं यों यौं यं: ।
AAKASH PRANA KRIYA हा ही हू हे है हो हौ ह: ।
AAKASH TATTVA KRIYA हां हीं हूं हें हैं हों हौं हं: ।

The shat chakras similarly have two such kriyas . The following table shows the letters.

CHAKRA PRANA KRIYA	CHAKRA KRIYA
Muladhara Muladhara	
व श ष स ।	वं शं षं सं
वा शा षा सा ।	वां शां षां सां ।
वी शी षी सी ।	वीं शीं षीं सीं ।
वू शू षू सू ।	वूं शूं षूं सूं ।
वे शे षे से ।	वें शें षें सें ।
वै शै षै सै ।	वैं शैं षैं सैं ।
वो शो षो सो ।	वों शों षों सों ।
वौ शौ षौ सौ ।	वौं शौं षौं सौं ।
व: श: ष स: ।	वं: शं: षं: सं: ।

Form the above table we can infer the modes of
SVADHISHTHANA PRANA KRIYA CHAKRA KRIYA ब -
-भ--म-य-र--ल

Vowelisation in pranakriyaand बं -- भं--मं--यं--रं--लं
vowelisation in chakra kriya. Then Manipurakapranakriya
ड--ढ--ण--त--थ--द--ध--न--प--फ are to be vowelised in
pranakriya. And in the MANIPURAKA CHAKARA KRIYA
has the vowelisation of डं--ढं--णं--तं--थं--दं--धं--नं--पं--फं Then
comes the ANAHATA PRANA KRIYA it has the vowelisation
of क--ख--ग--घ--च--छ--ज--झ--ट--ठ

And the ANAHATA CHAKRA KRIYA has the
vowelisation of कं--खं--गं--घं--चं--छं--जं--झं--टं--ठं

Then comes the VISHUDDHI PRANA KRIYA and
Vishudi Chakra Kriya. The pranakriya has only अ--आ--ई--
ऊ--ए--ऐ--ओ--औ--अ:

And the CHAKRA KRIYA has अं--आं--ईं--ऊं--एं--ऐं--ओं-
-औं--अं:

AJANYA PRANA KRIYA (ह--क्ष) (हा--क्षा) (ही--क्षी) (हू--
क्षू) (हे--क्षे) (है--क्षे) (हो--क्षो) (हौ--क्षौ) (ह:--क्ष:) And the AJANYA

CHAKRA KRIYA has (हं--क्षं) (हां--क्षां) (हीं--क्षीं) (हूं--क्षूं) (हें--क्षें) (हैं--क्षैं) (हों--क्षों) हौं--क्षौं) (हं:--क्षं:)

It should be noted that the whole set of letters must be in each in-breath , out-breath and retentions. One may notice omissions of some literal letters such as

इ, उ, ऋ, ॠ
ऌ, ॡ, ङ्, ञ

These are omitted in prana kriya and tattva kriyas. But however they may occur in Samantraka pranayamas appearing in the body of mantras.

Then there are DESHA—PARI DRUSHTA KRIYA, KALA PARIDRUSHTA KRIYA AND SANKHYA PARI DRUSHTA KRIYA to effect regulations in shvasa or prana. Then there are combinations of them. This has been considered in an earlier chapter.

Then in nasal pranayama there are left nostril breathings or right nostril breathings or dual nostril breathing. Thus there are :-

IDA NADI KRIYA
PINGLA NADI KRIYA
SUSHUMNA NADI KRIYA.

Then in digital pranayama there are ANULOMA KRIYA and PRATILOMA KRIYA and CHANDRA BHEDHANA KRIYA, SURYA BHEDANA KRIYA and NADI SHODHANA KRIYA. There is a huge subset of this with combinations of prana tattvas and chakras. Today we are familiar with shvasayama in digital shvasayama which are so called pranayamas.

Then without finger –thumb usages there are UJJAYA KRIYAS, VILOMA KRIYS, SARPIL-LOMA KRIYAS,. Thus by KAKI MUDRAS of mouth and tongue there are SHEETALI ---SHEETAKARI KRIYAS.

Thus there are BHRAMARI NAD KRIYAS in Bhramari pranayama. The exhalations are done here with vocal sound of a bee which is a humming sound. Then there are Samantraka pranayamas. There the prominence is to AUM Thus there is that PRANAVA KRIYA. Then in Samantraka pranayamas there are Mantra-prayogas. Thus there is MANTRA-PRAYOGA KRIYA, then NAAMA—PRA-YOG KRIYAS, then for meditation there are seisnological kriya or PRATYAHARA KRIYA. There is reference to sense-part in breathing as mentioned below.

EYES =   outer eye corner
          Inner eye corner
          Upper eye
          Bottom eye
          Centre eye –references.

EARS =   Hind ear
          Fore ear
          Top ear
          Bottom ear
          Centre ear –references.

NOSE -=   Nasal gate awareness
          Nasal floor awareness
          Septum awareness.
          Membrane awareness
          Roof nostril awareness.

MOUTH =   Lip awareness
          Cheek awareness
          Tongue awareness
          Palate awareness
          Teeth awareness.

The training about this is accomplished in yogasana-pursuits. There are sensological kriyas and pratyahara kriyas in asanas. By these kriyas the LAYA KRIYAS come in the horizon.

As seen on an earlier occasion, the act of breathing has a rich fabric of karmayog. Thus comes up KARMAYOG SANSKRUTI KRIYA. By ethereal, sublime and philosoplised state of mind in pranayama there is JNANAYOGA SANSKRUTI KRIYA and by meditation there is DHYANAYOG SANSKRUTI KRIYA.

Since Prana in Brahmasutra and Brahmopasana and pranayama has profused religious consciousness, there is BHAKTI SANSKRUTI KRIYA because of upasana in it. Because of metaphysical ambience in chitta, the "I" is now a principle than petty ego. Thus comes up AHAM—TATTVA—CHAYANA[CHURNING] —KRIYA.This "AHAM"is transcendent—not determined by birth—decay—age—death—gender—class—caste—creed—status—ethnicity etc. Then out of such sublime and philosophical process there are :=

STHITAPRAJNA VRITTI KRIYA

GUNATEETA KRIYA

And

BHAKTI VRITTI KRIYA.

The following passage from the Gita will shed light on those.

Yogi: (chapter 18)

"Endowed with untarnished Buddhi and
partaking of light –Sattvik and regulated in diet,
living in lonely and in undefined, having rejected
sensuality objects, having controlled the mind,

speech and body by restraint of chitta.
And firmly founded in Sattva, taking a resolute stand
On dispassion, after having got rid of attachment
And aversion completely, and remaining ever devoted
To yog of meditation, having given up Ahankar Himsa,
lust
Anger, and luxuries, devoid of feeling
Of pleasures and tranquilled in heart, such
Man becomes qualified for oneness
With Brahman who is TRUTH, CONSCIOUSNESS
And bliss. Established in that Brahman and
Contented to the brim in the chitta. The yogi no
Longer grieves or craves for any thing.
He is same to all the
beings. Such a yogi attains Supreme devotion
For ME"

(51—54)

Sthitaprajna (Chap 2)

"Arjuna , when one thoroughly dismisses
all cravings of mind, and is satisfied in the
self through (the joy of) the self, then he is
called stable in mind.

The sage whose mind remains unperturbed
amid sorrows, whose thirst for pleasures
Has altogether disappeared and who is free
From passion, fear and anger is called a
Stable mind.

He who is unattached to everything, and
meeting with good and evil without rejoice or
recoil is stable-minded.

When like a tortoise, which draws in
all its senses and organs from their objects,
He too withdraws them similarly
and is said to be stable-minded"

(55-58)

Bhakta (chapter ´ v)

He who is free from malice towards all
Beings and friendly and compassionate
To all, is free from Ahankar, mineness,
And is balanced in joy and in sorrows.
Forgiving all and being ever-contented,
And mentally united with Me, who has
Subdued his mind, senses and body,
Has firm resolve, and surrendered his
Mind and reason to Me,--that devotee
Of mine is dear to me.

He who is not a source of annoyance
To anyone and is not annoyed by
Anyone, and is free from delight and
Envy, perturbation and fear, is
Dear to Me.

He who wants nothing, who is both
Internally and externally pure, is wise
And impartial and has risen above all
Distractions, and who renounces the feeling
Of doership in all undertakings—
That devotee is dear to Me.

He who neither rejoices nor hates, nor
Grieves, nor desires and who renounces
Both good and evil actions and is full of

Devotion is dear to Me.
He who is alike to friend and foe,
As well as to honor and ignominy,
Who remains balanced in head in heat
And cold, pleasure and pain and other
Contrary experiences and is free from
Attachment, he who takes praise and
Reproach alike, and is given to contemplation
And contented with any means of subsistence
What so ever, entertaining no sense of
Ownership and attachment in respect of his
Dwelling place and full of devotion to Me
That man is dear to Me.

Those devotees, however, who partake
In a disinterested way of this nectar of pious
 Wisdom set forth above, endowed with faith
And solely devoted to Me, They are extremely
Dear to Me !!

(13-20)

Gunatita (chapter 'iv)

Arjuna, he who hates not light born of
Sattva and activity born of rajas and even
Stupor born of tamas when prevalent, nor
Longs for them when they have ceased.

He who is sitting like a witness, is not
Disturbed by the gunas, and who,
Knowing that the gunas alone move
Within themselves and thus remains
Established in identity, with the Atma,
And never falls off from that state.

He who is ever established in the self
Takes woe and joy alike, regards the
Clod of the earth, a stone, and a piece
Of gold in equal value, is possessed of
Wisdom, receives the pleasant as well
As the unpleasant in the same spirit
And views censure and praise alike.

He who is indifferent to honor and
Ignominy, is alike to the cause of a
Friend as well as that of enemy, and
Has renounced the sense of doership
In all undertakings is said to have
Risen above the three gunas.

One who constantly worships Me
And is in union and devotion for Me
Transcends the gunas.

(22—26)

Now coming to the next of the kriyas is the PRANAYAMA KRIYA. Again we have to turn to Gita for it. The fourth chapter while describing various yajnas says the following about pranayama yajna.

"Other yogis offer apana into prana
or exhalation into inhalation, even so
others , the act of inhalation into
exhalation or prana into apana.
There are still others given to
Practice of pranayama who have
Regulated their food and life style,
Offer prana into prana. All these
Have their sins consumed away by
Yajna and understood the meaning
Of sacrificial worship !!

(29—30)

Then finally there is Dhyana transformation kriya, because the way of pranayama is in meditativity. Thus are nearly seventy kriyas in classical pranayama. Just as in music a veteran and maestro does not dabble in those 78,000 ragas but masters a few in some tens of ragas but a mediocre carries a sack of several ragas, similarly modern pranayama seeker is interested in as many pranayamas as possible and creates a shallow pond of each of those. Here is a list of some of the pranayamas in vogue.

1) Ujaya
2) Bhaya viloma.
3) Antara viloma.
4) Bhhyabhyantara viloma
5) Sarpil-loma
6) Paryanka pranayama
7) Sarpil- Pranayama
8) Mala –Pranayama.
9) Chandra masa pranayama
10) Vartul pranayama
11) Kankana Pranayama
12) Kundalakara pranayama
13) Suchiparni pranayama
14) Padma Pranayama
15) Pushpakara Pranayama
16) Bhistaka Pranayama
17) Nasika pranayama
18) Gayatri Pranayama
19) Anuloma—Pratiloma
20) Surya bhedan (set)
21) Chanda bedhana (set)
22) Nadishodana (Set)
23) Samantraka
24) Naama Pranayama

25) Bhramari
26) plavini etc..etc...

Every Pranayama has an astonishing range of hierarchies. It will not be proper that some of the pranayamas are of neophyte and some others are of superior hierarchy. But the fact remains that Pranayama commences with Ujjayi. All aspects of conditioning, such as volume, velocity, density, confinement, deployment modules, graphic modes, breath designs etc. or Dosha—Kala—Saukhya Pardrushtata and Sukshmata and Deerghata can be attempted for orientation, training and experimentation. Thus all kinds of Ayama can be learnt. The viloma pranayamas teach pauses—suspensions for retention. The spiraloma or sarpila-loma pranayama has incradible concessions. During deep and and long inhalation there are micro and magna doses of exhalation which is a 'release'. So all inhalation of great length has an intermittent but tiny exhalations which again come as a "release". A naïve doubt comes up

When there is a long-long inhalation
Is there not a lack of of lapse of
De-carbon-di-oxilation and in a
Long-long-long exhalation is there
Not a deprivation and starvation in the
Oxigination!

But this doubt won't come with the spiral breathing.

Then in deep breathing usually inhalation starts at the pelvic pit and ends at the brim of the throat or even brain. Then exhalation is a return journey. This is a highly mechanical process. Mechanically, where the exhalation ends the inhalation begins. But the paryanka—pranayama has an astonishing break-through. It needs a very good aclematisation of uddiyana kriya. Then comes up the incredible breathing mode which is thus -

Take a deeper inhalation of pelvic location
And exhale towards the back ending at the
Diaphragm and inhale at the diaphragm to
Subsequently exhaling backwards towards the waist.
Thus this diagram will be as under like
A crater along the spine.

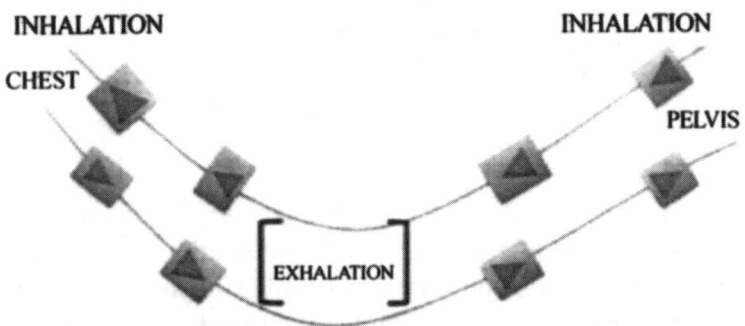

Thus one inhalation ends at the pelvis and the next at at the diaphragm or thoracic, and all exhalations end in between towards the back because of exhalative uddiyana. The inhalations will alternately end at the pelvis and thoracic.

Then the serpentine pranayama teaches negotiating turns in the breath drives. Thus the breath will go along and across the trunk.

Then let us consider the mala pranayama. In breath and out breath are mutually contrary in act and movement. These are movements such as :-

come x go
In x out
Fill up x empty out
Inflation x deflation
Up x down etc.

The breathing is almost a ""'sit—up"of breath. How can quietude, placidity, relaxation, sedation come about? Secondly, breathing is an internal drive and if you have a skilful driver you don't get a jerk, jolt and oscillations. Similar thing is possible in breath.

Inhalation to exhalation is a long and long "U" turn. So is the case in exhalation to inhalation. Thus an oval is drawn between the anterior and posterior of the body forming a "Mala" (not round the neck) Thus the above mentioned oscillation is Averted.

Then there is chandramasa pranayama. The moon has a crescent during two fortnights. The moon orbits of the earth gives us the lunar month with new moon to full moon fortnight with fourteen crescents and full moon to new moon another set of crescents.

Since there is an orbit the 'mala'- mode is very much there.But there is an additional fact to form a crescent moon. There is a part of the orbit which goes along with front of the trunk (anterior) and other half along with back of trunk (posterior). Thus there are two fortnights.(!). Now let us see the process.

The breathing should be close to being Normal but voluntary. But however it Should be commenced after deeper Exhalation to pelvic pit.The normal Breathing cycles will form a circle. These circles must be slowly mobilized Upwards along the back heading Towards base of the throat and then Roll over to anterior of the trunk by

'U" turn and come down gradually
cycle by cycle of breathing. Reaching
the pelvic pit roll-over to the back.
This will complete one orbit of the mala.
Several cycles of normal breathing will
Complete one orbit. This will be like a lunar
Month. Since each cycle comprises of
Exhalation and inhalation, the graphic
Effect in the mala will be as the phases of
The moon in a month.

The mala can be moved in both directions
Which may be called clock wise and
Anti clock wise.

If the orbital normal breathing is given a static confinement then there can be a rotary movement as shown in the diagrams below:-

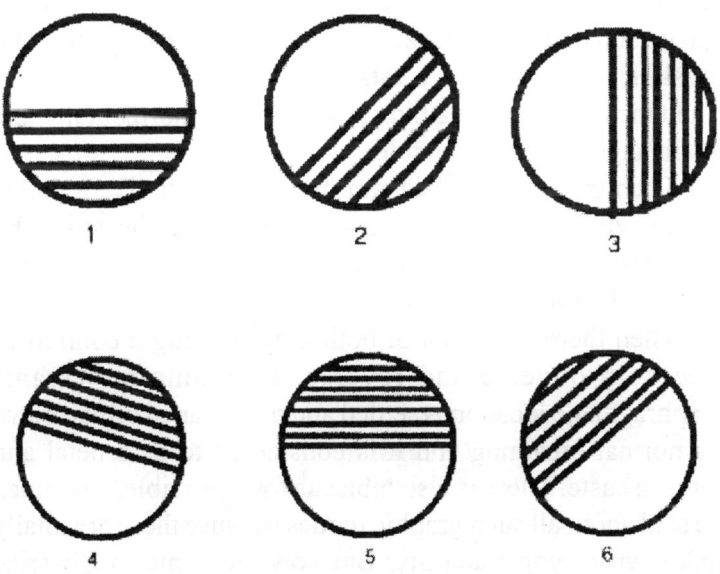

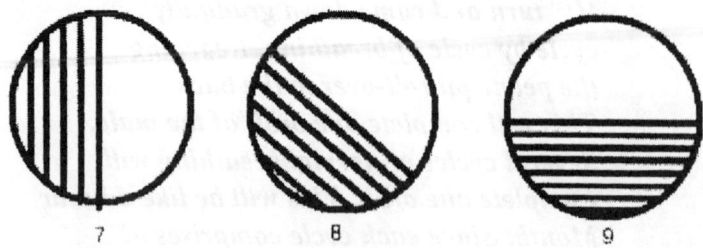

7   8   9

Here, the lined half indicates exhalation. If we look at phase 1 to phase 9 we see the exhalation mobility creates a rotary movement and the phase 1 returns in phase 9. This is how inhalative hemisphere and exhalative hemisphere are rotated. The circumference can be modified by volume of breathing.

Then there is Kankanakruti (Bangle) breathing. Here the breathing cycle should caste a bangle-shaped cycle over the spine. Then it should be angulated as far as it goes. Then retrace and come back to original angle and start angulating on the other side and go on angulating as long as long as one can go and then come back. In course of time, by practice and by skill, it can become a rotary movement of 360 degrees. Then the bangle of breathing may be drawn horizontally and again angulate on either side.

Then there is Kundalakara breathing. It is like a coiled snake when it sleeps. This is done along the spine by progressive uddiyana kriya. It can be exhalative uddiyana and alternately inhalative uddiyana.

Then there is viloma of both kinds casting a coniferous tree both obverse and reverse. In Padma pranayama diaphragmatic location is settled and oval shaped orbits drawn by normal breathing and it is considered to be a petal and lotus in caste. There is also hibiscus form possible. Not much be said about all such graphic modes because these are totally unknown to yog-fraternity. But now we come to Bhasrika which is perhaps the most popular Pranayama in the present set up of yog.

When it comes in a consumer package it marvelously works for making the head light, brain light and fresh and overcomes any conjestion by cold. It also helps to overcome chronic cold problems. It is good to counter hypertension. Those with a cold perform Bhasrika in mode of blowing the nostrils successively and overcome congestion and feel comfortable. Consumers of yog have made it extremely popular (!!)

Any way, in Bhasrika there is a rapid succession of inhalations and exhalations with high density sharp breathing. In one go there are 8—10—15---20---25---30 cycles. Then there is a respite of a few cycles and then there is a second round similarly. There can be 8—10 rounds. It is advisable to cut short the round when the breath loses the force and the flush in exhalation has dwindled. The flushing of the brain that takes place in Bhasrika is just incredible.

Then there is Kapalabhati kriya. It works for yog-kriya, Tattvakriya and chakra kriya long with Uddiyana and Agnisara. Some of the neo-yogis consider it as pranayama itself. Although in shasstras it is not a pranayama but a kriya. Of course we have considered this in an earlier separate chapter. In the classical mode it works as contributory to Uddiyana kriya and its profundity.

Then it is rightly worthy to mention Gayatri Pranayama. The Gayatri mantra is ' _-

When it is normal breathing there is viniyoga of Chatushpada Gayatri and in deeper breathing there is Dvipada Gayatri. (i. e. of four parts and two parts)
The divisions are as under.
1) --------in breath
2) ---------out breath

3) ---------in breath
4) ----------out breath
1) ॐ भू: । ॐ भुव: । ॐ सुव: ।
2) ॐ मह: ॐ जन: । ॐ तप: । ॐ सत्यम् ।
3) ॐ तत्सवितृवरेण्यंभर्गोदेवस्थधीमही धीयो योन: प्रचोदयात् ।
4) ॐ आपी ज्योतिरस: अमृत ब्रह्म भुर्भुवसुवरोम् ॥

The phase 2 can be an inner retention and phase 3can be exhalation and phase 4 can be retention as an alternative mode.This is Chatush-pada –Gayatri.

The Dvipada Gyatri I is as under
1) -----------in breath
2) ----------out breath

ॐ भूभुव: सुव: तत्सवितृवरेण्यंभर्गोदेवस्थधीमही । (in breath)
धीयो योन: प्रचोदयात् । (out breath)

Then Tripada Gayatri is with retention

1) --------out breath   ॐ भु: ......
2) ---------in breath   ॐ तत्सवितृवरेण्यं ......
3) ----------retention.   ॐ आपी ज्योतिरस: ......

Now coming to nasal pranayama kriyas we had several chapters to delineate. Thus we shall not consider those here.

In Chandrabhedana in-breath is by left nostril and exhalation by the right nostril. The Suryabhedana has opposite handling. The outer and inner retentions can be incorporated in them. In Nadi shodhan the process is as under "-

1.	exhale	through	the	right
2.	inhale	through	the	right
3.	exhale	through	the	left
4.	inhale	through	the	left
5.	exhale	through	the	right

Then either inner retention or outer retention may be done or both may be done . The prana kriyas should be used after asvasayama preperatories are over. These pranayamas too are in pop-yog packages, however what is done is shvasayama and called pranayama. Thus the details are not given.

But now we come to unfamiliar pranayam which is "Tattvabhedana pranayama" These are the five tattvas viz

Prithvi (Class of ल)

Aap (Class of व)

Tej (Class of र)

Vayu (Class of य)

Akash (Class of ह)

Suryabhedana can be done with each of the five tattvas using their class of literal letters and beejamantras or pranakriya and tattva kriya considered on an earlier occasion. So in the case of chandrabhedana and Anuloma and pratiloma and nadishodhana pranayama which will then become tattva bhedan or shodhana pranayama.

This becomes the ocean of pranayama by permutations and combinations. Thus it will be effected

+, −, x, ÷; of tattvas with the help of

Puraka (+)

Rechaka (−)

Antara kumbhaka (x)

Bahya Kumbhaka (÷)

This has been described in an earlier chapter on Puraka—Rechaka___Kumbhaka –dvayas. It may be given as information that there are 30 prithvibhedana/shodhana pranayamas. And after four tattvas too have 30 each pranayamas. By permutation and combinations in Puraka—Rechaka__ two Kumbhakas, there are nearly 1800 pranayamas

Then there are chakrabhedana and shodhana pranayamas by viniyoga of petal—**(Dala—)**. Following table indicates chakras, dalas (pettles) and useable letters.

CHAKRAS	DALAS	USABLES-
Muladhara	4	4
Svadhisthana	6	6
Manipuraka	10	10
Anahata	12	10
Vishuddhi	16	10
Ajna	2	2
Six chakras	50	42

These prnayamas are really countless. Then there are Mantra-pranayamas by using the beeja mantras (etc) and Panchakshari, shadakshari, Dvadashakshari etc mantras. Then there are Nama pranayama based on Bhagwannama, Raamanaama, Harinaama,and Ishta Devata namas.

Chapter : 50

A BASIC LESSON!

Basically there are two kinds of breathing in pranayama. This division is based on the *gati* of shavasana - meaning direction of breathing.

1) Mechanics of pranayamic breathing
2) Physiology of pranayamic breathing.

The first one is very natural to a person who has not been trained in pranayama nuances. But those who are influenced by pranayamic culture adhere to the second mode quite naturally because of certain inculcations by dedicated and long practice s of pranayamic technique and art.

In the mechanics of pranayamic breathing, the inhalative flows are from pelvic floor to thoracic brim i. e. bottom of the trunk to the top of the trunk. The exhalations are in opposite directions i. e top of the trunk to bottom of the trunk. Thus, as described earlier, these are 'sit ups' of breathing. The deeper the exhalation, the more the infiltration of the brain by the in-breath.

So also in the inhalation the source movement
Is the pelvis and the terminal movement is in the brain.
Then the source movement in exhalation
Is in the brain and terminal movement in the pelvis.
Thus the gati of in-breath is upwards
and exhalations is downwards.

But pranayama has a Hi-Tech process. There is an effective alternative to mechanics of breathing. Here the inhalation will end in the pelvic—pit rather than the brain and the exhalation will end in the brain-end rather than pelvic—pit.

There is a huge difference between
The brain treated by initial part
Of exhalation than tail end of exhalation.

So also pelvis dealing with initial part
Of inhalation than the tail end of inhalation.

To conceive the importance and efficacy of Pranayama, the following example can be given.

It is a school scenario when the bell rings at the end of the school hours at the last period. The naughty students prefer the last benches in class to enjoy the school hours. But the serious front benchers have the joy of escaping the first while the last benchers are deprived of this inexplicable pleasure.

In the case of mechanical process of breathing,
The brain has to face atrocity when it is
extra-ordinarily deeper inhalation. While in
the second mode of breathing deeper, the
Inhalation gives greater solace for the brain
because it goes away from the brain.

The following table will indicate breath flows in two processes.

EXHALATIONS
BY MECHANICS OF PRANAYAMA BY
PHYSIOLOGY OF PRANAYAMA
EVACUATIONS

Head	Pelvis
↓	↓
Throat	naval
↓	↓
chest	abdomen

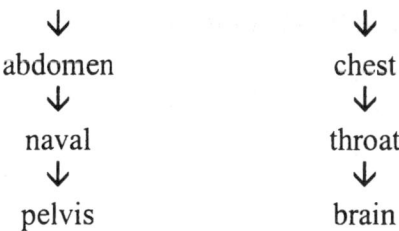

abdomen	chest
↓	↓
naval	throat
↓	↓
pelvis	brain

Thus the two columns give the comparative understanding of the two processes. If the brain is flushed at the end of exhalation rather than at the beginning of it, it is of exalted effect in terms of relaxation. The following table will indicate inhalations:-

INHALATIONS
BY MECHANICS OF PRANAYAMA BY PHYSIOLOGY OF PRANAYAMA EVACUATIONS

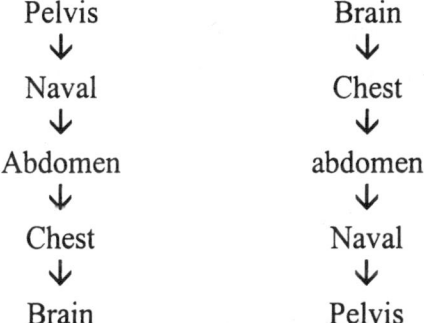

Pelvis	Brain
↓	↓
Naval	Chest
↓	↓
Abdomen	abdomen
↓	↓
Chest	Naval
↓	↓
Brain	Pelvis

The mechanical process of in-breath creates atrocity when breathing deeper while in the second process deeper inhalations work in the opposite way by bestowing relaxation. The deeper the inhalation, the greater the relaxation of the brain!

In pranic kriyas there are formulae for these breaths. The breathing will become in the above process. The breathing should be done in six stages and it will naturalize the above process.

FORMULA FOR INHALATION

Inhalation by mechanics

लं→वं→रं→यं→हं→ ॐ

Inhalation by physiology of Pranama

ॐ→हं→यं→रं→वं→ लं

Exhalation by mechanics

ॐ→हं→यं→रं→वं→ लं

Exhalation by physiology of pranayama

लं→वं→रं→यं→हं→ ॐ

Alternatively the formula are the follows for physiology of pranic inhalations which is advanced—level—formula

(ॐ) (ॐ---हं) (ॐ---हं ---यं) (ॐ----हं ---- यं ----रं)

(ॐ--- हं --- यं ---रं ---वं) (ॐ---हं ---यं ---रं ---वं ----लं)

Then for exhalation it is reversed i.e.

(वं) (लं --- वं) (लं ---वं ---रं) (लं --- वं --- रं --- यं)

(लं ---वं ---रं ---यं --- हं) (लं ---वं --- रं ---यं ---हं ---ॐ)

All these things are complicated and incomprehensible for non-student practitioners of yog. Today we have world wide fraternity of yog, who do not want to be students of yog but want to be practitioners of yog !

Chapter : 51

CONCLUSION

It is paramount that we understand that pranayama is not primarily and basically breath-control or breath-regulation or shvasayama. Pranayama needs a lot of study of breath usages, applications and Addressals by---on—in—with breath. Asanas provide an incredible field, lab and academy for that purpose.

It is important to note that there is a big difference in physiology of respiration that comes in body-science and physiology of breathing that occurs in the science of yog. The respiratory system is one of the many systems of human anatomy and physiology. But according to physiology of breathing of yog, the entire human embodiment is a breathing organism.

"Even inner, outer, physical, psycho-mental, Psychic, gross and subtle and esoteric and esoteric organs, senses and constitution are breathing organs."

Thus it is a marvellous precept of the science of yog. Thus even our mind becomes a breathing organ which even the modern science is accepting whereas yog postulates that conscious, subconscious, infra-conscious mind is a breathing organ.

The neo-yog and all its mockery are an outcome of feverish propagation of yog on a huge scale and thus becoming victims of Maya (delusion).

To call what is being considered as
Pranayama today is wholesale
Defamation of classical, authentic
and timeless yog.

Anyway, Shvasayama provides a realm of spiritualism for atheists. These later schools do not believe in anything that is metaphysically true or sublime and transcendent. But they take recourse to breath; strangely they believe in the shadow of Divinity –breath (which is a big part in their spiritual practice such as *vipashyana* of Buddhism) Breath is a great solace for those who are averse to God and Divinity.